C

The Old French Johannes
Translation of the
Pseudo-Turpin Chronicle

The Old French Johannes Translation of the *Pseudo-Turpin Chronicle*

A Critical Edition

BY RONALD N. WALPOLE

UNIVERSITY OF CALIFORNIA PRESS
Berkeley • Los Angeles • London

University of California Press
Berkeley and Los Angeles, California

University of California Press, Ltd.
London, England

Dis est mes conte et finis mes labeur.
Or m'en irai et Deus m'en doint bon eur,
Regracijant le dame de me vie,
Inspirement et de mon bien auteur,
Siege de grace, me feme et si m'amie.

Contents

Foreword

Johannes has proved to be a figure as elusive as his literary progenitor, the Pseudo-Turpin himself, and it has been an arduous chase to hunt him through the libraries and archives of western Europe. But a merry one; as I look back at the long criss-crossing alleys down which he has led me, I find again those keepers of the forest who with trained and practised expertise and utmost kindliness have guided me and helped me on. To the keepers of books, manuscripts and archives from the British Museum to the Vatican Library, from Paris, Saint-Omer and Valenciennes to Copenhagen, too numerous to name but none of them forgotten, I offer my grateful thanks. And I have found, hunting in the same forest though pursuing a different quarry, Dr. Ian Short, the editor of William de Briane's Anglo-Norman *Pseudo-Turpin Chronicle,* in whose cheerful companionship I have found scholarly aid and a most generous interest: *cil qui ne puet vivre sanz paine e sanz travaill.*

For a more material aid, itself issuing however from a purely humanistic persuasion, I acknowledge in duty and pleasure the aids afforded to me by a Guggenheim Fellowship and by a Humanities Research Fellowship of the University of California at Berkeley. My thanks are due also to the University of California Press, which has furnished the means, financial and other, to publish Johannes.

The form in which he is published demands a word of explanation. The essential elements of the edition are to be found in the main volume: the list of the manuscripts, their classification and the conclusions as to authorship and date to which this leads, the text, with readings rejected from the basic manuscript appended, notes to the text, an index of proper names and a glossary. The supplement provides auxiliary detail; it is intended not only to enlighten readers further on the character and literary life of the Johannes translation, but also to show its role in the whole developing *Turpin* tradition. It contains a full description of all the

FOREWORD

manuscripts, palaeographical, historical and linguistic. This is
followed by an appendix, with page references to the foregoing,
listing words which occur as variants in the manuscripts and which
offer particular difficulty or interest. Here too will be found the
variants of the four controlling manuscripts, a bulky section but
one which shows what scribes, slavish or inventive, could do
down the centuries with a prose text, undisciplined by meter or
rhyme. Here too is the Bibliography which in no way pretends
to cover the vast subject of the *Turpin* but simply draws together
the works to which the reader is referred throughout the edition.

Introduction

The *Pseudo-Turpin Chronicle* is an offshoot of the legend of
Charlemagne which is known to us in a learned form as it appears
in the pages of mediaeval historians and panegyrists of the
Emperor and perhaps more familiarly in its popular form as pre-
served in the Old French *Chanson de Roland* and the royal cycle
of old French heroic poetry. By 1145, at about which time the
Chronicle was written, the learned and the popular imagination
had magnified its vision of the Emperor into that of the ideal
suzerain and monarch, a strong and just ruler in his own domin-
ions and the effective servant of the divine will in his effort to con-
quer and convert the pagans beyond the frontiers of his realm.

This development was in great part a spontaneous growth
rooted in the esteem and devotion of contemporaries of the
Emperor who saw what a contrast he presented with those rulers
who had preceded him, and nourished in the memory of those
who suffered in the political disintegration which followed so
quickly after his death. To the voices of men trained in the
schools and active in the councils of state was added the voice of
the people. The third estate had not been forgotten by the medi-
aeval theoreticians as they outlined the qualities and duties per-
taining to the Christian king. They insisted, as did their authorities
in classical literature and in the Old and New Testaments, that the
ruler must among other things protect the humble and cast down
the proud. According to Jeremiah, whose words they heeded, this
was indeed the very word of God, and Charlemagne sought in this
as in all his policies, to follow the admonitions of his advisers and
his own practical bent by doing what he could to protect the
defenceless and help the poor, the "widows and orphans" of the
biblical phrase. And so, alongside of the learned tradition which
sustained and embellished the memory of Charlemagne as the ideal
ruler there developed a popular legend, this too a spontaneous
growth, rooted in the general affection which the Emperor's
benign governance had aroused among the common folk.

INTRODUCTION

The early form and development of the popular legend of
Charlemagne is not so easy to trace as is the learned legend. It was
not written and has to be inferred mainly from the extant epic tra-
dition which survives from the eleventh and later mediaeval cen-
turies. Needless to say, the popular and the learned legends were
not entirely distinct, but it is impossible to define the influences
exerted by the one upon the other. The later historical tradition
shows unmistakable influences of the popular legend, and there
can be no doubt that the seed of the legend which took root in the
popular mind was the one matured in the thoughts and scattered
in the writings of the scholarly clerics whom the Emperor gathered
about him as aids in his purpose to christianize and civilize his
kingdom. For the clerics, Charlemagne became the guardian and
the symbol of their high concept of empire in its abstract sense of
power to impose the law, the natural and the divine law. In the
memory of the people he lived on as the ideal of the beneficent
ruler, the exemplar of their simple faith, the hero victorious in bat-
tle against the enemies of his state and of his religion. That the
popular and learned legends were never wholly separate can be
seen in the *Chanson de Roland* where, in the uncertain years of the
eleventh century when the Capetians were striving to restore the
power and prestige of the French monarchy, French national feel-
ing in all its intensity and longing seems to have crystallized
around the legendary figure of Charlemagne.

In a sense, the *Pseudo-Turpin Chronicle* is part of this legend. It
tells us the same story, though in its own particular way and with
its own particular details, as the *Chanson de Roland,* that is, the
legendary story of Roncevaux: Ganelon's betrayal, the defeat of
the French rearguard, Roland's death and the final French victory
at Saragossa. More than this, it purports to chronicle the events of
the long crusade in Spain to which the *Chanson* makes merely
passing reference: *Set anz tuz pleins ad estét en Espaigne. . .*
Though the *Pseudo-Turpin Chronicle* is almost entirely made up of
these fables, it claimed to be a true history of Charlemagne and its
appeal was so persuasively made that it was generally esteemed
throughout the Middle Ages as no less authentic than Einhard's
Vita Karoli Magni. But this reputation did not, with a few spo-
radic exceptions, survive the early years of the Renaissance, and
more recent critics have exposed the hollowness of its pretensions

INTRODUCTION

and the mendacity which hides under its protestations of trustworthiness.

It is indeed a forgery, pious or impious according to one's view. We must look upon it not as a natural outgrowth of the Carolingian legend but rather as an alien shoot grafted on to that indigenous stock whence it drew a parasitic life. Of course, truth and falsity are relative terms when applied to mediaeval historiography. Intrinsic exactitude, a critical approach, objective judgment are qualities which even modern historians find difficult to sustain and which, in the nature of things, cannot be demanded of a mediaeval chronicler. An excessive credulity is a form of the mediaeval mentality, and we are not put out when we find it in a Bede or in a Limousin Astronomer. Naïveté is not reprehensible in those for whom sophistication is out of reach. However, we find the Pseudo-Turpin not only using traditional fables but manufacturing for interested purposes some of his own.

He claims to be writing an account of Charlemagne's crusades in Spain — *qualiter noster famosissimus Karolus Magnus tellurem yspanicam et gallecianam a potestate Sarracenorum liberavit.* Charlemagne's fabulous crusades in Spain are the extraordinary magnification which Carolingian legend made of the far less imposing facts we learn from history: his harrying incursions into northern Spain undertaken with no further purpose and achieving no greater effect than the setting up of a buffer zone along the Spanish march to serve as defence against the menace of Islamic power. The legend gave the Pseudo-Turpin the gist of his account of Roncevaux and also the events with which he filled in the supposedly long years of campaigning which preceded Roncevaux: the series of wars against Aigolandus in northern Spain and southern France, against Furre, against Ferracutus and against Altumaior of Corduba and Ebrahim of Seville. But he invents the great fiction, totally new, totally unfounded and thoroughly impudent, according to which Charlemagne's long and arduous wars in Spain were undertaken at the behest of St. James for the purpose of freeing the saint's burial place in Compostella from the Saracens and of liberating the pilgrim roads leading to his shrine. He weaves this false theme into the manufactured fabric of his chronicle in the impertinent assurance that it would win credence by its inclusion among the elements of the live and accepted tradition which was handing on the fabled biography of a beloved and admired Charlemagne.

That the love and admiration felt by laymen and clerics alike for the Charlemagne of legend were genuine there can be no doubt. The enhanced portrait of the Emperor and hero was the image of a cherished ideal and the virtues which it personified evinced a moral which was pervasive in the thought and feeling of the times. It is the crime of the Pseudo-Turpin that he pays false tribute to this ideal, and it is in this sense that his chronicle must be considered extraneous to the legend of Charlemagne. It has been described as the ecclesiastical form of the legend of Charlemagne, but this is not justified. The truly clerical legend of Charlemagne, fused with the popular legend, had by this time become a myth with a poetic truth of its own, endowed with the lasting reality of human experience and of national and religious ideals. *The Pseudo-Turpin Chronicle* is indeed the work of a cleric; it was no doubt composed in a monastic scriptorium; but it represents the perversion of Carolingian legend to use as propaganda for the crusade in Spain and the pilgrimage to Compostella.

Its self-advertisement is a mark of this perversion. It presents itself very explicitly to the reader as the unique account of Charlemagne's triumphant exploits in Spain, as a part of his biography neglected by other chroniclers but here told in full and for the first time by Turpin, Archbishop of Reims, *sedulus Karoli Magni imperatoris in Yspania consocius,* an eyewitness of all the great deeds accomplished by the Emperor during his fourteen years of war in the Peninsula. We do not know who the impostor was who thus assumed the name of Turpin, but it is obvious to us that he passed himself off as that appealing hero of the *Chanson de Roland,* Turpin, the fighting Archbishop of Reims

le guerreier Charlun

. . .

Deus li otreit seinte beneïçun

seeking thereby to extend to his chronicle the popular esteem in which that poetic figure was held. To answer the anticipated question: "Why have our history books not told us this before?," the Pseudo-Turpin declares that this is because the other historians of Charlemagne could not find a place for it in their too abundant subject matter or because, not having been with the Emperor in

Spain, they knew nothing about what he had done there: *auctorem . . . aut pro tantorum actuum scriptura prolixa aut quia idem absens ab Yspania ea ignoravit.* The Pseudo-Turpin, incorporating in his chronicle so much matter taken from the vernacular poetic tradition, reveals his purpose to reach out beyond a learned audience to a wider and more credulous public, a public with little schooling, more active in deeds than in council, composed of men like Potton de Sainte-Traille who, in Chastellain's *Chronique,* speaking from the beleaguered walls of Crespy, addresses the Burgundians: "Nous ne sommes pas du conseil de cour; nous sommes de l'exploit des champs." The better to impose upon this public, he took the popular stories and redacted them in Latin prose, knowing that the prestige of that language would of itself confer upon his work an authority as history which vernacular poetry could not command. His work is in form and purpose a forgery, a counterfeit of the common currency, loudly advertized as genuine and foisted for interested clerical purposes upon a public for the most part unable to criticize and no doubt delighted to read in this for them authentic form so much of what they wanted to believe.

How shrewd the Pseudo-Turpin's calculations were is proved by his success. For three centuries after it was written, his chronicle was accepted as authoritative. It was copied in hundreds of manuscripts, it was included in Latin historical compilations and, above all, after the beginning of the thirteenth century, it proliferated in a number of vernacular translations, some of them made to be included in Old French renderings of Latin chronicles, others done separately, a mark of the special interest the chronicle had for so many whose inherited interest in Charlemagne was enhanced by the image it presented of the Emperor as the forerunner in their own heroic and pious adventures as crusaders and pilgrims. Among the vernacular translations that of Johannes has a specially important place. It is preserved in thirty-two known manuscripts and their classification reveals that there were others which have been lost. The manuscript tradition shows by its scattering over a wide area in place and time that the Johannes translation was far more persistently and widely sought after than the other vernacular translations. Three factors would seem to explain this special popularity.

In the first place Johannes announced his translation in a prologue commending it to the public in terms attuned to the general interests and outlook of the times. Most people, he says, have been and still are interested in the history of Charlemagne's conquest of Spain and Galicia, but whereas among former sources of information some matters were left out and others added, here can be found the whole truth according to the Latin history written by Archbishop Turpin of Reims from which the present translation was made. To keep faithfully to the truth of the Latin, the translation is made in prose, because in verse the very search for rhyme entails a derogation from literal exactitude. Archbishop Turpin's Chronicle itself is an eye-witness's account of Charlemagne's conquest given exactly as Turpin experienced it while he kept the Emperor company throughout his campaigns. It is, then, a story which all gentlemen should cherish and heed not only because of its truthfulness but also because the memorable deeds which it recounts offer high moral examples to an age in which neglect of such reading is causing virtue to decline and courage to falter. So Johannes, in complete good faith, presented his French *Turpin* to the public as the authoritative history of Charlemagne's conquest of Spain, the sort of history which interested people had been looking for to replace the poems and rhymed chronicles now falling into discredit. He launched his French prose translation on a strong current of favorable opinion.

In the second place, Johannes, addressing himself to *toz hauz homes,* that is to the lay nobility for the most part ignorant of Latin and largely unschooled, rewrote the Latin *Turpin* to some extent as he translated it, the better to accommodate it to the mentality and taste of his prospective audience. The structure of the Pseudo-Turpin's chronicle is careless and lax; his style is verbose and pedantic. He uses matter drawn from poetic legend but often destroys the poetry in his borrowing. Engrossed in the purposes for which he was brewing his false concoction, the Pseudo-Turpin shows no real understanding of the legend he was misusing. He seems to have looked upon it as a nebula of incoherent particles, without a principle of unity, without a soul of meaning. Johannes, a naïf perhaps, yet a believer in the great legend, saw it in its poetic truth as an emanation of a deeply felt ideal, the expression of the needs, the interests, the hopes of his own as of previous generations. Johannes makes the structure of the chronicle more orderly and clear, the style more natural and convincing, and he restores much of the poetic life lost in the Pseudo-Turpin's insensitive narration. In his sincerity and with his warmer feeling, Johannes in his French comes nearer than the Pseudo-Turpin in his Latin to the drama and realism of epic poetry and so undoubtedly nearer to the minds and hearts of the lay people whom he had in mind as he made his translation. His popularity is due in part to the way he told the story.

But the Johannes translation seems to have won most popular favor when a redactor, a year or two after it was made, added to it at the beginning as complement to the Pseudo-Turpin's chronicle of Charlemagne's crusade in Spain, a short version of the legend of his crusade in the Holy Land. This legend, even more than the *Turpin*, remains obscure in its origin and development. It appears suddenly fully formed towards the end of the eleventh century, in that other pseudo-chronicle which resembles the *Turpin* like a brother, the anonymous *Descriptio qualiter Karolus Magnus clavum et coronam Domini a Constantinopoli Aquisgrani detulerit qualiterque Karolus Calvus hec ad sanctum Dionysium retulerit.* Without preamble of any kind, assertively and in great detail, the *Descriptio* tells us that at the moment when Charlemagne had reached the summit of his power in Europe and been crowned Emperor in Rome, news came to him of the persecution of the Christians by the Moslems in the Holy Land. The Patriarch of Jerusalem appealed to the Emperor of Constantinople for help, and Constantine, unable to provide it, turned for aid to the renowned Emperor of the West. Charlemagne undertook the task and passing through Constantinople went on to Palestine, relieved the Christians from oppression and restored to their keeping the Holy Sepulchre. Thence he returned to Constantinople where, refusing Constantine's offer of a rich reward, he accepted instead a gift of relics, some of them most precious relics of the Passion.

The *Descriptio* tells in detail how these were found in Constantinople and describes the miracles performed as they were brought to light and as they were borne home to Aix. There they were deposited by Charlemagne who organized the festival of the Lendit for their display during the summer Ember Days. Later, the chronicle concludes, they were given to Charles the Bald who distributed them among his favored churches in France, above all Saint-Denis, to which he presented a nail used in the Crucifixion and a piece of the Holy Cross itself. And there in Saint-Denis Charles the Bald organized a Lendit in imitation of the one established at Aix, during which the Abbey could display its relics to the people. The legend is also and no doubt more generally known in its poetic form, *Le pèlerinage de Charlemagne,* a product of the same tradition yet differing from the portentously serious *Descriptio* in the variety of its picturesque details and in the frivolity of its tone. Few of the questions surrounding this fabulous tradition have been definitively answered, but it seems that in all its extant forms it is the outgrowth of a concern on the part of interested clerics to win, by fair means or foul, credence for relics in their possession which they sought to authenticate as true relics originating in Jerusalem and whose value they sought to enhance by asserting that they were brought from the East to France by Charlemagne himself, whom for this purpose they thus made the great exemplar of crusader in the Holy Land and pilgrim to Jerusalem.

Here, as in the case of the *Turpin,* history offers but a slight basis for the story. It tells us only of Charlemagne's interest in protecting the holy places and the pilgrims who visited them, of the friendly relations which he maintained at a distance with the Patriarch of Jerusalem, with the Caliph Harun al-Rashid and, though here matters were more complicated, with the Emperors of Constantinople, relations of which the cordiality was marked by the exchange of honorific gifts. The legend changed the gifts to relics and replaced the journeyings of state emissaries with a journey to Jerusalem undertaken by Charlemagne in person. This was the framework of the fabrication. It was used at different times in various places and filled out in each case with details further invented to suit local needs and circumstances. The author of the *Descriptio* did the same, but on a much more imposing, one might say national, scale. The unknown author, who was certainly a monk of Saint-Denis, wrote as did those who used the legend before him, with the particular concern to publicize the famous relics which the abbey claimed it possessed. But, writing in Saint-Denis, that focal point of French national consciousness, he had in mind ideas of wider and deeper scope: the great movement of the crusade and all that it involved in politics at home and abroad, relations, pragmatic and ideological, with the German empire, with the Papacy, and with Alexis Comnenus and the Eastern Empire.

INTRODUCTION

And so, weaving the whole fabric of the *Descriptio* out of his own imagination, he created and succeeded in imposing upon his contemporaries this new image of Charlemagne as crusader in Palestine, exemplary in his saintliness, *omnino ecclesiastice doctrine deditus,* and as the defender of the faith to whom the Emperor of the East turned for succor in humility and gratitude. The *Descriptio,* like the *Turpin,* was almost at once accepted as authentic by responsible historians of the day and found its chronological place in their chronicles just antecedent to the Pseudo-Turpin's account of Charlemagne's crusade in Spain. At the beginning of the thirteenth century, Pierre de Beauvais, the translator into verse and prose of a number of didactic Latin works, found the *Descriptio* in a Latin manuscript at Saint-Denis. He was familiar with the Johannes *Turpin* and, declaring that it was timely and appropriate to make also available in French the little known but no less interesting chronicle of the *voie que Charles fist outre mer,* he translated the *Descriptio* and copied the Johannes *Turpin* as its proper sequel.

The *Descriptio* is for a modern reader excruciatingly long-winded. Pierre, though not easily bored, evidently found it tedious himself for, in his translation, he cut out some of its excessive verbiage. The *Descriptio,* thus revised in its French form and followed in the manuscript by the Johannes *Turpin,* came very quickly after it was done into the hands of a redactor who, energetically eliminating all the pietistic expatiation, reduced the *Descriptio* to the simple story of what happened and slipped it into the *Turpin* where it appears in his text as our Chapters II to V. The redactor draws no attention to his interpolation; implicitly but no doubt intentionally he leaves the impression that the Pseudo-Turpin was the author who truly chronicled all of Charlemagne's crusades against the Saracens in Palestine and Spain.

Nothing could have been better calculated to increase the interest of the *Turpin* for the barons and bourgeois of northern France at the beginning of the thirteenth century than this brief and rapidly moving story of Charlemagne's crusading journey to Constantinople and Jerusalem and his acquisition of relics which were never so avidly sought after as at that time. Here in this redaction of the *Descriptio-Turpin* was an omnibus, written in the language which the three estates could understand, embodying the

traditional and beloved image of the national hero but made more
actual by its appeal to interest in current events, for it was pub-
lished at the moment when, under Philip Augustus, that *alter
Karolus,* the persistent thought was being maintained with height-
ened optimism that through Charlemagne the old Empire had been
renewed and that it was, and was to be for ever, Holy, Roman and
French, at the moment too when the full tide of the crusades
seemed to be borne on in Capetian France as in the France of
Charlemagne by unanimous patriotic and religious feeling.

These, then, were the characteristics which won for the
Johannes *Turpin* in general and for the *Descriptio-Turpin* redac-
tion in particular, the unique favor with which it was received by
its mediaeval audience, and it is the fact of this popularity which
constitutes the main reason why it is the text of the redaction
rather than the text of the original translation which is printed
here. It has been thought that the translator, Johannes himself,
brought the *Descriptio* into conjunction with his *Turpin* and that
the manuscripts which lack the *Descriptio* matter are copies made
by more critical scribes who eliminated that story as inauthentic
and unacceptable. Proof that the text printed below is indeed a
redaction of the original translation is offered in Chapter II where
the evidence is provided by the classification of the manuscripts.
The whole Johannes tradition is represented for us by thirty-two
manuscripts. It is possible that there are others lying undetected in
manuscripts of which the last details, not surprisingly, have escaped
the notice of cataloguers. I stumbled upon our B2 when reading the
Chronique de Baudouin d'Avesnes in Brussels MS 10233. The Chro-
nicle was widely known in the translations which proliferated in the
early and later thirteenth century, and in the manuscript copies
made of them, so that scribes translating general Latin histories or
making historical compilations in French, could choose among the
translations and copies according to taste or to the availability of a
text. Anyone may then, with a good fortune equal to my own in
Brussels, come upon a Johannes *Turpin* thus introduced into some
"Chronique francaise des rois de France." Such chronicles, and
the manuscript copies in which they are preserved, are too numer-
ous and too scattered for me to have scoured them systematically
in search of another Johannes *Turpin.*

In Chapter II will be found recorded also the process by which
the Johannes translation passed through the hands of Pierre de

INTRODUCTION

Beauvais to be linked with his *Descriptio*. The broad division of
the manuscripts into three main groups: the original translation,
Pierre's *Descriptio* followed by the Johannes *Turpin* and the redac-
tion represented by our printed text, has determined the order of
the presentation of the manuscripts which forms the subject mat-
ter of Chapter I. Such an anticipatory organization will, I hope,
help the reader to begin to form from the start a mental picture of
the manuscript stemma which will issue finally from the study
undertaken in Chapter II. The detailed description of the manu-
scripts, along with the palaeographical and linguistic evidence
which allows us to date them and to know as far as possible their
history, forms a bulky chapter consigned to the supplement. I
have dealt in its pages not only with the palaeography and lan-
guage of each manuscript but also with the important textual
deviations which mark the individuality of some manuscripts
among their fellows and give us clues to filiations and contamina-
tions into which we see at the moment so imperfectly.

The subject matter of the *Turpin* is not only interesting to us in
itself but also in the fact that it was interesting to so many medi-
aeval people. The story of its manuscript tradition is a window
for us opening upon the mediaeval mind. The story is extremely
complicated and has to be painstakingly unravelled like a tangled
and broken skein. If we are to chart the multiple branchings of
the *Turpin* in order, as it were, to see its geography on the literary
and historiographical maps of Western Europe and to know the
particular forms it assumed at the hands of individual patrons and
scribes or under the influence of centers of propagation, we must,
I think, begin with studies as definitive as possible of isolable ele-
ments of the whole vast problem. So it has seemed necessary to
me to deal thoroughly with the story of the Johannes manuscripts
and with the problem of their relationship.

It seemed to me necessary also to keep together in this single
work all the various facts pertaining to this study because they
belong together. To relieve the book of some of its weight by
publishing separate articles on some of the controversies involved
or on some of the problems of detail, would take them out of their
context, necessitate much repetition in their presentation and add
bibliographical problems to those, tantalizing enough, which are
inherent in the subject. M. André de Mandach has said that studies

of the *Turpin* undertaken before his own all suffered from the narrowness of their scope and their failure to take in the panorama of the whole *Turpin* scene. They are, he says, like parts of a clock, never assembled into a working mechanism. M. de Mandach has made a great and valuable attempt to do just this; but it remains very doubtful whether his clock tells the right time. His *Geste de Charlemagne* is, with all its qualities, proof of the fact which must now be clear that it can hardly be expected of a single craftsman engaged in this enterprise to reconstruct perfectly the broken pieces of the *Turpin* and to put them perfectly together. Gaston Paris, Joseph Bédier, Pierre David, attempted total solutions of the problem but failed. The late Professor Adalbert Hämel saw their lack and ours: a proper knowledge of the manuscript tradition and the possession of reliably edited texts.

This edition therefore is offered as a contribution to what must be a corporate endeavor. For those who have no need or interest to bother with the *Turpin* as a problem, the text itself may have its attractions. Johannes's translation is one of the very earliest examples of French prose. It was soon followed by more racy chronicles of contemporary events such as those of Robert de Clari and Henri de Valenciennes, but already we come nearer in it than we do in the poetic literature of its time to what we should so much like to hear: the language of mediaeval French people talking among themselves.

Chapter I

The Manuscripts

A full description of the manuscripts is given in the supplement. It will present the palaeographical, linguistic and historical evidence which allows us to date and localize them, together with notices of their more important textual variations and a discussion of their lexical peculiarities where these offer some interest. A list of the words so treated is given in the Appendix to this description. The manuscripts are listed in groups and in a certain order which will be established in Chapter II. This arrangement is made here in order to give at once a panoramic view of the manuscript tradition which may help to keep clear our later progress through the details of collation and classification.

Group I.   MSS M, P, L1 form our Group I of the Johannes manuscript tradition. Their prologue mentions no sponsor of the translation and they contain no matter drawn from the legend of Charlemagne's legendary journey to the East. MS D is now lost, but there is evidence in a surviving catalogue to show that its place in our classification is here.

M   Munich, Bayerische Staatsbibliothek, MS Gallicus 52, fols. 102-114. The folios are of paper. A watermark and the character of the language suggest that the manuscript was written in Hainaut about 1470. The *Turpin* in M is appended as Chapter LXX to the *Chronique de Baudouin d'Avesnes.* It begins with the prologue which is proper to our sub-group of manuscripts, III M (see below, p. 3), but breaks off in the middle of this prologue and starts anew with the prologue proper to Group I.

P1   Bibliothèque Nationale, French MS 1621, fols. 208-225. The copy was written in the south-western

part of Picardy ca. 1250. In its account of Roncevaux, the text of
P1 has a long passage borrowed from the *Roman de Roncevaux.*

L1   British Museum, MS Harley 273, fols. 86-102 v°.
                  L1 was written in England, probably at Ludlow, at
the end of the thirteenth century.

D   A manuscript now lost, formerly Dover, St. Mar-
                  tin's Priory, MS H. VII, 6.

Group II.   MSS P2, P3, Br 1, P4, M0 form our Group II of the
                  Johannes manuscript tradition. In P2, P3, Br 1, the
Turpin is preceded by a French translation, made by Pierre de
Beauvais, of the *Descriptio,* the Latin account of Charlemagne's
legendary journey to Constantinople and Jerusalem. P4 is muti-
lated and preserves but a fragment of the French *Descriptio.* M0
contains Pierre's *Descriptio* but no *Turpin.*

P2   Bibliothèque Nationale, French MS 834. The
                  Descriptio-Turpin occupies fols. 15-31. The manu-
script was written and decorated with brightly embellished initials
in the region slightly to the north of Paris about the turn of the
thirteenth century.

P3   Bibliothèque Nationale, MS nouv. acq. fr. 13521.
                  This is the La Clayette manuscript, highly orna-
mented with miniatures and decorated initials. The *Descriptio-
Turpin* is written on fols. 42-56. The language is Francien, with
Picard and Champenois influences. The decoration and the lin-
guistic forms suggest that the copy was made in the Ile-de-France
in the early fourteenth century.

Br 1   Brussels, Bibliothèque Royale de Belgique, MS
                  10437. The *Descriptio-Turpin* is written on fols.
1-30 v°. It was copied in the Burgundian territory of north-
eastern France in the middle of the fifteenth century, probably
before 1454.

P4   Bibliothèque Nationale, French MS 2168. P4 is
                  mutilated and now contains of Pierre de Beauvais's

Descriptio-Turpin only a broken fragment of the *Descriptio*. It was copied in Picardy in the latter part of the thirteenth century. P4 is alone in asserting in its prologue that Pierre de Beauvais made his translation of the *Descriptio* for *son bon seignour Williaume de Caieu.*

Mo   Modena, Biblioteca Estense, MS N. 5. 12. Mo is a paper manuscript containing on folios 1-5 a text of Pierre de Beauvais's *Descriptio* but no *Turpin.* It was written in northern France at the end of the fourteenth century.

Group III.   The twenty-three manuscripts which follow form Group III of the Johannes manuscript tradition. They preserve a redaction of Pierre de Beauvais's *Descriptio-Turpin* in which the *Descriptio,* much shortened, is inserted in Chapter I of the Johannes *Turpin.* The *Descriptio* matter forms Chapters II to V of the text printed in this edition. Among these manuscripts, Br 2 stands apart. Of the others, eight, P5, P6, A1, P7, L2, L3, O, B1 form a sub-group defined by a prologue which declares that their "translation" of the *Turpin* was sponsored by Count Renaud of Boulogne who, for this purpose, borrowed a Latin *Turpin* from the library of Saint-Denis. This sub-group will be referred to as III R. The next fourteen manuscripts form another sub-group defined, except in the case of Br 3 and P11, by a prologue which makes a contradictory claim, namely, that their *Turpin* is a "translation" sponsored by Michel de Harnes who had it made from a Latin text treasured in Renaud de Boulogne's library. This sub-group will be referred to as III M.

Br 2   Brussels, Bibliothèque Royale de Belgique, MS 10233-36, fols. 57 v° - 78 v°. The *Turpin* here forms part of the *Chronique de Baudouin d'Avesnes.* It was written in Hainaut c. 1425. The text as used by the compiler of the *Chronique* begins with our Chapter XI and then, though with some omissions, follows our second redaction to the end.

Group III R

P5   Bibliothèque Nationale, French MS 2464, fols. 61-108 v°; incomplete at the end and lacking Chapter

XXVIII of the text printed below. P5 was written in or near
Paris in the second quarter of the thirteenth century.

P6　　　　　Bibliothèque Nationale, MS nouv. acq. fr. 10554,
　　　　　fols. 2-40 v°. P6 is a copy of P5, written in or near
Paris in the third quarter of the fifteenth century.

A1　　　　　Paris, Bibliothèque de l'Arsenal, MS 5201, pp. 189-
　　　　　225. A1 is decorated with historiated and highly
ornamented initials. Its *Turpin* was copied about 1270 in the
western part of Burgundy.

P7　　　　　Bibliothèque Nationale, French MS 5713, fols. 13-
　　　　　68 v°. P7 has gracefully ornamented initials. Its
Turpin here forms the major part of a more general *Gestes de
Charlemagne*. It is a rather free copy and has interpolations which
show filiation with the *Grandes Chroniques de France* and with
the *Fleur des histoires* of Jean Mansel. It was written in the Île-de-
France about the middle of the fifteenth century.

L2　　　　　British Museum, Royal MS 4 C. xi, fols. 280-
　　　　　286 v°. The manuscript formerly belonged to the
Benedictine abbey of St. Martin at Battle in Sussex. Its *Turpin*
was written in England ca. 1225.

L3　　　　　British Museum, Additional MS 40142. The manu-
　　　　　script, of 14 vellum leaves, is wholly taken up by
the *Turpin* and a genealogy of the kings of France. It was written
in England towards the middle of the thirteenth century.

O　　　　　Oxford, Bodleian Library, Hatton MS 67, fols. 1-
　　　　　17 v°. Written in England in the second half, per-
haps towards the end, of the thirteenth century.

B1　　　　　Bern, Bürgerbibliothek, MS 115, fols. lxxiii-
　　　　　lxxxvi v°. A lively miniature, and an equally lively
historiated initial, both at the beginning of the Turpin, depict epi-
sodes narrated in the chronicle. B1 was written in Artois in the
second half of the thirteenth century.

Group III M

P8   Bibliothèque Nationale, French MS 1444, fols.
119-126. The copy was made in the north-eastern
part of the Picard region towards the end of the thirteenth century.

V   Vatican Library, MS Regina 936, fols. 1-13 v°. V
has handsomely ornamented initials. It was written
in Artois towards the end of the thirteenth century. Its *Turpin* is
followed by two supplementary chapters, printed below as an
Appendix to the Text, the first on the "amiraus," or the "aumaçor
de Cordres," the second on the Navarrois. The latter ends with a
colophon containing the mention, unique in V and in the copy of
V, P9, of *Maistres Jehans* as the translator.

P9   Bibliothèque Nationale, French MS 906, fols. 250-
277. An indirect copy of MS V, written in north-
ern Lorraine in 1462. It preserves the appendices which we have
noticed in V, and also the mention of *Maistres Jehans.*

Br 3   Brussels, Bibliothèque Royale de Belgique, MS
12192-94. The manuscript was written in the third
quarter of the fifteenth century in the Burgundian possessions in
the Low Countries, perhaps in Brussels. The scribe's orthography
is mainly central in character but shows some Picard features. The
scribe replaced the prologue proper to Group III M with another,
in which no mention is made of Michel de Harnes or of Renaut de
Boulogne.

F   Florence, Biblioteca Medicea Laurenziana, Ash-
burnham MS 125, fols. 121-135 v°. F is illumin-
ated with miniatures and ornamented initials. It was written in
the north-eastern part of Picardy early in the fourteenth century.

P10   Bibliothèque Nationale, French MS 573, fols. 147-
161 v°. P10 in its text and in its ornamentation is
a direct copy of F. It was written in the mid-fifteenth century by
a scribe whose orthography shows some Picard influences.

P11 Bibliothèque Nationale, MS nouv. acq. fr. 10232, fols. 83-113 v°. Its *Turpin* was written towards the middle of the fifteenth century, probably in the northern region, though there are markedly few dialectal features. P11 is a rather independent copy of F. It makes no mention of Michel de Harnes or of Renaud de Boulogne in its prologue, and shows borrowings from the *Chronique des rois de France* of the Ménestrel d'Alphonse de Poitiers.

A2 Paris, Bibliothèque de l'Arsenal, MS 3516, fols. 284-290 v°. The manuscript was originally highly illuminated with miniatures and historiated initials but many of these have been removed. It was written in 1268, probably at Saint-Omer.

C1 Copenhagen, Royal Library, Old Royal Collection MS 487 in-folio, fols. 61-78. Written about 1300, probably at Corbie.

T Turin, Biblioteca Nazionale Universitaria, MS L. IV. 33, fols. 15 v°- 29 v°. The manuscript was badly damaged by the fire of 1904 but has been partially restored and much of the *Turpin* is legible. It is a copy of C1, written early in the fifteenth century in Artois or Western Hainaut.

B2 Bern, Bürgerbibliothek, MS 41, fols. 4-14 v°. The manuscript is ornamented with large initials in blue and red with filigree and marginal flourishes. It was written shortly after 1250 in the Île-de-France or in the neighboring region to the north or north-east.

C2 Copenhagen, Royal Library, Thott MS 571 in-folio. C2 is a manuscript of twenty-four folios containing only the Johannes *Turpin* and two genealogies of the French kings. It was written shortly after 1300 in Artois or western Hainaut.

A3 Paris, Bibliothèque de l'Arsenal, MS 2995. The manuscript, separated at some time in the eighteenth century from the present Arsenal MS 3152, contains thirty-three folios which are taken up with the *Turpin* and two genealogies of the French kings. There is a miniature at the head of the *Turpin;* the initials are colored and decorated with filigree and marginal flourishes. The manuscript was written in Picardy shortly after 1285.

S   Saint-Omer, Bibliothèque Municipale, MS 722, fols. 92-107. The manuscript is adorned with miniatures, now rather faded, and historiated initials. It was written shortly after 1300 not far from Saint-Omer.

Chapter II

The Classification of the Manuscripts

The manuscript tradition has preserved the Johannes translation in three distinct forms, which come before us in three groups of manuscripts. Group I is made up of the three manuscripts M, P1, L1. They have in common a Prologue which begins as follows: *Chi commenche l'istore que Turpins li archevesques de Rains fist du bon roi Charlemaine, comment il conquist Espaigne et delivra des paiens.*[1] Then comes the explanation that the translation is made in prose *pour ce que histoire traitie par rime samble menchongne,* followed by an appeal to heed the moral lessons which the Chronicle offers. The French text then renders Chapter I of the Latin Chronicle down to the first mention of Charlemagne (89, vii),[2] at which point it adds material descriptive of Charlemagne's early history transposed from the Latin, Chapter XX (179, i-xi). The passage as rearranged in our French *Turpin* reads to the following effect: After St. James suffered martyrdom in Jerusalem, his body was miraculously borne to Galicia which he had long before converted to Christianity by his preaching. But after his death the Christians abandoned their faith and fell into their old pagan ways until the time of Charlemagne (so far, this corresponds to the Latin, Chapter I; what follows is brought in from Chapter XX). Charlemagne, when a youth, had had to seek refuge in Toledo where the Emir Galaffre befriended him. In return, Charlemagne fought against Galaffre's enemy, Braimant, and slew him. Later Charlemagne conquered many lands and

---

[1] I give the text of M. In this manuscript but not in P1, L1 the Prologue proper to Group I is preceded by the first half of a different Prologue which will be noted later as peculiar to Group III M; see below, pp. 11 and 54.

[2] References to the Latin Chronicle are by page and line to the edition by C. Meredith Jones.

acquired great power. He regained the Holy Sepulchre for
Christendom and brought home to France some of the wood of
the Holy Cross. He honored many saints by enshrining them in
gold and silver, and built abbeys and churches far and wide *par
le monde.* He was Emperor of Rome, and reigned over
England . . . At this point, making the transition very neatly, the
translator resumes Chapter I of the Latin which tells how, when
Charlemagne had reached this summit of his power, he would
willingly have rested awhile but was summoned by St. James to
undertake the liberation of Spain. After this the French text,
with some adaptations, follows the Latin down to the death of
Charlemagne (Chapter XXXII; 235, xi). It omits Chapter
XXXIII, which tells of the miracle which befell Roland at Gra-
tianoplis and concludes with the supplementary chapter on the
finding of Turpin's grave near Vienne and his reburial "citra
Rodanum in urbem" (Appendice A, pp. 241-43).

Group II is made up of MSS P2, P3, P4, Br 1, M0. Its distin-
guishing feature is the juxtaposition with the *Turpin* of Pierre de
Beauvais's translation of the Latin *Descriptio,* the chronicle of
Charlemagne's legendary journey to Constantinople and Jeru-
salem. The French *Descriptio* is quite explicitly put here as a
preliminary to the *Pseudo-Turpin's* narrative of Charlemagne's
crusading wars in Spain. MS P4 has lost a number of gatherings,
and odd leaves in the remaining fragment. The whole of the
Turpin has been carried away and only a small part of the
Descriptio remains. MSS P2 and P3 are closely related copies
made from a common source in which the end of the *Descriptio*
and the beginning of the *Turpin* were lacking. Br 1 is a late,
fifteenth-century manuscript, much altered in forms and word-
ing, yet complete, so that we have to rely on it heavily for
identifying the place of Group II in the Johannes tradition. MS
M0 has the text of Pierre's *Descriptio* but no *Turpin.*

In MSS P2 and P3 we seem to have copies of an original
which contained the collected works of Pierre de Beauvais.
Before the Prologue to the *Descriptio* in these manuscripts
comes the explicit to Pierre's translation of the *Translatio et
Miracula Sancti Jacobi: Ci fine la tranlacion*[3] *monseigneur saint*

---

[3] I quote MS P2.

Jaque et si miracle que Calixtes li apostoles traita en latin por s'amor. Et Pierres par le commendement la contesse Yolent mist en romanz cest livre as .m. anz et .ii. cenz et .xii. de l'incarnacion Nostre Seigneur, ou regnement Phelipe le poissant vesque de Beauvais en qui cité cis livres, qui doit estre chiers tenuz, fu tranlatés de latin en romanz. The Prologue to the *Descriptio* names as the translator *Pierres,* with no identifying epithet. But it is undoubtedly the same *Pierres* who in the explicit just quoted says he made his translation of the Jacobean texts in the year 1212 in Beauvais, under the patronage of Countess Yolande and under the governance of its famous Count-Bishop, Philip of Dreux. There is no justification however for jumping to the conclusion that the same date and circumstances hold for the translation of the *Descriptio* which presents its own problem in this regard and will call for treatment below.

In his Prologue to the *Descriptio-Turpin,* Pierre tells us how appropriate the association of these two texts was. Though many people, he writes, were interested in the history of Charlemagne, few knew anything about *la voie qu'il fist outre mer.* So he translates this Latin chronicle into French, and puts it in its chronological place before the *Turpin . . . commant et par quel achoison Charles ala outre mer devant la voie d'Espagne.* The incipit announces the composite chronicle but seems to be careless of the order of the events as to which the Prologue is so explicit: *Cy commence l'istoire Charlemainne commant il conquist Espaigne et la sainte terre de promission en laquelle est Jherusalem, et aporta la sainte coronne de coy Dieu fu coronnés.* The translation of the *Descriptio* is an abridged version of the text published by G. Rauschen,[4] re-arranged here and there in a way which improves on the order of the Latin narrative. It ends with the distribution among various shrines in France by Charles the Bald of the relics brought home to Aix-la-Chapelle by Charlemagne. Its explicit reads as follows: *Cy fault l'istoire comment Charlemaine fu oultre mer,* and this is followed without a break by the incipit to the

---

[4] *Die Legende Karls des Grossen im 11. und 12. Jahrhundert,* Leipzig, 1890, pp. 94-125. The text of the *Descriptio* as it appears in the *Vita Karoli Magni,* the compilation sponsored by Frederic Barbarossa on the occasion of the canonisation of Charlemagne, is printed on pp. 45-66 by Rauschen. Castets has printed the text of the Montpellier manuscript in *RLR,* XXXVI (1892), pp. 417-474.

Turpin: Et aprés commence comment il conquist Espaigne si comme Turpins l'arcevesque traitta et ouÿ la verité.[5]

In the first chapter of the *Turpin* we find here, as in Group I, the passage transposed from the Latin, Chapter XX. The rest of the *Turpin* follows much as in Group I, ending with the reburial of the Archbishop inside the walls of Vienne.

Group III is represented by twenty-three manuscripts. Like Group II it contains the *Descriptio,* but reduced to a very brief summary and incorporated in Chapter I of the *Turpin.* Here again we find the passage in Chapter XX of the Latin transferred to Chapter I of the French text. Since the transposition is found in all our manuscripts, it must be looked upon as the work of the translator. We shall see later, when we make a close comparison of the French with the Latin text, that he made a number of such re-arrangements in the text of his original, quite obviously and quite effectively with a view to improving the Pseudo-Turpin's exposition of his subject matter. Except for MS Br 2, Group III falls into two sub-groups which differ mainly by their prologues. The first, comprising eight manuscripts, P5, P6, P7, A1, B1, L2, L3, O, has a prologue attributing the translation to the patronage of Count Renaud de Boulogne: ... *ci poez oïr*[6] *la verité d'Espaigne selonc le latin de l'estoire que li cuens Renauz de Boloigne fist par grant estuide cerchier et querre es livres a monseignor Saint Denise.* The second, made up of fourteen manuscripts, P8, V, P9, Br 3, C1, T, B2, C2, A3, S, F, P10, P11, A2, has an almost identical prologue but claims a different sponsorship as follows:[7]
... *ci poés oïr le verité d'Espaigne selonc le latin de l'estoire ke Mikius de Harnes fist par grant estude cerchier et querre es livres Renaut le conte de Bouloigne.* These contrasting assertions would suggest that in the two sub-groups, which I shall henceforth call III R and III M, we have two translations of a Latin *Turpin* which Count Renaud had found in Saint-Denis and which Michel de Harnes had later borrowed from Renaud's library. But III R and

---

[5] I quote both explicit and incipit from MS Br 1, the only manuscript in Group II to give the text at this point. The lost portion in MSS P2, P3 corresponds to Br 1 fol. 8 r°, 1. 31 - fol. 9 v°, 1. 15.

[6] I quote from the Prologue in MS P5.

[7] I quote from the Prologue in MS P8. MS Br 3 has its own prologue introducing the *Turpin* only in general terms as part of the "Chroniques de France." In MS P11, the prologue is shortened and omits all details as to sponsor and date.

III M, apart from their particular version of the *Descriptio,* contain essentially the same text of the *Turpin* which we find in Groups I and II. On the face of it, Michel de Harnes would seem to have done nothing more than engage a scribe to copy the translation of which Renaud is named as the patron. But this particular problem must wait, for we can see that its solution will depend in great part on a thorough collation of the manuscripts. As to this the most pressing question of priority and relationships concerns the presence and form within our groups of the *Descriptio,* Group I having only the *Turpin,* Group II having Pierre's *Descriptio* preceding the *Turpin* and Group III having a very abridged *Descriptio* inserted in Chapter I of the *Turpin.* Did the translator join the *Descriptio* to the *Turpin* or is this the work of later redactors? Do we have the original translation in the text of Group I, Group II or Group III?[8]

Let us look more closely at Chapter I of our French *Turpin.* The translator has combined here Chapters I and XX of his original to give in orderly sequence the outline of Charlemagne's life up to the moment when St. James calls upon him to undertake his last and most arduous enterprise, the conquest of Spain, which is the *Pseudo-Turpin's* theme and to which therefore this opening chapter serves as an appropriate introduction. Here, in columns to facilitate comparison, are the texts of the Latin *Turpin,* and those of our Groups I, II and III.[9] As we turn to them I would recall that in Group I we need have in mind as context for this Chapter I of the *Turpin* only the rest of the *Turpin* which follows it, in Group II the *Descriptio* which precedes it as well as the rest of the *Turpin* which follows it, in Group III an expanded Chapter I which belongs to the *Turpin* but which is adapted to include the *Descriptio.*

---

[8] It has been suggested that Group III with its version of the *Descriptio* represents the original Johannes translation of the *Turpin* and that Group I represents a late redaction of this from which, because of its recognized inauthenticity, the *Descriptio* element was removed. Cf. Mandach, *Geste de Charlemagne,* p. 141.

[9] MSS Br 3 and P11 are here in conformity with the other manuscripts of Group III.

Latin   MS M - representing Group I, fol. 102,b

89, v-x

eandem Galleciam praedicaverunt. Sed
ipsi Galleciani postea, peccatis suis
exigentibus, fidem postponentes usque
4 ad Karoli magni imperatoris Roman-
orum, Galliorum et Theutonitorum
ceterarumque gencium tempus perfidi
retro abierunt. Hic vero Karolus . . . 179,
8 i-xii: Quemadmodum Galaffrus, admir-
andus Toletae, illum in puericia exul-
atum adornavit habitu militari in pal-
acio Toleti, et quomodo idem Karolus
12 postea amore eiusdem Galaffri occidit
in bello Braimantum magnum et sup-
erbum regem Sarracenorum, Galaffri
inimicum, et qualiter diversas terras
16 ac urbes adquisivit (see variants) et
trino nomini subiugavit, et quomodo
abbacias multasque ecclesias per
mundum instituit, et quomodo mul-
20 torum sanctorum corpora et reliquia
a terra in auro et argento collocavit, et
qualiter Romae imperator fuit et dom-
inicum sepulcrum adiit, et qualiter lig-
24 num dominicum secum attulit (see
Chap. III, n. 3, below), unde multas
ecclesias dotavit, scribere nequeo.
89, ix-xviii: (Hic vero Karolus) post-
28 quam multis laboribus per multa
climata orbis diversa regna, Angliam
scilicet, Galliam, Theutonitam, Baioar-
iam, Lotharingiam, Burgundiam, Ytal-
32 iam, Britanniam ceterasque regiones
innumerasque urbes a mari usque ad
mare. . . adquisivit. . .gravi labore ac
tanto sudore fatigatus, ne amplius
36 bellum iniret, et ut requiem sibi daret,
proposuit. Statimque intuitus est in
celo

En icelle meisme Galisce preschierent
li apostle. Mais li Galatiien laissierent
puis par leur pechiés leur foi desci au
4 tans le bon roi Charlemaine. Cil Ch.
fu grant tans en sen enfance a Toul-
ette quant il fu de France escilliés, et
Galafres li amiraus de Toulette le fist
8 chevalier en son palais. Aprés se com-
bati Charles pour l'amour de lui a
Braimant le roi de Cesaire qui estoit
anemis a Galafre et l'ocist en bataille.
12 Mout de terre conquist par son grant
pooir et reconquist le sepulcre Nostre
Signeur et aporta le fust de le sainte
crois dont il departi a mout d'eglises
16 et mist mout de cors sains en or et en
argent, et mainte abeie et mainte
eglise fist par le monde. Il ot
l'empire de Romme et d'Engleterre,
20 Tiesceterre, Baiviere, Loheraine, Bour-
gongne, Lombardie, Bretaigne, et
pluiseurs autres contrees de l'une mer
desci a l'autre. Et puis aprés les griés
24 travaus et les grans paines des batailles
que il ot faites par le monde, il se
tourna a repos et ot pourpos que il
n'ostieroit mais.
28   En son proposement, esgarda une
nuit vers le chiel

MS Br 1 - representing Group II, fol. 9,b

En icelle meisme eglise (*sic*) prescher-
ent les apostres. Mais les Galiciens lais-
sairent puis leur foy jusques au temps
4 que Charles que Galaffres (*sic*) fist
chevalier en son palais a Toulette quant
il fu de France essilliez. Et se combaty
pour s'amour a Braymont ung fort roy
8 de paiens occist en bataille (*sic*). Ce
Charles eust puis Engleterre, Denn-
emarche, Baviere, Lorraine, Bourgon-
gne, Lombardie, Brethaingne, et plus-
12 ieurs autres terres de l'une mer jusques
a l'autre. Aprés les grans travaulx et
les grans paines des batailles qu'il avoit
faictes par le monde, et son voyage
16 d'oultre mer, se tourna a repos qui il
(*sic*) se reposeroit. Mais en son propos-
ement regarda une nuit vers le ciel

MS P5 - representing Group III, fol. 62

Icele meismes Galice prehecherent li
apostre. Mes li Galicien leisserent puis
lor foi par lor pechié desi au tens lo roi
4 Charle. Cestui Charle fist Galafres
chevalier en son palés a Tolete quant
il fu de France essilliez. Et puis se com-
bati Charles por s'amor a Braiman, un
8 fort roi de paiens, et ocist en bataille.
Aprés conquist mainte terre. Cist Char-
les fu empereres de Rome, rois de
France, et ot Engleterre, Danemarche,
12 et Tiescheterre, Baiviere, Loherroine,
Borgoigne, Lombardie, Bretaigne, et
plusors autres terres de l'une mer desi
a l'autre.
16   En cest grant pooir que Charles ert
si cremuz et si renomez par les batailles
dont il avait eue la victoire, en Sessoigne
et en autres terres, fu assise Jerusalem. . .
20 (The *Descriptio* follows; then, as Ch.
VI, fol. 65):
Emprés les granz poines et les granz
travauz que Charles avoit eu en Con-
24 stantinoble et en Jerusalem et en plus-
ors autres terres loing et pres, se torna
a repos et proposa qu'il n'ostoieroit
mes. En son proposement esgarda une
28 nuit vers le ciel

We note at once in the transposed passage that the mention made there of Charlemagne's journey to the East is retained in Group I (1.13) but omitted in Groups II (1.8) and III (1.8). The omission is obviously due to the fact that in Group II the journey to the East has just been narrated; and that in Group III it is about to be narrated. At 1.27 in Group I the transposed passage merges again into Chapter I of the Latin text by describing Charlemagne as weary of campaigning but aroused to new endeavour by the vision of St. James. Here, among the *griés travaus et grans paines* which Charlemagne has endured, Group II (1.15) and Group III (11.23-24) add a specific mention of the *voyage d'outre mer,* again because they narrate that story at length. In contrast to Group II and III, Group I shows close conformity with the Latin text as it is in Chapters I and XX: it has neither of the adaptations made in the text of the other groups to fit the *Descriptio* to the Turpin. If for a moment we consider Group I as a redaction of Group II or Group III, we shall have to think that the redactor removed the *Descriptio* from his French source, that he collated this source with a Latin text and carefully obliterated at 11.15 ff. and 11.23 ff. these adaptations. We shall have to think too that though his collation with the Latin text involved comparison between his French source and the two separate chapters, I and XX, of the Latin, he nevertheless left the transposed passage where it was in his French original. This is a possible but improbable hypothesis. The only reason such a redactor could have for removing the *Descriptio* from the "Chronicle of Charlemagne" which he was copying, would be his doubt as to the authenticity of the *Descriptio.* But this cannot have been his motive, for he found the mention of this episode in his trusted Latin *Turpin* and he left the reference to it in his opening chapter with its fundamental details concerning the conquest of the Holy Sepulchre and the relics of the Passion. The truth of the matter seems to be that Group I does not represent a Johannes *Turpin* from which the story told in the *Descriptio* has been excised, but rather that the mere mention of the journey to the East which we find in Group I has been elaborated and associated with the Johannes *Turpin* in different forms in Groups II and III.

If we now consider this view and look upon Group I for a moment as representing the original Johannes translation, we can see in the translator's Chapter I with its transposed passage a text ready-made for such innovations as we see in Groups II and III. In the rearranged Chapter I, the mention made thus early of Charlemagne's previous crusade in the Holy Land was an open invitation to one familiar with that story to link it as prelude to the *Turpin*, its chronological sequel in the Carolingian legend as this legend was generally known at the end of the twelfth century.[10] In making the transposition the translator obviously had no intention of expanding any of the mentions of Charlemagne's early exploits into a detailed narrative. He left the recapitulation of these exploits just as they were listed in his Latin original. The transposition itself is to be explained as a logical one, improving on the Pseudo-Turpin's inconsequent arrangement of his material by assembling in this introductory chapter the facts of Charlemagne's earlier biography dispersed in the Latin text over Chapters I and XX. The Emperor is thus presented to those about to listen to the *Turpin* as one who has grown to the stature required by what is to be his last and greatest undertaking. In its methodical re-ordering of the Latin text, the present passage is in conformity with a number of other rearrangements made by the translator with a view to improving the Pseudo-Turpin's exposition of his subject matter. These will be examined in Chapter III below; the point to be made here is that the transposition made in Chapter I of the French text is both logical and characteristic of the translator's method. The evidence so far adduced from Chapter I of our French *Turpin* suggests very strongly therefore that Group I represents the original translation which is characterized by some structural reorganization of the Pseudo-Turpin's subject matter, and that the reorganization which we see in Chapter I led to interpolated redactions of this original which are represented by Groups II and III.

Certain details in the text of Chapter I as it appears in Group III give support to this view. Chapter I in Group III looks like a redaction based on the text of Group II. Like Group II, Group III omits 11.13-19 in the text of Group I, that is above all the mention of the journey to the East. But then, as it repeats with Group II that Charlemagne had conquered many lands from sea to sea

[10] See Walpole, *Charlemagne and Roland*, p. 397.

and so attained great power and renown, it breaks off before the mention of the *voyage d'outre mer* which in Group II (1.15) is a reference to the story which this redaction has just told, and goes on to narrate, not the vision of St. James which follows in Groups II and I, but the journey to the East itself. After which (1.22), it returns to Chapter I as given in Group II (1.13), picks up the reference to the *voyage* (11.23-24), and makes this the point at which St. James appears to Charlemagne. We can see that the redactor of Group III brought the *Descriptio* into his *Turpin* between the sentence which ends and the one which begins in 1.13 of the text of Group II.

To this I may add a further point. The redactor of Group II had been careful to add his mention of the journey to the East among the achievements which preceded Charlemagne's crusade in Spain (1.15). With a similar insistence on chronological sequence, in a Carolingian tradition still in the formative stage and in which this sequence had not as yet been generally accepted, the redactor of Group III adds his mention of the Saxon Wars (1.18) as coming before the journey to the East. In doing this he seems quite clearly to be imitating the redactor of Group II.

Let us look at the texts again. In the transposed passage as we read it in Group I (11.13-18), the mention of Charlemagne's journey to the East (1) is followed by references to his honoring of saints by reburying them in shrines of gold and silver (2) and to his founding of abbeys and churches far and wide "par le monde" (3). Items (2) and (3) are lost in the texts of Groups II and III (1.8, 1.9). All these items are given in the Latin (11.17ff.) but in the Latin they occur in the reverse order (3), (2), (1). This seems to be another example on a minor scale of the translator's consistent purpose to improve on the arrangement of the material in his original. As he translated the passage and wrote of Charlemagne: *Mout de terre conquist par son grant pooir* he put here among the conquests that of *le sepulchre Nostre Seignor,* treating it as belonging to an order of things incommensurate with the honoring of saints and founding of churches. Further it would seem that the order in which these details are given in Group I would explain why in the other Groups the omission of item (1), which was deliberate, should have caused the loss of items (2) and (3), for it is more likely that items (2) and (3) would have been inadvertently

carried away if they had followed rather than preceded item (1).
And here again it must be added that it is not easy to understand
why, if the text of Group I is to be considered a redaction of that
of Group II or Group III made with the purpose of restoring the
latter to conformity with the Latin *Turpin*, the redactor should
have restored the passage but changed the order of its exposition.

It is interesting now to turn to the incipits to the Chronicle in
our various groups. Group I, with all three manuscripts in agree-
ment except for irrelevant details, reads: *Chi commenche l'istore
que Turpins li archevesques de Rains fist del bon roi Charlemaine
comment il conquist Espaigne et delivra des paiens.* Group II,
represented by P2, reads: *Cy commence l'istoire Charlemaine
commant il conquist Espaigne et la sainte terre de promission.*[11]
In Group III the incipits make no mention of the *Descriptio*.[12]
They describe the Chronicle as the Life of Charlemagne or as the
History of Charlemagne by Turpin or as the story of how Charle-
magne conquered Spain and Galicia. This corresponds to what is
said in the Prologue: . . . *comment (Charlemaine) conquist
Espaigne et Galice . . . ci poez oïr la verité d'Espaigne.* We note
that in Group II the only manuscript which mentions the journey
to the East, mentions it after the conquest of Spain. This suggests
that the inclusion of the Holy Land in Group II is an addition to
an original title which referred only to the conquest of Spain and
that the addition was made by a redactor who linked the *Descrip-
tio* to the *Turpin*. In Group III, where the *Descriptio* has been so
closely, and one may say so inconspicuously, integrated with the
Turpin, the original title announcing only the conquest of Spain is
left unchanged with this advantage, that the whole composite his-
tory of Charlemagne was thus brought under the authority of
Archbishop Turpin.

All this gives added weight to the hypothesis that we have the
form of the original translation in Group I. Such a conclusion

---

[11] P3 reads: *Ci après commence l'estoire Charlemeinne qui mult bien fait a oïr et a
entendre;* P4: *Ci après commence la vie C. si com il ala en Espaigne et delivra le
sepulcre monseigneur saint Jaque l'apostle de Galisse des paiens.* Br 1: *Ce livre cy
que nous trouvons en escript parle de France;* but on fol. 9 Br 1 has the explicit to
the *Descriptio* and the incipit to the *Turpin* as follows: *Cy fault l'istoire comment
Charlemaine fu oultre mer, et après commence comment il conquist Espaigne si
comme Turpins l'arcevesque traicta et ouÿ la verité.*

[12] There is one exception, MS B2, which has the following: *Ci commence toute la vie
Charlemaine translatee de latin en romanz puis qu'il vint a aler en Jerusalem et en
Espaigne et la conquist.*

would allow us moreover to understand better one of the statements which Pierre makes in the Prologue to his *Descriptio: Voirs est que plusors qui volentiers oient de Charle ne sevent nient de la voie qu'il fist outre mer, car li bon clerc qui les estoires ont en us ne cuident mie qu'il soit escrist en .iii. lieus en France fors a Ays la Chapele [et] a monseigneur Saint-Denis.* In writing of the good people who loved to hear about Charlemagne he must certainly have been thinking of the laymen to whom he was addressing himself, and he writes of them as of amateur historians familiar with a French *Turpin* but knowing nothing about the Latin *Descriptio.* His statement suggests that a French *Turpin,* probably our Johannes Turpin, was abroad and well-known when he wrote, and that he felt the need to supplement it with his own translation of the *Descriptio.* It does not suggest that the *Descriptio* and the *Turpin,* both out of reach of the layman because written in Latin, were simultaneously translated but rather that the already established popularity of the *Turpin* called forth the translation of the *Descriptio* as of a related part of the History of Charlemagne having a similar appeal.[13]

So we come to the conclusion that our manuscript groups show a developing tradition in the vernacular historiography of Charlemagne. First the Latin *Turpin* was translated into French to satisfy the growing interest of lay readers and audiences. Because of the immediate popularity of the French *Turpin,* Pierre de Beauvais translated the *Descriptio* as a natural and necessary adjunct to it. The *Descriptio* finds its appointed place in the text of our Group II, where for Pierre's quite explicit reasons it is joined as a preliminary chronicle to the *Turpin.* Finally, the long, composite chronicle thus formed was more closely unified by a second redactor who reduced the *Descriptio* to proportions at once more amenable to sophisticated laymen and more conformable to its subsidiary rôle in a chronicle attributed in its entirety to Archbishop Turpin who wrote this "History of Charlemagne" *tut si com il le vit et oït* (Prologue, MS P5).

---

[13] Pierre may have had in mind as he wrote this passage not only the Johannes *Turpin* which he was about to take into his compilation, but also the translation made by Nicolas of Senlis for Yolande, Countess of Saint-Pol, some time after she became Countess by her marriage to Hugh, Count of Saint-Pol, in 1198, and some time before the death of Hugh at Constantinople in 1202.

If these conclusions are sound, they will be borne out by the readings of the texts. The greater fidelity of the text of Group I to the Latin, relatively to Groups II and III, already visible in its rendering of Chapter I, should, if indeed its text is that of the original translation, show throughout the *Turpin Chronicle*. And if Group III is really a late redaction based on the text of Group II, then we should expect to find in it traces of its derivation from the particular texts of the *Descriptio* and the *Turpin* which we have in Group II. I give below first (pp. 20-23) some representative passages from the Latin *Turpin* according to the "C" manuscripts in Professor C. M. Jones's edition, from one unidentified member of which manuscript family the Johannes translation was made. With this as the best possible representative of the Latin original, I give for comparison the corresponding passages in Groups I, II and III. In a second series (pp. 24-27) I give some representative passages from the Latin *Descriptio* as printed by Rauschen, and with these set out for comparison the corresponding passages in Pierre's translation as it survives in Group II, and those in the summary version as it is given in Group III. In taking a single manuscript to represent each group (M for I, P2 for II, P5 for III), I give variants where they are relevant, but ignore them where they are not. I use italics at times to bring verbal concordances into relief.

1. Latin 179, i-iii	: Quemadmodum Galaffrus, *Admirandus Toletae, illum in puericia* exulatum adornavit habitu militari in palacio Toleti
Group I	: Cil Charlemaine fu grant tans *en sen enfance* (en son e. *lacking* P1) a Toulette quant il fu de France escilliés, et Galafres *li amiraus de Toulette* le fist chevalier en son palais.
Groups II, III	: Cestui Charle fist Galafres chevalier en son palés a Tolete quant il fu de France essilliez.

(Here, and in passages 2, 3, 4 and 5 below, Group II can be represented only by MS Br 1; the relevant parts of the text are lost in MSS P2, P3 and P4.)

2. Latin 179, v	: Galaffri inimicum
Group I	: qui estoit anemis a Galafre
Groups II, III	: qui . . . Galafre *lacking*

3. Latin 89, xi : Angliam scilicet, Galliam, Theutonicam, Baioariam . . . adquisivit

   Group I : Angleterre, Tiesceterre, Baviere . . .

   Group II : Engleterre, *Dennemarche,* Baviere . . .

   Group III : Engleterre, *Danemarche* et Tiescheterre, Baiviere . . . [14]

4. Latin 89, xviii : quendam caminum stellarum

   Group I : une voie d'estoiles

   Group II, III : un chemin d'estoiles en semblance de feu

5. Latin 99, i-iii : ad cuius sepulcrum arbor olivae divinitus florens maturis fructibus honestatur

   Group I : Un arbre qui est appellé oliviers (qu'on apele olivier P1) croist a sa tombe verdoiiens et chargiés de meur fruit

   Groups II, III : ungs arbres d'olives croist . . . [15]

6. Latin 99, xv-xvi : quasdam scilicet sine pugna, quasdam cum magno bello et maxima arte

   Group I : les unes par bataille, les autres sans bataille

   Groups II, III : les unes par miracles, les autres par bataille

---

[14] The presence of *Tiescheterre* in Group III in spite of its omission in Group II calls for an explanation. It must be remembered that the manuscripts which constitute Group II are late and very corrupt. I would say that Tiescheterre was lost to them during transmission by homoioteleuton with *Engleterre* and that Group III goes back to a representative of Pierre's redaction which included the name.

[15] The phrase *qui est appellé oliviers* in Group I is a strange one, for the olive hardly needed such a presentation to the audience of the Old French epic at the turn of the twelfth century. What we have here, it seems to me, is the translator's mistaken rendering of *divinitus*. The Pseudo-Turpin took this whole passage about the olive tree which grew on St. Torquatus's tomb and miraculously bore fruit on the saint's feast day in mid-May from the Martyrology of Ado (Migne, P.L., CXXIII, 267), where we may read as in the *Turpin: Nam eadem solempnitate apud praefatam Accitanam urbem, ad sepulcrum sancti Torquati arbor olivae divinitus florens maturis fructibus onustatur.* The adverb *divinitus,* "miraculously," which the Pseudo-Turpin borrowed has not passed with this meaning into our translation. *Divinitus* is formed on *divinus.* Already in the classical authors *divinus* had the meanings "divine" and "foreknowing" which were later in French made the separate semantic functions of *divin* and *devin* (cf. Horace: *imbrium divina avis imminentium, Carm.* III, 27, 10). It would appear that we have in Group I our translator's rendering of a phrase which he read as *arbor olive divinitus,* misconstruing *divinitus* as a p.p. masc. with *arbor,* having the meaning "known as," "called." A redactor, whom we may see here and in this series of readings revising the text of the Johannes *Turpin* omitted this inappropriate phrase.

7. Latin 123, xiii : Estultus comes lingonensis, filius comitis Odonis, cum tribus milibus virorum

Group I : Estous de Lengre, le fiu Oedon . . . (Estous . . . Oedon *lacking* L1)

Groups II, III : E. de L. (li fiu O. *lacking*)

8. Latin 141, xi-xiii : . . . et Aigolandus in medio illorum extitit. Quod ut Christiani viderunt, accinxerunt illos undique

Group I : et A. en mi iaus. Quant ce virent li Crestien, il les encloïrent

Groups II, III : et A . . . aus (Quant . . . Crestien *lacking*). Et nostre Crestien les acinstrent

9. Latin 141, xiv-xv : ex alia Arastagnus cum suo
Group I : d'autre part rois Arestans avec la soie (*lacking* L1)

Groups II, III : *lacking*

10. Latin 147, iv-vii : Quos ut vidit Karolus, mox retrusit illos in *oratorio* suo ne morerentur in bello (quam . . . plura *transposed in the translation*). Peracto bello

Group I : Quant il vit ce, il les fist aler en un sien *oratore* et commanda qu'il ne se meussent. Il vint a la bataille

Groups II, III : Quant il vit ce, il fu molt dolanz por la pitié de tanz preudomes. Il les commanda devant lui a venir, et conjura por s'amor qu'il alassent en une *chapele* qui dejoste ce liu ert, et qu'il l'atendissent iluec tant qu'il fust revenus de la bataille. Il i alerent et Charles vint a la bataille.

11. Latin 149, xviii-xix : Rotolandus tamen, vix impetrata a rege licencia, accessit ad gigantem bellaturus

Group I : Donc demanda R. congié au roi de combatre au paiien

Groups II, III : Donc vint R. au roy et demanda congié de . . .

12. Latin 151, xi-xii : Tunc Ferracutus, gladio amisso, percutere putans pugno clauso Rotolandum

Group I : Quant le paiien ot sen espee perdue il cuida ferir R. dou puing

Groups II, III : . . . perdue, *il corut Rolant seure* et le cuida ferir . . .

13. Latin 193, xv-xvi : (Karolus) qui erat hospitatus *cum proprio exercitu* in Valle Karoli

    Group I : qui avoit fait fichier ses tentes *a toute son ost* (a t. son ost *lacking* L1) ou val que on dist le Val Charle

    Groups II, III : a t. son ost *lacking*

14. Latin 199, iv-v : Ilico accepit propriis manibus pellem et carnem

    Group I : Dont prist Rollans sa char et sa piel (sa piel et sa char P1, L1)

    Groups II, III : et sa char *lacking*

15. Latin 203, xxv-205, i : invenit prius Karolus Rotolandum exanimatum iacentem, eversum

    Group I : Premierement trouva Charles Rollant gisant envers (envers *lacking* L1)

    Groups II, III : gisant envers *lacking*

16. Latin 205, xviii : quid faciam?

    Group I : que ferai je? (*lacking* P1)

    Groups II, III : que ferai je ore de toi?

17. Latin 215, x-xi (variant) : pro animarum eorum salute duodecim milia uncias argenteas, totidemque talenta aurea

    Group I : .xii. m. onches d'argent et autretant de besans d'or

    Groups II, III : .xii. mile onces d'or et autretant d'argent

18. Latin 219, xxi-xxiii : delictorum omnium suorum veniam . . . impetravi

    Group I : ont pardon de leur pechiés

    Groups II, III : sont sauvé

19. Latin 225, v-vii (variants) : Rethorica quae *convenienter placide* et recte docet loqui. Rethos graece dicitur facundus. Verbis enim facundum et *eloquentem* ars reddit.

    Group I : R. qui aprent *plaisamment* a parler et droit. R. dist otant comme plentius en parole *et bien parlans* (R. qui aprent de parler *pleisaument*. R. est dit atant que plentive en parole et *parlant* L1, R. qui ensaigne *plaisanment* a parler . . . parole et *parlans voir et discerneement* P1)

    Group II (Br 1; P2, P3 lack the chapter) : R. qui enseigne a parler droit. R. vault autant comme plaine parole

    Group III : R. qui enseigne a parler pleinement e droit. R. dit autretant come planteif en parole.

It is evident that we have in the *Turpin* of Group II a copy of
the *Turpin* of Group I, a copy moreover in which a number of
modifications were made, some of them clearly meant to emend
the original translation. One of the clearest cases of emendation
occurs in a passage which I have not quoted in the collation made
above, because it occurs in our Chapter X, the list of towns, a
chapter which has been omitted or lost in all the extant manu-
scripts belonging to Group II except Br 1, and in Br 1 the passage
is omitted.

Latin 95, xvii	:	Brachara metropolis
Group I	:	Brakaire Metropople M; B.
		Metropole L1; B. Metrope P1
Group III	:	B. mere des cités

The reading lost in the extant manuscripts of Group II was most
probably *B. mere des cites,* an emendation of an original *B.
metropole* in Group I in the form of a translation made for easier
understanding. The *Turpin* of Group II, then, is more than a copy
of the *Turpin* in Group I; it is a redaction, and the redactor who
brought the *Descriptio* into association with the *Turpin*, namely
Pierre, sought to improve the original Johannes *Turpin* as he
copied it.

This arouses our curiosity as to the relationship between Pierre's
Descriptio in Group II and the abridged version of this narrative
which we have in Group III. Pierre re-arranged here and there in
his translation the material of his Latin original. We note at once
that it is his re-ordered text which appears in Group III. Many
examples could be quoted; one will do. We read in the Latin
text[16] that the Patriarch of Jerusalem, in despair at the persecu-
tion suffered by the Christians in the Holy City, went to Constan-
tinople to get help from the Emperor Constantine. Constantine
could only deplore his own weakness; but as he and the Patriarch
talked together, they thought of Charlemagne, as famous in the
East as in the West. So they sent messengers to him, bearing let-
ters describing their predicament and urging him to come to their
aid. The letters, one from the Patriarch and one from Constantine,
are given in full. In the second, Constantine explains his action by
describing how Charlemagne appeared to him in a dream as the

---

[16] Rauschen, p. 104.

ruler ordained of God to protect the faithful against the unbelievers. Pierre changes all this to a more natural and dramatic sequence. He tells us how the Patriarch came in his distress to Constantine, who simply did not know what to do. It is now that Constantine has his dream in which an angel tells him to send for help to *Charle le Grant,* and shows him a vision of the Emperor of Rome imposing in physique, venerable in age and resplendent in bright armor, and it is in response to the angel's advice that Constantine forms with the Patriarch his plan to send an embassy to Charlemagne. Group III follows the order of events as given by Pierre.

To this and many other examples of its kind, may be added verbal concordances showing in their detail that the text in Group III is an abridgment of Pierre's translation of the *Descriptio*. I give examples of the relevant readings here, quoting the Latin from Rauschen's edition, Pierre from MS P2, the text of Group III from MS P5, again ignoring irrelevant variants.

1. Latin, p. 103, 1.23 : discordia exorta est maxima adeo, ut patriarcha

   Pierre : avint que la sainte terre de Jerusalem fu destruite de paiens et essillie et li Crestien ocis et enchainé (escaitivé P4, et e. *lacking* Br 1) et la sainte cité prise ou Nostre Sauverres sofri mort por nostre redempcion. Moult fu li sains lius traitiez laidement si que li patriarches (*Pierre has brought in some of these details from* p. 105, 11. 7-11)

   Group III : fu assise Jerusalem de paiens et li païs environ essilliez et li Crestien enchaitivé si que li p.

2. Latin, p. 103, 1.23 : ut patriarcha, vir perfectissime religionis, de civitate vi expulsus

   Pierre : si que li patriarches de Jerusalem qui Jehan avoit nom (*Pierre brings in the name "Jean" from* p. 104, 11. 19,22)

   Group III : si que li p. qui avoit non Jahan

3. Latin, p. 104, 1. 3 : lacramabiliter
   Pierre, Group III : complaignentiment

4. Latin, p. 104, 1. 4 : que et quanta sibi sint illata turpia
   Pierre, Group III : l'essill et la dolor de la terre

5. Latin, p. 104, 11.15ff : Johannes Neapolis sacerdos et David

	Jherosolimitane ecclesie archipresbyter. Sed J. Neapolitanus vir scilicet columbine simplicitatis et D. Jherosolimitanus homo quoque iustus et timoratus ac timens Deum in omnibus
Pierre	: Jehan de Naples, prestres et hom de grant simplece, li autres David de Jerusalem, justes hom et crement Dieu
Group III	: J. de N., hom de bone vie et de grant simplesce, li autres D. de J. justes hom et religieus
6. Latin, p. 106, 1. 30	: meditans quid agerem
Pierre	: commença a penser comment il porroit secorer la terre
Group III	: entra en pensee comment il p.s. la t.
7. Latin, p. 109, 11. 30-33	: (*Charles reaches Constantinople, goes on to defeat the Saracens in Palestine and then, though the Latin is not explicit here – cf. p. 118, 1. 3 – returns to Constantinople*) Tandem rex cum exercitu suo Constantinopolim pervenit. Postea vero fugatis paganis ad urbem que vexilla vivifice crucis Christique passionis, mortis ac resurrectionis retinet monimenta, letus et supplex advenit.
Pierre	: D'iluec erra tant li rois et s'ost qu'il vint en C. *et fu receuz de l'emperere (sic) a grant sollempnité et de tout l'empire.* Charles rois de France, empereres de Rome, se parti de Contentinoble quant il ot ses oz assamblees, et ala tant qu'i entra liez et joians en la terre de Jerusalem ou Nostre Sires jeuna la quarantaine et soffri mort por nos. Li rois et li empereres *esploita tant par la vertu de Dieu qu'il delivra toute la terre des paiens* en .v. mois et .iii. semaines, et rendi as Crestiens *le sepulcre Nostre Seignor,* et mist toute la terre en pais et conferma sainte eglise et (en P4) toutes ses droiture[s.] Quant Charle ot la terre a crestienté rendue il la laissa seure *et retorna s'en en Contentinoble.*
Group III	: (Charles) vint en C. *Li empereres le reçut molt honoreement atot son pooir et atot son empire et* li patriarches a grant joie et a grant solempnité. *Puis*

esploita tant par la volenté de Deu qu'il delivra tote la terre et le sepulcre Nostre Seignor. Aprés s'en vint en C.

8. Latin, p. 110, 11. 14-15 : animalia multi generis tam bestiarum quam volucrum

   Pierre : bestes de molt de manieres *et chiens* et oiseaus a merveilles

   Group III : bestes de diverses manieres *et chiens* et oiseaus

9. Pierre : (Nothing corresponding to what follows is in the Latin; cf. p. 118, 11. 1-2). Et quant il ot atorné si haut saintuaire ainsi com il convint, il prist congié a l'emper-eor et a toz bonement, et repaira s'en a toute s'ost

   Group III : Et quant il ot si grant saintuaire receu, dom iluec et en autres leus sont avenu maint miracle apert, puis s'en parti au congié de l'empereor et de toz et s'en vint

It is clear therefore that both the *Descriptio* and the *Turpin* in Group III derive from the texts of these two chronicles as we recognize them in the manuscripts of Group II. In only one of the manuscripts constituting Group II, M0, is the *Descriptio* unaccompanied by the *Turpin*. We can see that the separation was quite deliberately made in the text of M0. The redactor has omitted Pierre's Prologue explaining the interest of the *Descriptio* as prelude to the *Turpin;* he seems to have been interested in the *Descriptio* alone as a text similar in theme to the *Olympiade* and the *Histoire d'outremer* of William of Tyr and his continuators which form the major part of the volume he was compiling. MS P3 contains all of Pierre's works; MS P2 contains about half of them, so that these two manuscripts appear to be copies at some remove of an original in which Pierre's *oeuvre* had been assembled. Since the *Turpin* is closely joined to the *Descriptio* in both, we must conclude that this early compiler considered the French *Turpin* no less than the French *Descriptio* as one of Pierre's works. We have seen, however, that the *Turpin* in Group II is a copy of the *Turpin* in Group I; we must therefore conclude that Pierre, in order to make the compilation which he thought so appropriate, translated the *Descriptio* and copied the Johannes *Turpin*. This does not preclude the possibility that Pierre himself translated the *Turpin* some

time before he translated the *Descriptio*. But there is no proof at
all in what has been said above that he did. What our collation of
the texts of the *Turpin* and of the *Descriptio* in Groups I, II and
III does allow us to conclude surely at this point is that the original
Johannes translation rendered only the *Turpin*, that its popularity
gave Pierre the idea of translating the *Descriptio* and joining it to the
Turpin as its necessary complement, and that a second redactor
reduced this rather diffuse compilation to the more concise and
unified form which we have in Group III, a form in which, as the
more than twenty manuscripts comprising the group show,
obtained for this *Histoire de Charlemagne* its most widespread
popularity.

So much then is clear. But the relationships between the groups
show more complicated aspects than those which I have stressed in
order to give simplicity to my main argument. The three texts of
our *Turpin* are each represented by a manuscript tradition more or
less corrupted at the hands of various scribes and in which we find
the usual signs of contamination. It is understandable, therefore,
that in some passages, the correct text is to be found in Group II
or Group III, and here readers will want to know whether the
classification made above is proof against such seemingly contra-
dictory evidence. We must then proceed to a detailed classification
of all the manuscripts forming the Johannes tradition. And here,
perhaps, we shall find the solution to other problems, some of
which have been mentioned, some others of which must already
have crossed the reader's mind. There is no mention of the trans-
lator's name in the manuscripts of Group I. What then, given the
relationship of Group III to Groups II and I, of the importance to
be attributed to the ascription which we find in MS V of Group
III M: *Chi faut et finne li estoire Karlemainne que Maistres Jehans
tranlata* (fol. 13 v°, a)? What were the roles of Michel de Harnes
and Renaut de Boulogne, both named in their respective prologues
as sponsors of a translation of the Latin *Turpin*? Are we to trust
the assertion made in MS P4 of Group II that Pierre made his
translation of the *Descriptio* for his *bon seignour Williaume de
Caieu, qui volentiers ot verité*? What are we to make of the contra-
dictory statements as to the date of the translation, given as 1206
in III R, and, according to the manuscripts, as 1207, 1206, 1200 in
III M? If they refer, as the evidence so far adduced would suggest,
not to the original translation but to copies made of Pierre's redac-

tion for Renaud de Boulogne and Michel de Harnes, what then is the date of the original translation? Who was its patron? and who was its author? — questions as to which the manuscripts preserving the original translation are silent.

To turn our attention first to Group I. MS P1 is of the mid-thirteenth century, MS L1 is of the latter part of the thirteenth century, MS M belongs to the latter part of the fifteenth century. Yet the texts of P1 and L1 show much rehandling by the scribes while M is on the contrary quite conservative. A collation of the three manuscripts reveals two further matters of interest. First, a particular though not very significant affinity between M and P1, and secondly the fact that the scribe of M, who it will be remembered began by copying half of the Michel de Harnes prologue, consulted his Michel manuscript again at times and gave preference to its readings. Let us take these three matters in order and note first the freedom which MSS L1 and P1 show in their treatment of the original.

The scribe of L1 followed closely enough the general tenor of his original, but he constantly changes the wording, usually with an eye to abridgment, so that his readings are at variance in almost every line with the rest of the tradition. A few examples will be enough to show his peculiar quality (I refer by chapter and line to the text printed below):

1. VI, 11 M, P1   :   Le chemin des estoiles regarda Charles par pluiseurs nuis et commencha a (c. molt durement a P1) penser que ce pooit estre (p. senefier P1)

     L1   :   Cest chemin regarda Charle plusurs nuz e purpensa qe ceo pout estre

2. X, 1 M, P1   :   Les cités et les grans villes que il conquist adont en Galisce sont nommees par tes nons (par si fais n. P1) que vos orés chi

     L1   :   E les citeez e lé viles qe il conquist dona a Galice desquels ces sunt les nuns.

3. XLIV, 1 M, P1   :   Quant il orent couvert les ieux et les oreilles estoupees, si comme li rois l'ot commandé

     L1   :   E quant il urent ceo fet

The scribe of P1 on the other hand is expansive. First of all we may note that in contrast to the scribe of L1, our present scribe is wordy. Here are two examples:

1. Prol., 22 M, L1	:	et Turpins avoec lui qui tout mist en escript pour chou que la verité fust aprés iaus en memore.
P1	:	et T. avoc lui qui tot metoit en escrit les choses qui au roi et a chaus de l'ost avenoient et por che qu'il fust as vivans et as haus homes en mimoire et raconté qui a venir estoient et i presissent garde et lor sovenist des anchiseurs.
2. XXII, 19 M, L1	:	et rendoie le peuple fort et encoragiet (corajous L1) vers paiens.
P1	:	et r. le pule a foi et a creance e encorajoié de combatre envers les p.

In these and similar cases, he is trying to heighten the style of his original. This purpose is apparent throughout his copy. Thus, when Fernagu begins his conversation with Roland (XXXVI,3), he opens with the apostrophe: *Frere, saches tu por voir que je ne puis. . .*, and when, after Turpin had seen the vision of Roland's death, Baudouin came along with his tale of what happened, instead of the *ez vos Baudoin* of Johannes (LXII,19), the scribe of P1 writes: *ne demora pas l'esreure de demie leue que nos veismes B.*[17] Perhaps here the scribe changed the reading in his model because his chronicle was to be read silently and not publicly to an audience. The *Turpin* in XII, 14 says that the statue in Cadiz was as high as a crow can fly; our scribe more believably makes it *haute tant com on puet une petite piere geter.* In all this M and L1 read together and are faithful to the Latin text.

More striking, however, in this process of dramatization, is our scribe's particular insistence on what is for him the fact of Archbishop Turpin's having seen or heard of all that he narrates. Here are some examples:

1. LXIII, 29	:	. . .vesqui. Et jo Torpins qui la estoie oï che, qui tos tans estoie avoc le roi et le metoie tot en escrit et sans rime (!) sans mot de fauseté. Ains laissoie asés de l'estoire a metre en escrit par mal loisir (fol. 219 v°, col. 1).
LXVIII, 23	:	. . .a Paris. Et jo pris .ii. miens homes, si les envoiai aprés le roi a Paris, et lor priai qu'il me fesissent savoir tos les esremens

---

[17] The phrase "l'esreure de demi leue" meaning "a short while" is perhaps worth adding to *T.-L.,* III: i, 780, 11. 13-14. Cf. Chaucer's phrases: "They seten stille wel a furlong - wey," and "Thre mile-wey maken an houre."

Klm., car jo avoie tote se vie escrite, et le
voloie avoir de si en se fin, et tot ensi
com il li avenroit.(fol. 222, v°, col. 2).

This is taken up again later (LXX, 12):

. . .mut le costume des quatre deniers
doner.

Totes ces choses qui avenues estoient
a Charlemagne, manda il a Torpin
l'archevesque a Viane par les .ii. serjans
qu'il avoit envoié aprés a Paris, et T.
mist tot en l'estoire qu'il avoit fait
escrire. S'en fait meus a amer et a
croire que s'il ne s'en fust pas entremis,
et por ce li metoit . . . (fol. 223, col 1
and col. 2, this last mutilated).

At LXV, 4, where Johannes claims the authority of the Latin
to vouch for the miracle which stayed the sun until Charlemagne
had overtaken the Saracens, our scribe adds the words italicized in
the following: "ce tesmoigne le letre *et jo Torpins qui la fui et le
vi,* s'estut li soleil. . ."

Apart from his purpose to enhance the rhetorical effect, our
scribe's expansiveness is further characterized by his addition to
the Pseudo-Turpin's Chronicle of much material drawn from cur-
rent epic legends. The most important of these occurs at LXVI, 15
where he has a long interpolation describing the death of Aude as
narrated in the *Roman de Roncevaux* (fol. 220, col. 2): *Le cors
Rollant fist K. aporter a Blaives sor .ii. mules, son cor et s'espee
avoc lui. Iluec le fist sepelir mult honorablement et mettre en
biere, et Olivier dejoste lui desor une autre.*

*Charlemagne apela Basin le Borgegnon et Guion de Nevers et
Sanson son frere. Si les envoia por Gilain se sereur qui fu feme le
duc Milon, et puis le dona K. au conte Guenelon qui fist le traïson
des .XII. pers.*[18] *Chil troi qui chi vos ai només, Basins et Sanses
et Guis, monterent et alerent por le dame. Aprés envoia K. a
Viane por Girart et por Audain se niece. . .* The messengers, who
in this case are not named, bear with them Charlemagne's false

---

[18] Our scribe is carefully consistent in naming Charlemagne's sister, Roland's mother,
Gilain. When copying the chapter describing the leading barons in Charlemagne's
army (XXIII, 2-3), he omitted from the passage referring to Roland the words *nez
de Bertain la seror Charle.*

announcement of victory, of rewards to come, and of the wedding
ceremonies which he is preparing in Blaye for Roland and Aude.
Girart and Guiborc receive this message with great joy; but
Guiborc and Aude part company never to see each other again.
Girart sets out along with Bernart, Aymeri, Huon de Lon and
Guion de Moncenis, escorting Aude who is mounted on the mule
which Girart took from Clargis. Aude sees a vision, but a priest-
interpreter, Aude's *maistre,* Amangin, forbears to tell her what it
portends. At Charlemagne's command, there is great pretence of
joyful celebration in Blaye. The Emperor, accompanied by
Ogier, Richard d'Aspremont and Turpin, rides out to meet
Girart. And there, at their place of meeting, Charles tells the
disbelieving Aude his made-up story of Roland's and Oliver's
defection to the enemy, of their betrothals to the daughters of
King Floart and Baligant. Aude scorns the hand of the duke of
Normandy, whom Charles proposes to her as a husband. She is
sure Roland is dead. Turning secretively to Girart, Charles tells
him the true tale of what has happened, and then repeats it to Gil-
ain, who arrives at that moment with her escort of three knights.
Questioned anew by Aude, Charles at last avows all. Aude begs to
be taken to the bodies. She remains alone in the monastery, where
an angel comes down in answer to her prayer and tells her that her
death is imminent. A priest hears her confession and she dies in
Charles's arms. He and Girart are griefstricken; whereupon Turpin
intervenes with the following admonition and so brings the story
back to the Johannes text: *Quant jo Torpins oï ces plaintes et ces*
regrés qu'entre Girart et Charlemagne faisoient, jo ving a aus et si
lor dis qu'il faisoient trop mal quant il menoient tel doleur en
chose ou il ne pooient riens conquester, mais presissent les cors et
les fesissent enterrer. Adonc me respondi li rois que jo en fesisse
me volenté. Nos presismes les cors et les enterrasmes a molt grant
honor et le cor Rollant et s'espee mesisme a son chief en l'onor de
Deu et se proëce. Puis emporta on le cors qui gisoit a Saint Droon
a Blaives gesir a Saint Seurin a Bordiaus. Mais l'estoire ne dist pas
par qui il fu portés.
    Aprés l'enterrement de Rollant se departirent de Blaives et s'en
alerent a Belin. Et la fu enterrés Gondrebuef. . .
    There is another interesting interpolation at LXX, 17, where the
mention of Charles's return to Aix-la-Chapelle has prompted our

scribe to add a summary account of the Saxon wars as described in the *Chanson des Saines*.[19]   Unfortunately a corner of the folio has been torn off here, (fol. 223, col. 2) but enough of the text is left for us to learn the gist of the tale. Guitequin devastated Cologne and slew [Milon]. Charles summoned the Herupois to his aid, slew Guitequin, and gave [Sebille] to Baudouin, Roland's brother. Guitequin's sons then slew Baudouin, whereupon an avenging French army slew one of Guitequin's sons and baptised the other, leaving him to reign over the land. So Charles returned to Aix, "et par lui furent fait li baing d'aue. . ." (LXX, 18).

Our scribe's interest in the epic legends is shown also in other interpolated passages, less extensive than those just described, in which he adds to the Chronicle details drawn from other narratives of the same heroes and the same events. I quote the chief among them:

XXXI, 16 : Hernaus de Biaulande haoit sor tos homes Agolant. Car ja un jour qui passés estoit, li avoit tote vilonie faite, et por che metoit plus s'entente a lui encontrer, et tant le quist par le bataille ferant. . . (fol. 212 v°, col. 2)

L, 8 : Adont vint Rolant au roi et li dist que Guenes estoit molt bons chevaliers et molt sages hom, et bien feroit le message s'il li voloit envoier. Adonc l'apela Klm. et li envoia et manda Marsilion qu'il venist. . . (fol. 215 v°, col. 2).
Guenes s'apareilla et mist soi a le voie. Et molt avoit le cuer enflé envers Rollant de che qu'il avoit jugié le message sor lui. . . (fol. 216, col. 1).

LII, 1 : . . . en Franche, et demanda as barons et as prinches de se terre qui feroit l'ariere garde. Guenes sali avant et le juja sor Rollant et sor Olivier. Quant R. l'oï si en fu molt liés de l'onor que Guenes li faisoit.
       Quant Klm. vit jugié l'ariere garde sor Roll. son nevou si l'en anuia molt, et por le dotance li laissa . . . (fol. 216 v°, col. 1)

LII, 14 : Le bataille des .XX. mile paiens s'en vint durement vers nostre gent et fais-

[19]Cf. Gerard J. Brault's remarks on the text of Girart d'Amiens' *Charlemagne* in *ZrP, LXXVI*, 1960, p. 72.

oient outreement grant noise, et outre
lor volenté, car il pensoient nostre gent
a sorprendre.

Rollans oï le noise et apela un chev-
alier et le rova monter sor une montaigne
et prendre garde que c'estoit. Chil i
monta et vit venir les Sarrasins aprestés
de bataille, et vint a Rollant et li dist, et
si i estoit Olivers qui parloit a Rollant et
li disoit qu'il sonast son cor, si l'orroit
Klm. et retorneroit et il et tote l'ost car
il estoient traï. Et Rollans dist que no
feroit, car trop seroit grans hontes, n'en-
core n'estoit il ne plaiés ne navrés, ne
hom de se compaignie.

Paien qui molt se hastoient d'assem-
bler, vinrent et aprochierent les nostres
et lor bataille qui de .xx. mile . . . (fol.
216 v°, col. 1)

The last ministrations of Baudouin and Tierri to Roland as he
lies dying are much elaborated in P1. At one point, perhaps in an
outburst of enthusiasm for the truth such as urges him to make
Turpin intervene in the first person, he quotes Tierri directly:
Quant jo, Tierris, vit (sic) *si Rollant apressé a la mort* . . . (fol.
218 v°, col. 2). Roland pardons Ganelon all, and beseeches Tierri
to do likewise: *et me proia que jo jamais parole n'en meüsse dont
maltalens ne discorde peüst venir a cort, car ses oncles a mais meil-
lor mestier de lui garder qu'il n'ot onques mais* (fol. 218 v°, col 2).
Roland dies at length with the Lord's Prayer, in Latin, on his lips.

Many of the scribes who copied our *Turpin* show by the confu-
sion in their readings that they were very ignorant of geography;
they did not, for instance, know much about Arles or the Aly-
scamps. The scribe of P1 however seems to have known the town
and the cemetery very well:

LXVI, 2

l'un a Arle le Blanc que Gerbiers li fieus
Garin conquist sor le roi Annadas qu'il
baptisa el non de Gerin.[20] Chil Annadas,
aprés le bautesme fu merveilles prodom
et essaucha tote se vie sainte crestienté
et fist faire a Arle le Blanc cel chimentire
dont jo voil chi parler (fol. 220, col. 1).

---

[20] The details come from the Lorraine epics. Gerbiers is Girbert de Metz, son of Garin
le Lorrain. See the ed. of *Girbert* by Pauline Taylor.

*Below he adds (fol. 222 v°, col. 1; cf.
LXIX, 6):* por aus enterrer en Aleschans
dont Arle Blanc estoit pres a .iiii. leues.

Our scribe treats his original as freely by his omissions as by his
interpolations. He omits entirely chapters XLVI, XLVII, XLVIII,
that is, all that tells of the new dignities bestowed on Saint-James
of Compostella by Charles after his conquest of Spain. He has pre-
ferred not to interrupt his narrative here with Chapter XLIX which
gives the personal description of Charlemagne. Instead, he inserts
the rubric *Chi comenche l'estore de Renchevaus,* continues with
that story, and transposes Chapter XLIX to the end of the Chroni-
cle where it comes quite logically after the account of Charle-
magne's death and before the final chapter which describes that of
Turpin. It is presented with the scribe's characteristic insistence
that Turpin wrote it: *Torpins dist que Ch. estoit noirs de chev-
eus. . . Torpins dist que le rois K. portoit corone. . .* (fol. 228 v°).
P1 omits also, entirely or in part, most of the lessons pointing the
moral to some of the episodes in the Chronicle. I note them by
reference to chapter and line of the printed text: XVII, 7-10,
12-15; XVIII, 7-21; XXVIII, 10-14; XXX, 7-16; XXXII, 2-6, 15-
26; LIV, 21-25. In this last case, most of the long homily which
takes up Chapter LIV is given, but it is ascribed to Turpin: *Tor-
pins li archevesques dist que chi fait assavoir. . .* (fol. 217, col. 1).
At XXXIII, 17-21 the scribe goes a step further, making Turpin
deliver the homily, and in quite his own style: *Et jo Torpins li
respondi et si li dis: "Sire, il ne sont mie legier a savoir li jugement
Nostre Seigneur. Car se vos ne les menastes en la bataille por aus
eschaper de la mort et por lor vies respiter, por che n'ont il mie
laissié qu'il n'aient rechut corone de martire, et lor jor ne porent
il trespasser"* (fol. 213, col. 2). The last chapter describes the find-
ing of Turpin's body and is embellished to the greater glory of this
most admired chronicler: *(ses cors) fu trovés en char et en os en
terre, en son sarcus qui de marbre estoit polis entailliés a oeuvre
trifore, vestus de vestemens a vesque, si com il fu tesmoignié des
prodomes et des clers de le glise et des bones gens de religion qui le
virent et sorent chertainement, et le mistrent en mimoire come de
celui de qui on le devoit bien faire et qui maint bel servise et
mainte paine avoit faite et enduré por essauchier sainte crestienté a
l'onor Deu e mon seignor saint Jaqueme et le bon roi Charlemaigne
et saint Denise de Franche.*

It is clear then that the manuscript in Group I which best represents the original translation is M. Yet M is sometimes at fault; for example:

1. Latin 97, 1 (cf. X, 8)	:	Talavera quae est fructifera
M	:	T. qui n'est mie bien *grande*
P1, L1	:	T. qui n'estoit mie *plentieue*[21]
2. Latin 103, vi (cf. XII, 14)	:	*deorsum* latus et quadratus, desursum strictus
M	:	*dehors* et par en bas lee et quarree, deseure estroite
P1	:	lee *desos* et quarree, et estroit desus
L1	:	*dehors* lee et q., desus estrait
3. Latin 103, xvii (cf. XIII, 3)	:	per tres annos in illis horis commorans
P1, L1	:	en le demoree qu'il fist par .iii. ans
M	:	en le demoree *lacking*

In spite of their marked individuality therefore, P1 and L1 are important for the reconstruction of the text of the original translation.

A few readings suggest that M and P1 had a common source. They are as follows:

1. Latin 109, iii (cf. XV, 13)	:	Daemones vero eius corpus ibi eiecerant
L1	:	ileoc avoient deables la karoine portĕ
M	:	Illuec avoient (deables *lacking*) la carongne portĕe
P1	:	Iluec estoit la c. portĕe
2. Latin 109, iv-v (cf. XV, 14)	:	qui ... elemosynas ... retinent
L1	:	qe les almoines retiennent
M	:	... retiennent et reçoivent
P1	:	... retiennent et recolpent

There is little sense in M. It looks as if *recoupent* was added in our hypothetical common source and that the *reçoivent* of M is a corruption of it.

3. Latin 123, x-xiv (cf. XXIII, 5)	:	Oliverus ... filius Raineri comitis cum tribus milibus virorum bellatorum. Estultus, comes lingonensis, filius comitis Odonis, cum tribus milibus viroum, Arastagnus rex

---

[21] Why our translator added the negative is a problem. All our manuscripts have it. Perhaps he used a Latin text with abbreviations for *quae* (q^e) and *est* (ē) and misread the phrase as *quae est infructifera.*

As we saw above, p. 22 no. 7, Group I, which keeps the mention of Eudes, is thereby seen to be in the direct line of the translation whereas Groups II and III derive from Pierre who omitted it. Yet in Group I, L1 omits the sentence dealing with Estous and in M, P1 the sentence is given but is placed after *Arestans*. In Groups II and III the Latin order is preserved, though I must add that Br 1 and A1 omit the sentence about Estous. The passage with its repetition of *mile homes* lent itself to error by homoioteleuton. What we have to explain in M and P1 is a transposition common to them both. The omission in L1, as in Br 1 and A1, is due to the repetition of the phrase *a tot trois mile homes* attached both to Oliver and to Estous. The transposition in M, P1 seems readily explainable as being due to the same error, attributable here to the scribe of a manuscript from which they both derive, who, however, saw and rectified the omission after copying the sentence dealing with *Arestans*.

4. Latin, 177, 1, var. (cf. XLIX, 17)   : Parum panis comedebat
    L1   : Petyt mainjoyt de pain mes de char
                                              manjout bien
    M, P1   : Petit de pain mengoit et plus de char et
                                              ne mengoit que d'un mes

The phrase *et ne . . . mes* is an interpolation given only in M and P1. Some such statement was traditional, though Einhard (ed. Halphen, p. 71, ch. 24) says that Charlemagne kept to four dishes, not one.

5. Latin 219, xxii (cf. LXX, 6)   : In accordance with the Latin, our French
                                              Turpin has it that St. Denis assured
                                              Charles that subscribers to the abbey
                                              restoration fund were healed *gravioris
                                              sui vulneris, de leur greignurs pechiés*.
    L1   : *de lur greignurs mesfés sunt aquitee;*
    M, P1   : *seront quite de la quarte partie de leur
                                              pechiés (mesfais* P1*).*

6. Latin 225, ii (cf. LXXIII, 2)   : To what is said of dialectic, M and P1,
                                              but not L1, add: *Par ceste art puet on
                                              mout entendre des autres ars.*

7. Perhaps another example is to be found at 161, xi (cf. XL. 4). In his theological discussion with Fernagu, Roland, in order to prove that Christ ascended into heaven, used the comparisons of the millwheel falling and rising, of the bird flying down and up, of Fernagu himself walking downhill and up again, and lastly the setting and the rising of the sun. M and P1 use the sun twice, replacing the bird by the sun as follows:

    L1   : tant cum les oyseals volent en haut
                                              autretant descendent il en val
    M, P1   : tant comme le soleil monte otant
                                              descent il.

In group II, MSS P2, P3 have *oisiaus* in agreement with the Latin;
Br 1 omits the sentence. However, all the manuscripts in Group
III R except P7 which omits the passage, replace the bird with the
sun, and so do MSS P8 and C1 in Group III M. When these manu-
scripts make the comparison with the sun a second time they do
so, with the Latin, in very different terms, so that the scribes pro-
bably had no sense of needless or awkward repetition. The conclu-
sion to be drawn is that the setting and rising of the sun seemed to
a number of scribes to be a better proof of the Ascension than the
flying down and up of a bird. It is possible therefore that M and
P1 do not owe their common reading here to a common source.

However that may be, I think that the evidence in items 1-6
above, especially nos. 4, 5 and 6, assure us that M and P1 stem
from a common source, a lost manuscript intermediary between
them and the original text of the translation.

One further manuscript remains for consideration here, MS D,
the lost Dover manuscript. All that we know about it is provided
in its description given in John Wythefeld's catalogue of the manu-
scripts in the library of St. Martin's priory made in 1389. There,
the incipit to the *Turpin* and the first words on the probatory leaf,
in this case fol. 5, which are quoted, allow us to place D in our
Group I, but to go no further than this in its classification among
the Johannes manuscripts.

We may then, represent the relationship between the manu-
scripts composing Group I with the following stemma:

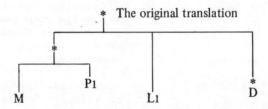

As we saw in the brief description of M in Chapter I, the scribe
who wrote M as Chapter LXX of the Chronicle of Baudouin
d'Avesnes, began by copying the prologue of a manuscript of the
type Group III M. Having reached the words *tut si com il le vit et
oï* (1.13) halfway through the prologue, he began again, starting a
new paragraph and copying from another manuscript the prologue

proper to Group I. The two prologues are not complementary; their transcription in sequence is a redundancy, the work of a scribe who had access to two redactions of the Johannes *Turpin* and who after some hesitation made his choice between them. There are a few passages in his transcription of the Chronicle which suggest that at times he used the rejected manuscript again.

1. Latin 177, iv (cf. XLIX, 22)	:	After *bibebat* M, but not P1 or L1, has the following interpolation: *Mout se delitoit a faire lire devant lui les histoires, les anchiennes giestes et les livres saint Augustin, ne nus ne lisoit devant lui l'espasse d'une heure de jour qu'il ne l'en rendist merite.*
Group II	:	Mout . . . Augustin (ne . . . merite *lacking*)
Group III	:	*(reads with M.)*

The passage is not in the Latin *Turpin.* From the reading in P1, L1, we may conclude that nothing similar was in the original translation. Judging by the readings in Group II, Pierre added the passage *Mout . . . Augustin.* The details which he brings in are traditional in the mediaeval historiography of Charlemagne. The source is Einhard's *Vita Karoli Magni,* where the context is the same as in our *Turpin: In cibu et potu temperans sed in potu temperantior . . . Inter caenandum aut aliquod acroama aut lectorum audiebat. Legebantur ei historiae et antiquorum res gestae. Delectabatur et libris sancti Augustini praecipue his qui De Civitate Dei praetitulati sunt* (ed. Halphen, c. 24).[22] The later redactor whose work survives in Group III, copying Pierre, added the jongleresque phrase about due reward for services rendered. It seems clear that M took the whole passage into his text from a manuscript belonging to Group III, no doubt from the manuscript of which he began by copying the Prologue.

2. Latin 213, xv-xvii (cf. LXVI, 21)	:	Sed et tubam postea alius in beati Severini basilicam aput Burdegalem indigne translatavit.

To this Johannes added the following sentence which is found in Groups I, II and III: *Mais l'istore ne dist mie par qui il i fu portés.* Groups II and III however extend the interpolation, and part of

---

[22] This passage, conflated with Einhard, c. 29. is found also in the *Vita Karoli Magni.* See Rauschen, p. 28.

this further addition is likewise in MS M. P2 : *Vous qui l'estoire oez, n'enquerez mie que l'espee devint, car Dieus ne vost mie qu'ele feust plus veue por ce qu'ele ert aornee des sains nons Nostre Seignor. Ne vost Dieus qu'ele fust trovee que desloiautez ne fust faite pour li avoir. Et qui vous en dira autre chose ne le creés mie* (*Ne vost . . . creés mie* lacking M).

Johannes's interpolation is a comment on *alius,* and expresses his regret that the *istore*, that is, his Latin *Turpin,* did not say who took Roland's horn from Blaye to Bordeaux. It was undoubtedly Pierre who brought in the cautionary elaboration *Vous qui . . . creés mie* which refers to the problematical fate of Durendal.[23] The whole interpolation passed on to Group III whence the scribe of M took with some discrimination what he wanted.

3. Latin, 233, iii-v (cf. LXXVIII, 4 ff.)   :   atque eadem die et hora qua visionem ego videram scilicet V Kalendas Februarii anno dominicae incarnacionis DCCC.XIIII, illum ab hac vita migratum fuisse

Group I, P1, L1   :   et en cel jor avoit Torpins veue la vision de le mort Karlemaine (de le m. K. *lacking* L1) en le quinte calende de fevrier. Tot droit au jor que Karlemaines trespassa estoient acompli (a cel jur esteient a. L1) .viii. cens ans et .xiiii. de l'incarnations Nostre Seigneur.

---

[23] The Song of Roland tells us that Charlemagne, on his return from Spain, put Roland's horn in the church of St. Seurin at Bordeaux (vv. 3684-87). But once Roland is dead, with the horn and Durendal drawn close to him, the poet is careless as to what happens to the sword. All he says is that Charlemagne gave it to Count Rabel in whose hands it is borne away into the final battle and out of our sight (vv. 3014 ff., vv. 3348 ff.). The *Guide du Pelerin* (ed. Vielliard, p. 78) likewise informs us that the horn is in St. Seurin, but is silent as to the destiny of Durendal. Mouskés seems better informed:

> Mais par tant qu'ele estoit si bonne
> L'en osterent puis li kannonne,
> Se l'envoiierent Carlemainne (vv. 9024-26)

But this is only one story among the many conflicting ones which remain to be gathered into a definitive treatment of the subject. Among the manuscripts of the Johannes tradition, Br 3 has the sage addition: *(char) Dieu et Charle le sceurent bien et fu perdue (ne ne vault mie Dieu . . .),* and MS P7 tells us surprisingly that the name *Durendal* was Hebrew: *Il avoit encore s'espee moult belle et bonne appeellee en ebreu Durendal* (fol. 55, 1.9).

M	:	et en cel jour et en celle heure meismes avoit Turpin veu la vision. Vrai est que au sextisme jour que Charle acoucha, il trespassa de cest siecle, recheue toute se droiture de sainte eglise en la quinte *(sic)* heure dou jour et en le quinte Kalende de fevrier. Tout droit a cel jour estoient accompli .lxxii. ans de son eage et .xlvii. de son regne et a .viii. c. ans et .xiiii. de l'i . . .
Group II	:	All three manuscripts have essentially the same reading as M, though the text is badly corrupted in Br 1.
Group III	:	Reads with Group II and M.

It is clear that P1 and L1 preserve more or less Johannes's text, and that elsewhere we have an interpolation made by Pierre, who added the details concerning Charlemagne's seven-day illness, his pious end, and the mention that he died in his seventy-second year, in the forty-seventh year of his reign. All these details were part of common knowledge among the clerics of Pierre's day. They knew of them from the historiographical tradition whose source was Einhard: *septimo postquam decubuit die, sacra communione percepta, decessit anno aetatis suae septuagesimo secundo et ex quo regnare coeperat quadragesimo septimo, V. Kal. feb., hora diei tertia* (ed. Halphen, c. 30).[24]

I do not think there can be any doubt that the scribe of M consulted at points 1, 2 and 3 above the Michel manuscript which he had read and rejected as the original from which to make his copy. The borrowed details are all topicalities which must have been of particular interest to him, to his patron and to his audience no less than they must have been to Pierre who had brought them for that reason into the Johannes tradition. For the rest, our scribe seems to have preferred to keep to his chosen source, the text of the French *Turpin* which he had obviously preferred as the most authentic one available.

Group II, the manuscript family preserving Pierre's *Descriptio* and the *Turpin* in sequence, is as we have seen made up of four manuscripts. These are the very fragmentary P4 of the mid-thirteenth century, P2 and P3 both of the late thirteenth century,

---

[24] This passage from Einhard was also borrowed by the author of the *Vita Karoli Magni;* see Rauschen, op. cit. p. 88, 11. 32 ff.

and Br 1 of the fifteenth. To these we must add Mo, of the early fifteenth century, which contains Pierre's *Descriptio* but here dissociated from the *Turpin*. The dissociation seems to have been made quite deliberately by the scribe. His incipit, which is introductory only to the *Descriptio,* reads: *Cy commence et s'ensieut l'istore du voiage que Charlemainne fist oultremer et dont vint et comment fu establi le Lendit.* The form of his explicit likewise excludes all thought of the *Turpin: Cy fine l'istore du voiage d'oultremer fait par le grand Charlemainne, et comme le Lendit vint a Paris.* It was no doubt with the same intent that he omitted the prologue in which Pierre explained why he brought the *Descriptio* and the *Turpin* together. The text in Mo seems in fact to be the work of a scribe compiling a codex of which the general theme was not Charlemagne or France, but rather the general history of Palestine: item 1, our *Descriptio;* item 2, the *Division des aages* (from Adam to the birth of Christ); item 3, the *Olympiade* (or *Les prises et conquestes de Jherusalem*); and finally item 4, a text of William of Tyre continued down to 1314.[25] Mo offers us a very free and somewhat abridged copy of Pierre's translation. P4, through the loss of an odd leaf and two whole gatherings lacks most of the *Descriptio* and all of the *Turpin.* Yet as far as it goes it gives us the oldest and best text we have of Pierre's *Descriptio;* it has too the particular interest that it contains in its prologue the unique mention of Guillaume de Cayeux as the sponsor of Pierre's translation, a statement which must be examined when the place of P4 in our classification has been made clear (see below, pp. 52 ff.). P2 and P3 prove at once upon examination to be very similar copies of a common and faulty model. They contain in their different miscellanies a number of identical articles, copies of works by Pierre de Beauvais: *L'oeuvre quotidienne, La translation et miracles de saint Jacques,* Pierre's *Descriptio* followed by our *Turpin, Le bestiaire.* At the juncture of the *Descriptio* with the *Turpin,* they show the same interruption of sense caused by the loss of the last part of the former and of the beginning of the latter, an interruption to which neither scribe paid any attention. Both copies are alike too in other notable omissions: our Chapter X containing the list of towns in Galicia and Spain supposedly captured by

---

[25] See my note on this manuscript in *RPh* VII, 1953-54, pp. 130-141 and the description in the supplement to this edition.

Charlemagne, our Chapters LXXI to LXXV giving the description
of the pictorial representation of the seven arts in Charlemagne's
palace at Aix, and a long passage beginning with *a cisel,* LXXVI, 5
and continuing to the end of Chapter LXXVII, here again a break
in the narrative which seems to have left both scribes unconcerned.
MS Br 1 is complete where P2 , P3 and P4 are deficient, but its text
offers a very degenerate copy of the *Descriptio* and the *Turpin.*
Pierre's composite chronicle indeed survives only in a very degraded
tradition. To make the best of it, we must establish the relationship
which exists among the manuscripts in which it survives.

Looking again at P2 and P3 , we find proof that neither is a copy
of the other, for there are aberrant variants in each where the
other has the traditional reading. I give a few examples chosen
from many; the references are to my edition of Pierre's *Descrip-
tio*[26] and, for the *Turpin,* to the text printed below. The follow-
ing readings show P2 to be independent of P3 :

1. *Descr.* VI, 13

    P3   :   choses que vos veez ci et qui ci sont
                                              amenees

    P2   :   que v. v. ci et *lacking; the phrase* que
                                              v. v. ci *does not occur elsewhere in the
                                              tradition; it is an addition made by the
                                                scribe of P3.*

2. *Turpin* XXXVIII, 2-3

    P2   :   Dieus, dist Rollanz, qui Adam sans
                                                semence d'autrui forma, fist nestre son
                                                fil de la Vierge sans semence d'autrui.
                                                Car

    P3   :   fist . . . autrui *lacking.*

The following readings show that P3 is not a copy of P2 :

1. *Descr.* II, 17

    P2   :   giete flambe sovent
    P3   :   giete toute flanbe s.

---

[26] Popper volume, 433 ff. When I made the collation at that time, the Clayette manu-
script, the present P3, had not been rediscovered, and I was using the copy of it made
by Mouchet for Lacurne de Sainte-Palaye. I may note here that the readings there
quoted hold for the Clayette manuscript except the one numbered II, 2 on p. 442
where the omission is due to Mouchet and not to the scribe of P3. In the present
work I have adopted different sigla for the manuscripts: P is here P2, C1 is P3, W is
P4, Br is Br 1.

The readings are interesting. Behind them undoubtedly lay the impf. indic. of *gieter.* The Latin (Rauschen, p. 107, 1.1) has *emittebat,* M0 has *getoit,* Br 1 *flamboioit* (the whole passage is lacking in P4). It seems certain that the model of P2 , P3 had *gietout,* the Western or Anglo-Norman form; apparently it was not recognized by our two late thirteenth-century scribes who dealt with the problem each in his own way.

2. *Turpin* XII, 13-16
P3 : une pierre . . . assise seur terre, desouz lee et quarree, deseure estroite et haute tant comme uns corbiaus puet voler haut, et siet seur ces piez
P2 : deseure . . . voler haut *lacking.*

We may be sure then that P2 and P3 are independent copies of a single model. This model is responsible for the many variant readings which P2 and P3 have in common. The aberrant character of these readings is shown below; for the *Descriptio* by comparing them with the text of P4 which at the given points is in agreement with the Latin text as represented by Rauschen's edition, and for the *Turpin* by comparison with Br 1 and the text printed below. I offer only a few examples and these not because further proof is needed that P2 and P3 derive from a common intermediary, but rather to characterize these copies and their model, and to facilitate comparison later with Br 1 and M0 .

I.   P2 and P3 show many cases of identical omission due to homoioteleuton. Such omissions can of course be easily made by any scribe and can occur coincidentally in manuscripts of different families. But the series of identical omissions which I exemplify here constitute fair evidence in the present argument.

1. *Descr.* I, 4
P4 : faisoit . . . cels qu'il sorpooit, tenir et garder ferme pais a sainte iglise, et toutes les gens qu'il pooit ataindre soumetoit il a sainte glise par force (cf. Rauschen, p. 103, 7-11).
P2, P3 : et toutes . . . sainte glise *lacking.*

2. *Turpin* XVIII, 9-10
P2, P3 : a la bataille . . . nos armes *lacking.*

3. *Turpin* XXII, 9-10
   P2, P3   :   qui . . . toz cels *lacking.*

These omissions leave the text glaringly corrupt, yet both scribes
were content to reproduce the model unchanged.

II.   Additions common to P2, P3 :

   1. *Turpin, LV, 23*
      P2, P3 *add after* cheval   :   et cest cop conduit li angle.

   2. *Turpin, LV, 27*
      P2, P3 *add after* a un seul cop
      entre les autres   :   Ilcel cop conduit Dieus.

III.   Inferior readings common to P2, P3 :

   1. *Descr.* III, 31   :   avec [lui n'] iroient
      P2, P3   :   avoic (avec P3) en iroient

The loss of the negative deprives the sentence of all meaning.
Rauschen (p. 108, 1.22) has *quicumque huius edicti mandata non
perageret.* Cf. Br 1 : *avec lui aler ne vouldroient;* M0 : *qui demor-
roient* (P4 lacks the passage).

   2. *Descr.* VIII, 15
      P4   :   este vous c'une si tres douce rousee
                                                 descendi
      P2, P3   :   Ez vos eue (hiaue P3) tres douce et (ou
                                                 P3) rousee d.

Rauschen (p. 113, 1. 27) reads: *ros celitus veniens.* The *eue* in P2,
P3 seems to be due to a reading in the model where *cune* had been
read as *euue.*

   3. *Turpin* XIX, 14 and 15
      P2, P3   :   .ix. somiers charchiez *lacking,* le disoit
                                                 lacking.

   4. *Turpin* XXXIV, 1
      P2, P3   :   Fernagu *lacking.*

   5. *Turpin* XII, 12-17   :   Sor la rive de cele mer est une pierre
                                                 enciene entailliee d'euvre sarrazine, asise
                                                 sor terre, desos lee et quarree, desus
                                                 estroite, et haute tant com uns corbeaus
                                                 porroit voler haut. Sor cele pierre est cele
                                                 ymage fete d'arain en la semblance d'un
                                                 home sor ses piez dreciee.

P2, P3 :   Seur la rive de celle mer est une pierre
faite d'arein en la samblance d'un home
d'oivre sarrazine, assise seur terre, desouz
lee et quaree, deseure estroite et haute
tant comme uns corbiaus puet voler haute
et siet seur ces piez (deseur . . . voler
haute *lacking* P2).

The confusion must be due to a jump, made by the scribe who wrote the model, from *pierre* in 1.12 to *pierre* in 1.15, and to his perception of his mistake when he reached *homme,* at which point, instead of rewriting the passage, he simply went on with the omitted words, allowing the description of the stone column *(pierre)* to apply to the statue surmounting the column *(ymage).* So he left in his text the silly phrase *une pierre faite d'arain.* Of such stuff are made the texts of our handsome manuscripts P2 and P3.

It is clear that the scribes of P2 and P3 copied their model with painstaking but unimaginative exactitude, even when what they read and copied made no sense. The two manuscripts are almost facsimiles of their model. Their division of the *Descriptio* into prologue and a single chapter, the *Turpin* into thirty-three chapters, is identical. Both scribes were equally unfamiliar with the geographical and personal names, and visibly tried to reproduce the forms in their original which reflect an ignorance equal to their own. Both write *Persis* for *Persans* (XIX, 3), a form which is however common in the epic poems; but for *Maiorgues* (XIX, 9), P2 writes *Mairiores,* P3 writes *Marciores. Agiens* (Agen) at XIX, 11 becomes *Engiens* in P2, *Angiens* in P3, and at XXIII, 12 both make Angelier *dus d'Aquilaine.* Yet we find in these two manuscripts at times the correct reading lost to all other manuscripts in the Johannes tradition. So at XVII, 12 both read *foillirent* corresponding to the Latin *fronduerunt* (111, xviii), while the other manuscripts read *florirent,* perhaps to be regarded as a *lectio facilior.* Of the two, P2 is slightly the better manuscript. P3 occasionally drops, adds, or changes a word or phrase, whereas the scribe of P2 keeps with more consistency to the letter of the text he was copying.

MS P4 shows no particular affinity to P2, P3. As we have seen, it does not share their variant readings in examples I, 1 and III, 2 on pp. 44 and 45 above. This is the case throughout the fragment of the *Descriptio* preserved in P4, of which the text in comparison with that of P2 and P3 proves to be much the truer representative of Pierre's translation. However, it too has its faults. The most striking occurs at *Descr.* IX, 23 where P4, instead of recording that the flowers were *muees en manne* (cf. Rauschen 115, 24, *conversi sunt in manna*) reads *muees en mainte maniere;* this in spite of the fact that the scribe found no difficulty with the word *manne* in 11.25 and 26. The reading in P4 seems to be due first to a scribe who read *manne* in his model as *mainte,* and then to a second scribe who emended the incomplete sentence by adding *maniere.* I think this more probable than that a single scribe was responsible both for the error and the emendation, for, if a scribe had hesitated over an obscure *manne,* the occurrences of the word in the text immediately following would have cleared up his difficulty. He must have written what he saw unthinkingly, leaving it to a later copyist to make some sense of the nonsense handed on to him. At II, 3 P4 reads *Sires* against all the other manuscripts which have *Sauverres.* At VI, 37 *(il li otroia bonement. Donc retornerent andui)* P4 omits *Donc retornerent.* The omission leaves the passage meaningless; it is obviously due to homoioteleuton which caused the scribe to pass unawares from the one *-ent* to the other. P4 then is as far as it goes, in respect to P2 and P3, an independent and more faithful copy of Pierre's text, removed from the original by at least one intermediary.

Comparing Br 1 with P2, P3 at the points where the latter two manuscripts have variants in common, we find that Br 1 almost invariably has the correct text, though often in corrupt form, and so shows itself independent of them. This is the case for example in all the readings set forth above on pp. 42-46. Elsewhere, however, there are two exceptions.

1. At *Descr.* I, 2, Br 1 along with P2 and P3, but against P4 and Mo, omits the word *Charles,* the necessary antecedent to the relative pronoun *qui:*

P2	: Mais qui s'ert donez
P3	: Mes qui set donnez
P4	: Mais Charles qui s'ert donnés
Br 1	: Mais qui cest donné
Mo	: Maiz Charlemaine qui s'estoit donné

The Latin reads (Rauschen, 103, 7): *Sed ipse vir illustris . . . deditus erat.* Whatever caused the loss of the word *Charles* - confusion perhaps of an abbreviation of *Charles* in the form of *k* with a following *ki* - it is not acceptable to attribute the error in P2, P3 on the one hand and in Br 1 on the other to a coincidence.

2. The other case is at *Turpin* VII, 4 where the Latin text reads as follows:

91, viii	:	Ego sum . . . Jacobus apostolus, Christi alumpnus, filius Zebedaei
Turpin		
VII, 4	:	Jaques li apostres, norriçons Deu, filz Zebedee
P2, P3	:	J. li a. Nostre Seigneur des .ii. fiux Z.
Br 1	:	J. li a. nourreçons des filz Z.

The *des .ii. fiux* of P2 , P3 and the *des filz* of Br 1 are errors arising probably from an earlier scribe's misreading of *deu* as *de .ii.* So we have to posit as common source for P2 , P3 on the one hand and for Br 1 on the other, a manuscript which probably read here: *J. li apostres norreçons de .ii. filz Z.* These readings 1 and 2 oblige us to assign as ancestor to Br 1 a copy of Pierre's *Descriptio-Turpin* which in another line of descent underwent the changes which culminated in the text of P2 and P3 . This copy was on the whole a good one, for though it suffered debasement in its later transmission, it handed down to Br 1 a text free of the blemishes inherited by P2 , P3 from their common model, and superior at some points to what we have in P4 . Thus Br 1 reads correctly where P4 was shown to be in error above on p. 47. Br 1 , then, in textual detail and in the fact that it is complete where P2 , P3 and P4 are deficient, has its uses; but it is a text which has deviated far from the original in the hands of unintelligent scribes who modernized the language and seem not to have understood or bothered to understand much of what they were copying.

Mo gives us a text of Pierre's *Descriptio* so changed in its wording that proof is needed that it is indeed a representative of that work. I have dealt with this in *RPh* VII, 1953-54, p. 133. As to its place in our tradition, we may note first that Mo has none of the variants which characterize P4 , nor, except in one case, does it share those which are otherwise peculiar to P2 , P3 . This point of resemblance with P2 and P3 calls for scrutiny. The reading is at *Descr.* II, 10 ff., a passage which Pierre has transposed to this context from its place in the Latin (Rauschen, p. 106, 11. 30 ff.). As Constantine wonders how he may succour the Christians of Jerusalem, a youth appears to him in a vision and tells him to turn to Charlemagne for help: *Pren en aide Charle le Grant . . . ,* and then shows him in another vision *quendam militem ocreatum et loricatum.* This phrase appears in Br 1 (the passage is *lacking* in P4) as: *Adonc lui monstra la semblance d'un chevalier armé.* But P2 and P3 read . . . *li monstra la forme Charle en semblance d'un ch. a.,* and Mo has the same interpolation: *forme Charle en.* I have no doubt that Br 1 has Pierre's text and that the *forme Charle* is an addition in P2, P3, Mo. But I would also say that the agreement here between Mo and on the other hand, P2 and P3 is coincidental. The youth in the vision knew very well that Constantine and our-selves would know who the knight was; but behind Mo, P2 and P3 we may discern scribes who wanted to tell us. Their interpolation, I would say, represents not a common source but a common mentality.

Br 1 and Mo have, as we have seen, diverged widely from Pierre's original text. The comparison of these two manuscripts throughout the *Descriptio* gives the impression that the scribe of Br 1 was struggling rather helplessly with a poor model while the scribe of Mo was quite purposefully adapting a good one. Let me give one illustration:

Descr. IV, 6-7. *Charles and his army on their way to Constantinople enter the forest from which they will emerge only under the miraculous guidance of a bird.*

P2, P3	: Mais ne dit mie l'estoire (l'estoire *lacking* P2) en quel assens il *("le bois")* ert ne combien loin ne combien pres de Con-stantinoble. Li rois entra en cest bois . . .
Br 1	: Mais l'istoire ne dist mie en quel lieu il estoit ne combien prez le Roy estoit. Et entra ou bois
Mo	: Maiz pas ne dit l'istore combien ce bost estoit pres ou loing de C. Le Roy entra

Yet among all the divergences which make Br 1 and Mo look like completely independent representatives of Pierre's original text, they have in common two readings which conflict with the Latin and with the readings in P2 and P3.

1. The first passage occurs in the description of a miracle wrought by the holy nail newly found in Constantinople.

Rauschen, *op. cit.,* p. 117, 11.12-15	: At multis praetermissis non est reticen-dum, quod factum est de quodam puero qui aridam manum sinistram et totum latus aridum a ventre matris habebat.
P2, P3, X, 14	: Entre les autres miracles dont Nostre Sires fist tant ileques par sa grace, avint qu'il ot .i. home qui le bras senestre et la

Br 1   : main dusc'au coude et le costé tout avoit sechié des qu'il fu nez

: ... avint que en la cité un home avoit qui sa main senestre avec le queute *et le pié* estoient si secq des qu'il fu nez

Mo   : Entre les autres malades y en fu .i. garis qui des qu'il fu né avoit le bras senestre *et li pié* si secs

The tale goes on to tell how, as the nail was taken from the shrine in which it had lain so long unknown, the man felt as if a nail were being drawn from his hand *and foot,* and a lance from his side. In the readings quoted above from the Latin text and from P2, P3, there is no mention of a withered foot; but the healing of the foot is told later in all our texts, Latin and French. So it is the addition in Br 1 and Mo of *et le pié* at the beginning of the story, which is interesting. Is the reading in Br 1 and Mo due to an independent impulse on the part of each scribe to mention *pié* in the sickness as it is mentioned in the healing? Or are we to attribute it to the intervention of an earlier scribe from whose copy both Br 1 and Mo derive?

2. The second passage occurs in the *Descriptio,* where Charlemagne, having made many conquests and conferred many benefactions on the Church, achieved the fame which led the Romans to make him Emperor.

Rauschen, p. 103, 11.16-19   : *Proinde postquam* tanti tamque famosi viri per totum fere orbem terrarum fidei probitatisve fama transvolvavit, Romani magno terrore perterriti potentissimum Romanum imperium ... ipsi prescripserunt.

P2, P3, P4, I, 8   : *Si tost comme* la renommee de sa proëce et de sa grant bonté espandi par les terres, *li Romain* s'espoënterent (R. qui espoenté furent de lui, le firent empereur

Br 1   : ... *si comme toute* la renomee de sa proësce et de sa bonté s'espandirent autres *(sic)* par les terres. *Et li Roumains* qui espoenté furent de lui, le firent empereur

Mo   : ... *tant que* la renomee de son bien et de ses proësces s'espandi par toutes teres. *Les Romains* le firent empereur

P2, P3 and P4 correctly render the Latin, whereas Br 1 and Mo show the same error: they have lost *tost,* given the clause beginning *si comme* Br 1, *tant que* Mo, a consecutive instead of a temporal meaning, linked it with the preceding verbs and begun a new sentence with *Et li Roumains* Br 1, *Les Romains* Mo. They would seem therefore to go back to a common source which read *si tost que* or *si tost comme.*[27]

---

[27] Br 1 uses *si comme* with consecutive force again at II, 4: *Moult fu ly sains lieux traitiés laidement, si comme li patriarche ... s'en ysy ...* Cf. G. Tilander. "Pourquoi vieux français *(aus)* si com, *(au)*tant com, tel com sont-ils devenus *(aus)*si que, au*(tant)*que, tel que en français moderne?" *Stud. mod. Språkv.* XVI (1946), 31-56, especially section ix, pp. 52-53.

I find no other readings in Br 1 and Mo which would afford further grounds for thinking that behind these two manuscripts lies a lost intermediary which was a common source for them. It is quite possible that evidence to such effect has been buried under alterations made in the transmission of these texts by liberty-taking scribes. As things are, my own opinion is that, while we cannot take the two passages examined as affording conclusive evidence of the derivation in question, yet we cannot dismiss this evidence as of no effect. Tentatively therefore I place Br 1 and Mo in our developing stemma of the manuscript tradition as derivatives of a common source.

This hypothesis brings us into difficulty. We have seen that two readings common to P2, P3 on the one hand and to Br 1 on the other, show a kinship which has obliged us to posit for them a common source. The first of these (see p. 47 above) showed the omission in P2, P3 and Br 1 of the name *Charle* as antecedent to *qui* in the sentence at *Descr.* I, 2. Mo has the correct reading here, and this disagreement with Br 1 seems incompatible with the fact just established that Br 1 and Mo derive from a common source. I think that the difficulty can be resolved. We must remember that Mo enters into our collation for the *Descriptio* alone. The seeming incompatibility to which I have drawn attention arises then from the single reading at *Descr.* I, 2. The omission in P2, P3 and Br 1 of the word *Charles* destroys the syntax of the sentence. We have seen that nonchalance in this regard is characteristic of the scribes of P2, P3 and Br 1. But such carelessness is not true of the scribe of Mo. I think that the model which served for Mo, confronted with the broken syntax of the sentence, inserted *Charles* as the obvious correction.

This does not exhaust the list of manuscripts representative of Group II. At *Turpin* VII, 4 we saw above on p. 48 that Group III has the correct reading which is lost in Group II. A similar case occurs at *Descr.* X, 8 where all the manuscripts of Group II are in error while Group III has the correct reading:

Descr., Rauschen, p. 116, 11.21-24	:	trecenti namque et unus curati sunt homines . . . iste unus viginti annos in infirmitate habens
Group II	:	furent sané en cele eure par la cité .iii. cens malade. Et .i. hom qui
Group III, IV, 15	:	furent sané .ccc. malades et un.

Here P2, P3, Br 1 and Mo (P4 does not have the passage) have lost the *et un* by haplology with the *Et un* which begins the next sentence – and the next miracle. The text used by our second redactor from which Br 2 and all the manuscripts in III R and III M derive must be considered a lost representative of Group II, a translation of the *Descriptio? – a tant cerkié es livres mon seignor* and Mo. It is perfectly understandable that the *Descriptio-Turpin* of Group III, which is to be dated in or just before 1206, and which was no doubt adapted from Pierre's composite chronicle soon after he had made it, should derive from a copy superior to any of those which survive in Group II. The redactor's model itself was no doubt a copy, for it is not likely that he had Pierre's own text at his disposal. So we must include the redactor's model as an independent member of our Group II, and draw up the stemma of this family of manuscripts as follows:

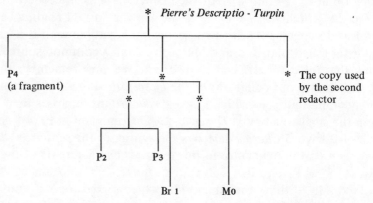

What now of the unique reading in the prologue of P4 which declares that Guillaume de Cayeux was the sponsor of Pierre's translation of the *Descriptio? – a tant cerkié es livres mon seignor Saint Denis Pierres qu'il a pour l'amour son bon seignour Williaume de Caieu qui volentiers ot verité mis de latin en romans comment et par quele ochoison Charlemaine ala outremer devant le voie d'Espaigne.* In *Romania* XXI, 1892, pp. 263-64, Gaston Paris accepted the assertion as Pierre's own, adding that Pierre must have called Guillaume "son bon seignour" only out of deference. Guillaume de Cayeux, like Hughes de Saint-Pol, Renaud de Boulogne, Michel de Harnes, Baudouin de Hainaut, Robert de Bethune, Garin Fitz Gerold, was one of the many barons of the

day whose interest in the history of Charlemagne and whose
patronage of those who made it available in the vulgar tongue,
were but aspects of their vigorous participation in the history –
making of their own times. Guillaume was a gentleman of Pon-
thieu, a vassal and close friend of Richard Lion Heart whose
companion-at-arms he had been on the third crusade. After the
death of Richard, he had won the equal confidence of King John,
to whose cause he remained faithful, eventually fighting on his side
at Bouvines where he was taken prisoner. This allegiance could
not have endeared him to the supporters of Philip Augustus,
among whom none was more staunch and active than the
warrior – bishop of Beauvais, the king's cousin, Philippe de Dreux,
who for so long was patron of Pierre de Beauvais. He had always
been the arch enemy of Richard of England, and he and Guillaume
de Cayeux were foes on the battlefield of Bouvines. The assertion
made in the prologue of P4, to the effect that Guillaume de
Cayeux was patron of Pierre's translation of the *Descriptio*, seems
then surprising on the face of it, for, if authentic, it would mean
that momentarily Pierre had found favor in a house that could
only have been inimical to the one which had constantly
befriended him. There is no sign in the biographical details we
know of Pierre that such a disruption of his quiet existence in
Beauvais ever occurred. The assertion does not then look trust-
worthy. Looking now at the evidence of the manuscript tradition,
we see that P4 is indeed the oldest of the extant copies of Pierre's
text, and although this is never in itself a guarantee of greater
accuracy, P4 proves to be, as far as it goes, the most faithful
among existing copies. Against it on this matter is ranged the evi-
dence of P2, P3, Br 1, which make no mention of a patron. P2
and P3 read simply: *a tant cerchié es livres monseigneur Saint
Denise Pierres qu'il a mis de latin en romans. . .* The scribe of Br 1,
in difficulty as he so often is, writes: *a tant cerchié es l. m. S. D.
par quoy il a mis de latin en françois.* Behind *par quoy* we may
with willing indulgence see the *Pierres qu'* of the tradition. P2,
P3 and Br 1 stem, as we have seen, from a common source and
they are the end products in a tradition of rather slavish and unin-
telligent copying. We must, I think, judge that their silence with
regard to Guillaume is due to the fact that their common source
did not mention him. The problem becomes qualitative therefore

rather than quantitative, one of deciding whether there was an omission in that source or an interpolation in P4. I think the latter alternative more probable. It is more likely that an interested scribe made a false claim to honor Guillaume than that a rival scribe denied a just claim by merely leaving it out of his copy. I would conclude therefore that Guillaume de Cayeux did no more than sponsor a copy of Pierre's *Descriptio-Turpin,* a copy which must have been made during Guillaume's lifetime in the first third of the thirteenth century and which served as model for the scribe of P4.

For the rest, our best surviving text of Pierre's composite chronicle lies in MS P2 which must however be supplemented by Br 1 and Mo where it is incomplete. There is little to choose between P2 and P3 which are, as it were, twin brothers and almost indistinguishable. P4 can be a useful corrective to them for that part of the *Descriptio* which is all that it preserves in its present mutilated state. Br 1 and Mo remain useful in spite of the rejuvenation and adaptation which they have undergone in transmission. They give us substantially the complete text of Pierre's *Descriptio,* Br 1 that also of the *Turpin* in Pierre's revised form. They can be taken at times as correctives to each other, and also to the more occasional lapses of P2 and P3. Behind the manuscripts of Group III lies another, independent copy of Pierre's *Descriptio-Turpin,* so that the joint testimony of these manuscripts has its part to play in the restoration of Pierre's text and, through this, of the original Johannes *Turpin.*

We come now to Group III with its summary version of the *Descriptio* grafted into Chapter I of the *Turpin.* There are twenty-three extant manuscripts in the group. As we have seen, they divide mainly into the two sub-groups which I have designated III R and III M according as they name in their prologues Renaud de Boulogne or Michel de Harnes as the patron of the translation. The classification is not quite so simple in the case of three manuscripts of Group III. Br 3 and P11 have each in its own way a shortened and reworded prologue making no mention of Renaud or of Michel. Their place in III R or III M has to be decided in accordance with the evidence afforded by their readings. Br 2 offers our Johannes *Turpin* only from Chapter XI on; the compiler of the chronicle of which the *Turpin* here forms part rejected the first ten chapters and with them whatever prologue his model may have had. The place of Br 2 in Group III must also be decided on the basis of its readings. Group III R is represented by eight manuscripts: L2 ca. 1225; P5 of the second quarter of the thirteenth century; L3 of the mid-thirteenth century; O, A1 and B1 of the second half of the thirteenth century, P7 of the mid-fifteenth century and P6 of the third quarter of the fifteenth century. Group III M is represented by fourteen manuscripts: P8, V, B2, A2, A3 of the second half of the thirteenth century; C1 of the end of the thirteenth century; F, C2, S of the early fourteenth century; T of the early fifteenth century; P10, P11, T of the mid-fifteenth century; Br 3 of the third quarter of the fifteenth century; and P9 which is dated 1462.

The readings bear out the division of Group III into two main families. Br 2 however stands apart; its place in Group III will appear when its readings can be compared with those which distinguish the subgroups III R and III M. Though the other manuscripts representing Group III are numerous and often vary very much in their treatment of the text (this being more true of III M than of III R), variants occur which show the two families at times unanimous within themselves and in disagreement with each other. I list some examples, rather numerous because we shall need them in later comparisons, and again paying no attention to irrelevant variants. The reading in III R is represented by P5, the reading in III M by P8.

1. II, 9	III R	:	l'essil de la terre
	III M	:	l'eschil e le dolor de le t.
2. II, 12	III R	:	ses armes erent totes vermeilles et ses escuz autressi
	III M	:	Ses escuz estoit tot vermauz (ses armes . . . vermeilles *lacking*)
3. III, 19	III R	:	honor
	III M	:	amor
4. V, 9	III R	:	et la fesse (et la corde dont il fu liez a l'estache P6)
	III M	:	et le loijen
5. VI, 7	III R	:	tendoit
	III M	:	aloit

6. VI, 8   III R   :   droit trespassant par Gascoigne
                  III M   :   et par G.

7. X, 10   III R   :   Segunce (Segobe *lacking*) qui
                  III M   :   Segonce, Segobe qui

8. XIII, 15   III R   :   rois d'Aufrike
                  III M   :   rois de Frise (d'Aufrique B2)

9. XV, 5   III R   :   en l'air
                  III M   :   en l'air *lacking*

10. XXI, 13   III R   :   ferirent premiers (alerent assembler P7)
                  III M   :   furent primes

11. XXVI, 15   III R *lacks,* III M *has the sentence:* Quant Agoulans
                          oï le sarrasinois qu'il parla si s'en esmer-
                          villa molt et esjoï (et si en out mout
                          grant joie V)

12. XXVII, 12   III R   :   Ce demostre (Sy d. P6; Laquelle chose
                              est grant demonstrance que P7)
                  III M   :   Je demoustre (*passage lacking* P11)

13. XXX, 7   III R   :   laidement
                  III M   :   malement

14. XXXII, 10   III R   :   que li rois ne le sot (sans le sceu du roy
                              P6)
                  III M   :   Mais li r. ne le sot mie *(variants in the
                              wording but not in the syntax).*

15. XXXIII, 27   III R   :   .XX. homes (.vii. h. P7)
                  III M   :   .XL. h. (.vii. h. A3)

16. XXXVII, 7   III R   :   ne nus ne l'engendra (*phrase lacking* P6)
                  III M   :   ne nului n'engendra (*passage in* 11.7-9
                              lacking F, A2, P10, P11).

17. XXXVII, 13   :   *Roland is explaining to Fernagu the
                              Three Persons of the Trinity. The
                              Latin reads,* 155, xvii: coaeternae sibi
                              sunt et coaequales
                  III R   :   pardurables en soi es ciels (soi. E celes
                              A1; es ciels *lacking* O)
                  III M   :   p. en soi et en eles (en soi et *lacking* P8;
                              et en eles *lacking* V; et en eulx Br 3).

In III R and III M the readings are probably corruptions of . . . *et
evels* or *et ivels.*

18. XLIX, 3   III R : bon oïr

       III M : bon savoir (or est il point de dire Br 3)

19. XLIX, 15   III R : Li ceinz dont il ert ceinz

       III M : Li c. d. il se caignoit

20. LI, 13   III R : de vos sivre (de v. servir B1)

       III M : de vos servir

21. LII, 8   III R : firent l'ariere garde (*sentence lacking* P7)

       III M : furent en l'a. g. (feroient, *but the passage is much altered* Br 3)

22. LIV, 13   : *The correct reading,* molt est despite chose *has become* m. e. petite (*or* de petite) chose *in* III R. (mult est grant li pechez cumpainie de femme O; perilleuse chose P7)

       III M : m. e. povre cose (que povre compaignie est de femme Br 3)

23. LIV, 29   III R : la ou luxure doit estre chastiee (*sentence lacking* P7)

       III M : la u l. ne doit estre mais caastés

24. LX, 20 (Roland prays God's blessing *super fideles tuos,* 199, xxii)

       III R : sor toz cels qui

       III M : sor tes fius qui P8, B2, C2; fieus V, F, A3, C1, S; feels A2 feaulx Br 3; filz P11.

There can be little doubt that the forms *fius, fieus* represent an understanding on the part of the scribes who used them that the sense was "fils" instead of "fideles," a poorer reading but one understandable in itself and no doubt induced in the Picard texts by confusion between *feeus* from *fideles* and *fieus* from *filios.*

25. LXIV, 5   III R : les uns morz et les autres demi vis

       III M : les uns mors et les autres demi mors

26. LXVI, 14   III R : sor un lit (.ii. mules en *lacking; passage lacking* P7)

       III M : sor .ii. mules en un lit (en un lit *lacking* B2; *passage lacking* V)

27. LXVII, 14   III R : el cimetire (Saint S. *lacking*) fu

       III M : el c. Saint Seurin fu

If we compare these readings with Pierre's text, as preserved in Group II, with the original translation as preserved in Group I and with the Latin text we may say that Group III R is in error at

nos. 1, 2, 3, 4, 7, 11, 13, 15, 16, 18, 19, 24, 26, 27 and that
Group III M is in error at 5, 6, 8, 9, 10, 12, 14, 20, 21, 23, 25.
Other readings, no. 17 for example, mark the distinctiveness of
the two groups relatively to each other in their treatment of what
seems to have been a common difficulty. We must then conclude
that the manuscripts in Group III R, and those in Group III M
derive respectively from two independent copies of the second
redaction through which our Johannes *Turpin* passed. This runs
counter to the facile assumption which has long been held by some
that the Michel group of manuscripts represents a copy of
Renaud's "translation" of the *Turpin*. It makes us wonder again
about the stories told in the Michel and Renaud prologues: here
that Renaud had a translation made from a Latin *Turpin* which he
found at Saint-Denis, and there that Michel had a translation made
from a Latin *Turpin* found in Renaud's library. The common
source of our Renaud manuscripts is clearly a faulty copy of that
same model which lies behind the common source from which all
our Michel manuscripts derive. It would seem, then, that both
Renaud and Michel, in spite of the claims made in their prologues,
did no more than sponsor a copy of the second redaction of our
Turpin, a redaction based on Pierre's composite *Descriptio-Turpin*
and made by someone unknown shortly before 1206, the date
ascribed to Renaud's "translation" in the prologue. MS Br 2,
although it belongs to ca. 1425 and offers on the whole a poor
text, nevertheless helps us to see more clearly into the elements of
this problem.

As we have seen, the *Turpin* in Br 2 lacks the prologue and
Chapters I to X. Lacking the prologue and early chapters, Br 2
does not fall readily into classification with Group I, II, III R or
III M; its place in the Johannes tradition must be determined by
its readings and here we must bear in mind that our collation is
limited to its curtailed text. The text of Br 2 is not that of our
Group I. Br 2 ranges itself with Groups II and III against Group I
in the list of comparisons drawn up on pp. 20 ff., except for
nos. 1-5 and 7, 14, 16, 19 where the relevant passage is lacking in
Br 2. Nor does Br 2 align itself in any particular way with either
III R or with III M. Here it agrees now with the one group,
now with the other, and in doing so almost invariably agrees

also with the text of Group II. Using the readings set out in the collation on pp. 55 ff. above, we find that Br 2 agrees with III R and Group II at nos. 8, 9, 10, 14, 20, 21, 25, with III M and Group II at nos. 11, 13, 15, 16, 18, 26, 27 *(Saint Sevestain).*

Before going on to draw the conclusion which must follow from these facts, I must add some details which complicate the simple situation as so far presented. A moment ago, I said that Br 2, as it agrees now with III R, now with III M, "almost invariably" agrees also with Group II. There are three cases showing a contrary situation.

1. At XXVII, 12, rendering the Latin *unde patet quia* (133, iii), the manuscripts in Group I, Group II and Group III R read *Che demonstre que* (*e Deu monstre que* L1; *laquelle chose est grand demostrance que* P7). Group III M reads *Je demoustre* and Br 2 has *Je mousteray.* Does this appear to be in contradiction to the evidence so far presented, and indicate a closer affinity between Br 2 and III M? I do not think so. The *je*, which is certainly an inferior reading, reflects the confusion so common in Picard between surds and voiced consonants. We find in Br 2 such forms as *venchance, charchiez, juchement, venchie;* they were common over a wide region in the north from Normandy to Lorraine. We also fine in Br 2 *porges* from *portĩcus,* a spelling which represents the graphical confusion resulting from the phonetic identity of *-che* and *-ge.* We find in MS P9 the spellings *cheussent, cheurent,* from *gesir,* occurring along with *geut.* In the scribal forms of *Jouffroi, che* and *ce* are written for *je,* and *je* for *ce* (ed. Fay-Grigsby, pp. 56, 22). The *je* for *che* or *ce* in Br 2, like the *je* in the III M manuscripts, may be explained as a graphical substitution of *je* for *che* which any Picard scribe could make as he mentally pronounced the phrase he was copying, especially as the change carried with it a perfectly acceptable sense. The agreement between Br 2 and III M at this point is not of a nature to disallow the conclusion to which the facts adduced above seem to point, namely, that Br 2 derives independently of III R and III M from their common source.

2. At XIII, 5 our *Turpin* is rendering the Latin *eamque tintinnabulis, palleisque, libris . . .* (103, xix). Group I has no word corresponding to *tintinnabulis.* In Group II, P2, P3 read: *lesqueus,* Br 1 lacks the phrase. In Group III R, P5, A1, P7 have nothing corresponding to *tintinnabulis.* B1 reads *Des coules,* O: *Desquelez,* L2: *desqueles,* L3: *Desqueles.* These last four manuscripts obviously reflect an original *D'esqueles,* which must have offered some obscurity in the common intermediary from which, as we shall see below, these four manuscripts derive. Group III M reads unanimously *cloques* and with this Br 2 agrees. There seems to me to be no doubt that the translator's phrase or at least that of Pierre's revised text, was *D'esqueles,* that the scribes of the mid-thirteenth century were unfamiliar with the word, and that the scribe of the source manuscript of Group III M sutstituted for *esqueles* the more familiar word *cloques.* The scribe of Br 2, writing ca. 1425, also used *cloques* which was alone current at that time; *esqueles* had probably been lost in transmission long before he wrote.

3. At XL, 20 Br 2 reads with Group III R: *Li paiens li trencha par mi le baston;* cf. the Latin: *absciso baculo* (161, xxiii). The phrase is lacking in III M and Group II. Its loss is due to homoioteleuton; the word *baston* ends the sentence quoted and the preceding one. This explains its loss also in MS B1 of the Renaud Group. The error was committed independently by the scribe of B1, by Michel's scribe and by one or more scribes who handed down the tradition preserved in the manuscripts of Group II.

We must conclude, therefore, that Br 2 does not belong to either subgroup III R or III M and that, in spite of its many deviations, it is at some important points a better representative of the second redaction than the manuscripts of III R and the manuscripts of III M. Is Br 2 to be placed then in Group II? The answer is to be found in a passage discussed above on p. 39. At XLIX, 22 ff., Pierre added in his revised *Turpin* a short passage drawn from Einhard: *Molt se delitoit en faire lire devant lui les estoires et les anciennes gestes et les livres de saint Augustin.* The second redactor copied this interpolation from Pierre but added to it a phrase of his own which appears, though with distortions here and there, in all the manuscripts of Group III: *ne nus ne lisoit devant lui l'espace d'une hore ou demi ore qu'il n'en receust la merite.* Br 2 has this sentence: *Moult se delitoit en oïr lire devant luy ystoirez et anchiennes giestez et les livres saint Augustin; nulz ne lisoit devant luy heure ne demye qui n'en recheust merite.* Br 2 therefore takes its place in our stemma as an independent derivative of the text of the second redaction alongside of the two other independent copies now lost, the one made for Renaud in 1206, the other made for Michel in 1206 or 1207, as to which date the III M manuscripts vary.[28] What Michel borrowed from Renaud's library was then not a Latin *Turpin* copied from one treasured in Saint-Denis, but a manuscript of the second redaction of the Johannes *Turpin,* the model which had served Renaud's scribe and now was to be used in turn by the copyist whom Michel set to work. Beyond the impudence of the assertions made in both prologues – they are excusable, being meant only to impose, as was the widespread fashion, the authority inherent in a Latin text – there would seem to be both rivalry and collusion, for while Michel clearly vied with Renaud in popularizing the *Turpin* in this form, the otherwise contradictory assertions made by his scribe do agree with Renaud's in allowing that the first initiative was Renaud's own and that it was by Renaud's courtesy that Michel obtained the text of the *Turpin* which he sought. In any case, both patrons achieved an impressive success, for the *Turpin*

---

[28] MSS V, C1, B2 and M in its first prologue give 1206. P9, a copy of V, gives 1106 – "duplici scribae errore" wrote Gaston Paris, *De Pseudo-Turpino,* p. 57, n. 2, but really with only one, the eleven for the twelve hundred. MSS P8, F with its copy P10, A2 give 1207. C2, A3, S, all springing from a common intermediary, give 1200 omitting *e. sis* or *e.vi.* P11 has no date.

which they promulgated was, more than all others in the vernacular, *chiere tenue et volentiers oïe* over a wide region and for a long time. Its popularity was no doubt due in part to Pierre's initiative in making a single chronicle of Charlemagne's legendary crusades in East and West, but perhaps above all to the author of our second redaction who, sensing the taste of the *haus homes* to whom his chronicle is addressed, reworked Pierre's *Descriptio-Turpin* into the unified, short and more pleasantly readable chronicle which survives in the manuscripts of our Group III.

Within the IIIR Group, P6 proves to be a copy of P5. The two manuscripts contain five identical texts, copied in the same order. A comparison of the *Turpin* text in both shows that P6 shares with P5 many variant readings, additions and omissions. Here first are a few examples of visibly erroneous readings common to both manuscripts:

Prologue, 7	:	le non del bon roi *(sc. Charlemagne)*
P5, P6	:	. . . roi Phelippe
VIII, 11	:	fist garder a vie
P5, P6	:	fist garder la vile
IX, 10-11	:	Li Galicien qui puis la predication monseignor saint Jaque et ses deciples erent repairié
P5, P6	:	Li G. qui puis la p. m.s.J. et ses d. qui puis erent r.
XXVI, 3	:	Agolanz s'en issi et ses oz. Il se rangierent
P5	:	*has a smudge left by an erasure corresponding to nine letters between* oz *and* se, *but* Il *is just legible after* oz
P6	:	Agolanz s'en issi et ses oz se r.

The other manuscripts of Group III R show no sign of difficulty here.

Further examples of variants which P5 and P6 share are Prol. 13: *recita* (others *traita*); IV, 6: *chanoines* (others *nonains, moines*); IV, 19: *Nostre Sires* (others *il* standing for *Deus,* 1. 17); V, 17: *Nostre Sires* (others *Deus*). The following additions to the text, here printed in italics, are common to both; III, 7: saluerent *de par le patriarche;* III, 9: plorer *mult durement;* IV, 7: .xii. *des plus prudomes et* des plus sains homes; V, 19: France *ou eles sont en plusors leus;* LXXII, 2: plus bel *et plus delitable a servir Deu.*

Lastly here are some examples of omissions common to both manuscripts, VII, 13: *corone;* LI, 10: *mort;* the whole of Chapter XXVIII; at XXXVII, 22 both omit the illustrations provided by the sun and the almond, whereas the other manuscripts of III R are complete here. In places, the scribe of P6 was attentive enough to see errors in P5 and to emend them. For instance, at IX, 13 P5 has *renoier* for *recevoir,* which P6 emends to *croire.* At XXXIII, 25, P6 changes the *.xx. Turs* of P5 to the correct *.xx. m. Turs,* and at LXXV, 10, P6 replaces the *estoire* of P5 with the obvious correction *estoille.* The question arises here as to whether these readings which I attribute as emendations to the scribe of P6 as he copied P5, are of such a nature as to suggest rather that P5 and P6 are copied from a common source. I do not think so. There are other cases of such emendations, all of them are, I think, cases where the obviously alert scribe of P6 tried to make sense of an erroneous passage in P5.

A second grouping within III R is to be seen in the three Anglo-Norman manuscripts L2, L3 and O to which B1 is closely related. All four manuscripts go back to a common intermediary. Significant readings are as follows:

1. IX, 4	:	The Latin, 95, iv, reads: *armis retro eiectis,* which appears in Group II as *lor armes getees puer,* and in Group III M: *lor armes puer gietees.*
P5, P6	:	lor armes gitoient jus
A1	:	l. a. laïs gitoient
L2, L3	:	l. a. pur getouent
B1	:	l. a. pur i getoient
O	:	par pour et en fauf *(sic)* lez porterent[29]
P7	:	*phrase lacking*

The imperfect of the verb as contrasted with the past participle elsewhere is characteristic of Group III R; the retention of *pur* is characteristic of the sub-group L2, L3, O, B1.

2. X, 30	:	Gilbadaire, Cartage, Septe qui est es destroiz d'Espaigne ou
L2, L3, O, B1	:	G. (Cartage . . . Espaigne *lacking*) ou

3. XIII, 6	:	Charlemagne built the Church of St. James and endowed it with gifts. The

---

[29] The reading, though not the meaning, is clear. The *fauf* would seem to be for *faus* and the phrase *en faus* an adverbial extension meaning "secretely:" "their arms, they bore them out of fear and secretly."

Latin, 103, xix, reads: . . . *in ea instituit, eamque tintinnabulis palleisque, libris ceterisque ornatibus decenter ornavit.* In III M *tintinnabulis* is represented in all the manuscripts by *de cloches.* In III R:

P5, P6, P7, A1	:	*phrase lacking*
L2, L3, O	:	desqueles
B1	:	des coules

This reading has been discussed in a larger context above on p. 59. Renaud's scribe must have written *desqueles,* the corruption of an original *d'escheles* or *d'esqueles.* Because of its unintelligibility, *desqueles* was omitted by the scribes of P5, P7 and A1, but evidently it has passed through a common intermediary to L2, L3, O and B1, where it shows quite surely through their variant spellings and punctuation.

4. XVII, 18 L2, L3, O, B1	:	(iiii *lacking*) mile
5. XIX, 7-8	:	L2, L3, O and B1, because of the repetition in this passage of *li rois de* all show a jump from *Osbins li rois* to *de Marroc,* omitting King Facins and King Aylis. Omissions thus caused are common, of course, and are often independently made by two or more scribes, but the exact correspondence of our four texts here seen in the present context impels me to attribute the error to a common source.
6. XXIII, 3	:	Bertain la seror Charle
L2, etc.	:	Bretaigne . . .
7. XXIV, 5 P5, P6, A1	:	Selins et Salemons qui fu compainz Estouz de Langres, Baudoin
L2, L3, O	:	Gelins et Salomuns ki compains esteit Baldoins
B1	:	G. et S. qui compaignon sunt Estout, B.
P7	:	Angelier et S. qui compaignon esteient, B.

L2, L3, O and B1 all seem to go back to a common source which had lost *fu.* It would appear that the scribe who wrote this source was an Anglo-Norman who read *Estout,* probably written in his model with a small *e,* as *estout,* the imperfect of *ester,* and understood the verb in this context as meaning "to be;" cf. *a cui estes?*

in Baudouin de Sebourc, quoted in T.-L. III: 2, 1382, 11. 29-34;
(see too L. Foulet, *Glossary of the First Continuation,* s.v. *ester*),
and so he made Salomons the companion of Baudoins. This was
copied without sense of difficulty by the Anglo-Norman scribes of
L2, L3 and O, except that the lexical emendation, *esteit* for *estout,*
that is, *estre* for *ester,* was evidently felt as needed by all three
scribes. The scribe of B1, a Picard, did not confuse *estout* the pro-
per name with *estout* the verb form; but he had to supply a verb
and so wrote *sunt* to go with the subject as he saw it, namely
Gelins et Salomuns. The reading helps to establish the fact that
our four manuscripts go back to a common source and it also
strongly suggests that this common source was an Anglo-Norman
text.[30]

8. XXVIII, 12	:	Quar si com cil furent mort qui foïrent, ausi moront cil laidemant qui retornent as vices.
L2, etc.	:	Kar si cum cil furent mort ki alsi muerent il laidement si retornent as vices.

The group L2 etc. all go back to a source in which *foïrent* was
omitted.

9. XXIX, 17	:	pou pain et poi a boivre devant els
L2, etc.	:	pou *lacking*
10. XLVI, 11 P5, P6	:	.ii. evesques
A1, P7	:	.ix. e. (so Group II and the Latin, 171, v, var: *novem*)
L2, L3, B1	:	nos e.
O	:	lez e.
11. LXIV, 7	:	.iiii. peus
L2, L3	:	quatre forz pels
O	:	q. f. postz
B1	:	q. f. pascons

---

[30] It may be helpful to note here the relevant details in what is said in the supplement
concerning the imperfect tense forms in MSS L2, L3 and O. All three manuscripts
show the ending *-out* in this tense and person for the first conjugation. L2, which I
have dated ca. 1225, does this regularly. O, of the second half of the thirteenth cen-
tury, also uses *-out,* but tends to replace it with analogical *-oit,* while the scribe of L3,
ca. 1250, though using *-out* occasionally, preferred *-oit.* There was some conscious-
ness that the form was archaic for in L2, the earliest of our Anglo-Norman manu-
scripts, *gisout* has been corrected by a contemporaneous reviser to *gisoit,* though here
of course, the case is one of the extension of the form to a verb of the second con-
jugation. B1 does not know the *-out* form at all.

| 12. LXV, 36 | : | li autre en eschieles sor lor cous |
| L2, etc. | : | et li altre en e. et li altre sur lur c. |

13. LXXII, 4	:	qui fait en parchemin torte ligne. N'est mie chanz qui n'est selonc musique et qui n'est escriz par quatre lignes
L2	:	N'est mie . . . lignes *lacking*
L3, O	:	N'est mie . . . et *lacking*
B11	:	*omits a still longer passage*

The source of the trouble here seems to lie in an omission in a common source caused by the repetition of *n'est.* L3 and O reproduce the faulty model, L2 omits the whole sentence probably because it made no sense, and so in his own way did the scribe of B1.

| 14. LXXVII, 17 | : | es pe*ises* tantes pierres et tanz merriens d'esg*lises* qu'il avoit fetes |
| L2, etc. | : | tantes . . . esglises *lacking* |

I do not think there can be any doubt therefore that L2, L3, O and B1 stem from a common intermediate source. Judging by example 7 above, this source was an Anglo-Norman manuscript. There is no consistent mark of a more particular relationship between any of the manuscripts comprising this family of four. Among them B1, although beautifully and intelligently transcribed, is the freest and therefore the least reliable copy.[31] Of the three Anglo-Norman manuscripts, L2 and L3 are certainly the most faithful and of these two L2 is the better.

P7 and A1 are independent copies of Renaud's text. P7, as the supplement will show in detail, is of little use as a representative of our Johannes tradition, though it is of much interest in itself. A1 on the other hand offers a good text obviously copied with care. There is little to choose between P5 and A1; after hesitation I give the preference to P5 since A1 has lapses like *et sa fille Lyon* for *et ses filz Leo* (II, 8), *la pointe devant gitoit* for *la pointe del fer g.* (II, 15), *le graindre froment* for *le grain de f.* (XXXIX, 6), *la dont tu venis* for *la dont tu meus* (XL, 7). But poor readings in each can be corrected from the other

To sum up, the manuscripts in Group III R represent Renaud's copy of the second redaction of the Johannes translation. The

---

[31] For example, at VI, 4: *proposa qu'il n'ostoieroit mes. En son proposement.* L2: *n'ostoireit* L3: *qu'il en ost ne irreit mes* O: *n'estoiroit mes* B1: *se porpensa qu'il n'isteroit mais hors de son pais. En sen porpensement qu'il faisoit.*

Group is best represented by MSS P5 and A1. The lost manuscript from which MSS L2, L3, O, B1 derive must be considered a good and independent copy of Renaud's text on a par with P5 and A1. It is best represented by L2. The relationship of the III R manuscripts are shown in the following stemma:

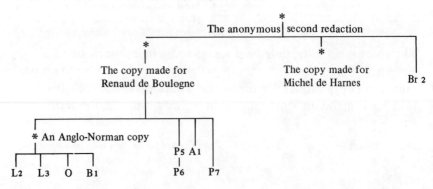

Turning now to the III M family of manuscripts, we may first note that MS P9, for Gaston Paris the "pessimus codex" of the Johannes tradition,[32] is an indirect copy of MS V. That P9 is a copy of V is at once suggested by the presence in both these manuscripts, though in no other of the tradition, of the two chapters supplementary to the *Turpin* printed below as Appendices to the text, the first describing the foray into Galicia by the "aumaçor de Cordres" and the second narrating the origins of the Navarrese, this latter concluding with the explicit which declares that Maistre Jehans was the author of the translation. The suggestion is strengthened by the conformity visible throughout the *Turpin* in the particular readings of both manuscripts. Here are a few examples of additions, omissions and particular readings common to P9 and V.

1. Additions; the relevant readings are here printed in italics:

II, 5	:	si que *li Crestien et* li patriarches
XX, 16	:	Dont dist Ag. qu'il repairaissent a Karlon *quil* (=qui) *parloit a lui*
LXXI, 1	:	gramaire *qui est bonne sienche* qui mere est

---

[32] *De Pseudo-Turpino*, p. 57, n.2.

2. Omissions:

III, 5	:	sages et discrez de lor loi *lacking*
XII, 4	:	Cadis, c'est li leus ou ele est *lacking*
LVI, 19	:	"Alpha" et "O" *lacking*

3. Particular readings:

XXVII, 4	:	Mahoumet qui fu *uns sages Diu*
XXXI, 22	:	Desi as kevilles fu u sanc *li vesques Turpins*
LII, 17	:	qui est de faim erragiés *de venir as brebis*

A still closer agreement between P9 and V is discernible in the following forms which are common to both manuscripts: *Nareth* for *Nazres* (X, 13); *Agalte* for *Algate* (X, 19); the *.xvi. home bien octodore* (for *ortodoxe*) of MS V at XLIX, 35 which appears in P9 as *.xvi. homes octodoreis,* the scribe of P9 having read *octodore* as a past participle and written *ei* for *e* < free tonic *a* as was his custom.

The agreements between P9 and V which have been exemplified above might be explained by supposing that the two manuscripts are copies of the same model. But conclusive evidence against this is provided by the fact that there are in P9 empty spaces left in the text and also corrupt readings which show that the scribe could not have been using the exemplar copied by the scribe of V, but rather that he was using a degenerate copy of V itself. There are many passages which are perfectly clear in V where the text of P9 shows that the scribe had difficulty in reading his model. On fol. 270 r°, and in the corresponding area on the verso, the scribe of P9 left blank spaces equal in each case to nine lines of his text; the omitted passages occur in MS V on fol. 10 r°, b (fifteen lines) and fol. 10 v°, a (eleven lines). The lacuna on the verso, I might add (details are given in the supplement), and some of the lesser lacunae which I shall bring to attention in a moment, have been filled in by the rubricator whose hand is perfectly recognizable and who drew on the text of some unidentified French *Turpin*. There are other lacunae in P9 where the scribe must have found phrases or words lost or obscured in his model which are present and perfectly clear in MS V. For example, at L, 11 ff., MS V reads (fol. 9 r°, a, ll. 41 ff.): *Marsilles l'onnera mout la nuit, et quant vins* (sic) *après mengier si l'apiela a conseil et li dist . . . que s'il le*

metoit en aaisse de Karlon. . . P9 (fol. 267 r°, ll. 26 ff.) leaves
blank spaces for *onnera, si l'apiela, metoit.* Other similar gaps
occur in P9 on fols. 262 v° and 263 r°. There are other places
where the text in V offers no difficulty but where in P9 it is cor-
rupt. We come upon one immediately in Prol. 17, where V has
que on n'ot mais si volentiers que on seut and P9 has *qui ont oye
maix si v.* At X, 5, V shows correctly and clearly *Bracare mere
des cités,* whereas in P9 we find *Bracaire, Credes, Cistes.* We must
conclude then that P9 stems through an intermediary from V.
However, quite often, where V is faulty, lacking single words or,
especially in the latter part of the chronicle, whole phrases, we
find in P9 an intelligent emendation. So at Prol. 19 he supplies
comment, lacking in V; at I, 4 where V lacks *portez,* he supplies
translatei; at VI, 7 where V has *entiere Franche* he emends to *en
terre de France.* At XXI, 17 when the scribe of V heedlessly wrote
reclamans la vie Nostre Seigneur, P9 finds the right word *l'aide,* the
scribe of V having obviously misread *l'aiue.* At times, indeed, the
scribe of P9 seems to have been more intelligent and attentive than
the scribe of V.[33] The details need concern us no longer. P9 is a
copy of a copy of V; yet, before we relegate it to the limbo where
copies of extant manuscripts lie, it may be well to remember its
linguistic interest as a fifteenth-century copy written in the lan-
guage of western Burgundy and based at one remove on a model
written in thirteenth-century Picard.

MS V itself stands in no particular relationship with any other
manuscript within the III M family. This is true also of MS P8,
which is a more carefully copied representative of the original
Michel text than V. MS Br 3 is also an independent member of the
family. It is, however, a late copy colored by the personal inter-
ventions of the scribe who wrote it. The remaining manuscripts,
C1, T, B2, C2, A3, S, F, A2, P10, P11, show more complicated
relationships. They form a group stemming from a lost interme-
diary, and within this larger group they resolve into minor groups

---

[33] At XLVI, 10-14, the scribe of V omitted all that comes between *Compostele* and
Compostele. But he noticed his mistake when he came to *Galice* in 1.15 and without
more ado inserted after *Galice* the passage he had overlooked, repeating the matter of
1.15 again when he reached it and then continuing correctly. P9 reproduces the con-
fusion but does complete the sentence which, upon realizing his error, the scribe of V
left incomplete at *Galice.* Almost immediately the absent-minded scribe of V made a
similar error, going back after *comenda* in XLVII, 1 to what follows *comenda* in
XLVI, 15. Here the scribe of P9 saw the error and avoided it.

which show our III M text in process of deterioration. To prove
first the existence of the larger group, I list the following sample
of significant variants which all these manuscripts, apart from
irrelevant details, show in common and in contrast to the rest of
the Michel family. The respective readings are represented by the
text of P8 on the one hand and by those of C1 on the other except
where P8 or C1 has a particular variant.

1. Prol, 10   :   et Loey sen fill
    C1 etc.   :   et Loeys son ainsné fil (*phrase lacking*
                              P11)

2. II, 16   :   *The readings in P8, V are variants but*
                              they do not have fu et
    C1 etc.   .   :   g. fu et flambe s.

3. IV, 2   :   Ains li pria
    C1 etc.   :   Ains rouva (ains requist P11)

4. V, 4   :   Illuec fu entr'eus si grans odors et si
                              grans clartés
    B2 etc.   :   I. fu e. li deliz si granz et li c. (le joie et
                              li deduis et le c. C1)

5. X, 4   :   Midone, Bracharie, mere des cités,
                              Vimaranne, Granie
    C1 etc.   :   M., V., B. . . . , G.

6. XV, 10 MS V   :   Navare et de l'Avare (et de l'A. *lacking*
                              P8)
    B2 etc.   :   N. et par dela Navare (par *lacking* C1)

7. XXII, 10   :   en prison mist hors
    B2 etc.   :   en p. il les desprisona (delivra C1)

8. XXVI, 18   :   tes peres ne tes aves ne tresaves
    C1 etc.   :   tes peres ne te mere ne . . .

9. XXIX, 18   :   Ce sont message Nostre Signor que nous
                              paissons cascun jor el non
    C1 etc.   :   que . . . jor *lacking*

10. LVII, 24 MS V   :   Guenes qui estoit consentans (consachanz
                              others) de l'uevre (qui bien savoit se
                              traïson P8)
    C1 etc.   :   G. qui toute savoit le male oevre (qui la
                              traïson avoit faite et la savoit P11)

11. LXV, 16 : tous cis malisces et toute cele traïsons estoit faite par Guenelon et que tout ce avoit il fait.

    B2 etc. : cist domages estoit avenu par G. et qu'il en avoit meserré contre Charlemaine *(C1 has a long omission here)*

12. LXVII, 32 : desissent .xxx. sautiers et .xxx. messes a toutes vegiles

    C1 etc. : ...xxx. messes et .xxx. comendasses et .xxx. vegiles

13. LXVIII, 5 : Ostreval, et avoient aporté lor mors
    C1 etc. : O. Si estoient venu veïr leur mors qu'on aportoit *(passage lacking C2, P1 1)*

14. LXXIII, 7 : Ceste ars aprent a mesurer les espasses
    C1 etc. : Chis ars enseigne terre (terre *lacking, others*) a mesurer, et (et *lacking, others*) les hauteches des tors par esgart et si aprent a mesurer les espasses

15. LXXV, 7 : conoissent par ceste art les ocoisons (l'ocission V) des gens et des batailles

    C1 etc. : (les oc. . . . gens et *lacking*) les b.

Within this larger family a smaller one comprising MSS F, P1 0, P P1 1, A2 is clearly defined. P1 0 is from beginning to end a direct copy of F, both in its texts and in its illumination. The reproduction of the textual errors in F by the scribe of P1 0 meets the eye on every page of P1 0. Proof that the copy was made directly from F is afforded by the following. At XLIX, 22 F reads: *toudis tempré a l'aighe.* In the word *aighe,* the shaft of the *h* is short and blurred at the top; the second stroke blends with the round of the following *e* and its prolongation in a backward curve at the bottom is left indistinct. So the *h* looks like an *r* and that is how the scribe of P1 0 took it, writing: *trempé a l'aigre.* For the reading in F at XVIII, 10-11: *Contre les uises* ("vices"), P1 0 has *Contre les juses,* a very nonchalant misreading of the first three minims of the word in F. The scribe of P1 0 indeed copied F directly, slavishly and unintelligently. For the rest, proof of the grouping is afforded by the many particular readings which F, P1 1 and A2 share, of which a few examples will suffice: IX, 1: for *s'atriva, perala;* IX, 4: *lor armes et lor covertures porgeteies de maint bel portrait;* XXXIII, 27: the addition (arme) *ki ja fust si trenchans ne tant dur temprei* F, (arme) *tant fust trencant ne t. d. t.* A2, (armeure) *tant fust dure ne trenchant* P11; LXXI, 12: *cil qui manie la clef del tresor et ne set ce qu'il a dedans le vaissel ou cele clef ferme et desferme.*[34] The same manuscripts also show many omissions in common, e.g. VII, 19: *des le . . . te di;* XXIX, 10-14: *de nostre loi . . . reguler;* XLVI, 8-10: *A Yrie . . . Compostele;* the whole passage concerning the dignities conferred upon Compostella from XLVII, 7 to the end of XLVIII; much of the moral in LIV, 8-25; and a great part of Charlemagne's lament over Roland, LXIII, 8-20. They have, too, the same additions to Michel's text, for example at LVIII, 8 ff. where they develop the account of the attentions bestowed first by Baudouin and then by Thierry on the dying Roland. MSS F, P10, P11 and A2 derive then from a single intermediary which handed down to them a much deteriorated text.

A2 and F are independent copies of this intermediary. As between F and A2, the latter reproduces the model more faithfully; the scribe of F committed many careless and unintelligent mistakes of his own. In many of these P11 agrees with F against A2 where A2 has the correct reading, and a thorough examination shows that P11 is indeed a copy, though a very free one, of F. The scribe of P11 borrowed matter from the *Chronique des rois de France* of the Ménestrel d'Alphonse de Poitiers, he sometimes adopted a style independent of that of his model, he altered some of the facts with a view to flattering a chivalric audience, he brought in details from other epic traditions and frequently added glosses to expound the sense of the narration as he went along (see the supplement for details). Yet the following collation of F, A2 and P11 will show that the text which he was using in this way was that of MS F. Where I do not give the text of A2, it is in substantial agreement with P5.

1. I, 5
   F, P11   :   par mer *lacking*

2. I, 12
   F   :   Apres qu'il l'ochist en bataille conquist
                                           mainte terre

---

[34] An interesting reading, which I have not been able to fathom, occurs at II, 6 where F and P11 read *Fenix* for *Jean* and A2 leaves a blank space. Could *Fenix* be a corruption of *Felix,* the name of one of two monks whom, according to the *Annales Regni Francorum,* the patriarch Thomas sent in 807 from Jerusalem to Charlemagne? See the edition of the *Annales* by Kurze, p. 123.

P11 : Et après ceu qu'i l'out occis et conquis, il c. m. t.

3. II, 1-2
F : si cremus et si redoutés
P11 : si c. et si doubtés

4. II, 6 : *For the name of the patriarch* Jehans, *F, P11 read* Fenix. *A2 leaves an empty space.*

5. II, 18 : *For* s'esveilla *F, P11 read* se leva

6. IV, 16
F, P11 : ... Daniel. Illeuc asambla molt de gent et K. fist proiere

7. VII, 12-14
F, P11 : rois terriens (autresi ... sarqueu *lacking*) et ke tu veus k'il t'aparaut coroune el chiel, ausi t'a eslit a delivreir mon sarcu. La voie

8. X, 6-7
F, P11 : De celes d'Espaigne sont ci li non en ordre *lacking*

9. X, 14
F, P11 : Urance ... Sarragoce *lacking*

A2 gives us the clue to explain the omission. After *Sarragoce,* A2 has an interpolated name, *Galatulie,* which must have been in the common source of F, P11, A2 and which by homoioteleuton with *Calagurie,* caused the omission in F and so in P11. Such omissions can, as is well recognized, be independently made; but the scribe of P11 was attentive, his independence here is suspect, and so I think that the omission common to F and P11 has its place in the evidence.

10. X, 24
A2 : croist sor sa tombe
F : c. en mi le tombe
P11 : en mi le temple

Temple in P11 seems to be a correction applied to F induced at once by the sense as determined by the preposition and by the Picard form of the fem. article.

11. X, 31
    A2   : Septe qui est un destrois d'Espaigne
    F, P11   : Septe qui est une des .iii. *(sic, in both)*
                                          d'E.

12. X, 31-32
    A2   : por les destors que li mers a iluec. Si
                                          conquist Gesit
    F, P11   : por les destrois que li m. a illeuc le con-
                                          quist (a illeuc comquis P11). Si c. G.

13. XII, 17
    F, P11   : et tient en sa main destre une cleif (une
                                          grant c. P11)

14. XX, 15
    F, P11 *add the words in italics*   : et parole a lui *se tu veus.*

15. XXII, 13
    A2   : Les sages d'armes et les escuiers dona
                                          armes et fist chevalier
    F   : Les s. d'a. ordena d'armes de chevaliers
    P11   : Les s. d'a. ordena d'armes et de chevaux

The three manuscripts inherited the erroneous repetition of *armes;* F and P11 both omit
et les escuiers.

16. XXXII, 1-2
    F, P11   : Toz cels que Charles trova en la cité fist
                                          occire *lacking*

17. LXVII, 25   : *For* apent F *reads* apert *(from "aparoir")*
                                          which makes little sense; P11 *reads* aper-
                                          tient *which makes better sense and seems
                                          to be an emendation of* apert *in F.*

To continue the collation into lesser detail: the proper names
in F, A2 and P11 are often very deformed, but F and P11 show fre-
quently the same or closely similar corrupt forms which contrast
with those in A2 . For example: I, 8: *Galifres (Golafres* A2); X, 4:
Madone (Midone A2); X, 13: *Abstenge (Astenge* A2); X, 23:
saint Orchaise (Orcaise P11 ; Orace A2).

It is certain therefore that P11 is a direct copy of F, but a copy
made with many modifications introduced by the scribe. Among
these his borrowings from the *Chronique des rois* of the Ménestrel
d'Alphonse de Poitiers are specially interesting and call for some
attention here. I cannot be exhaustive in my treatment of this
matter. There is no critical edition of the Ménestrel's *Chronique*

des rois de France, so that my collation cannot be thorough. But the fact that the scribe of P11 used the Ménestrel will emerge with certainty enough from a comparison of his text with the *Chronique des rois* as it is preserved in French MS 5700 of the Bibliothèque Nationale.

As is well known, the Ménestrel d'Alphonse de Poitiers composed his *Chronique des rois de France* in the third quarter of the thirteenth century. For some of his material on Charlemagne he used the *Turpin,* as to which it has generally been agreed that he made his own translation from a C text of the Latin chronicle.[35] Proof that the scribe of our MS P11 borrowed details from the *Turpin* in the Ménestrel's *Chronique des rois* appears in the following passages.

At XV, 17, P11 (fol. 88 v°) shows the interpolation italicized in the following: "en une terre qui a nom Sens sus un fleuve et en un pray moult bel et ouny *et en cel an mesmes y fu puis fondee une tres belle abbaïe et riche en l'ounor de saint Primien et saint Savinien en laquelle abbaïe les corps de molt bons martirs reposent, et en ce luy meismes a bonne ville et belle et riche.* A similar passage occurs in the Latin *Turpin* at 109, x-xiv, but with this difference that the saints in honor of whom the basilica was founded were saints Facundus and Primitivus. The passage as we find it in P11 occurs in the *Chronique des rois* of Bibliothèque Nationale MS 5700, fol. 52a. The Johannes translation has the Latin passage transposed to XVIII, 2-6 where in a very logical order of exposition the founding of the church of Saint-Fagon is made to commemorate the miracle of the lances and the victory over Agolant just recounted. On fol. 89, 1. 4 up, P11 has the passage corresponding to our XVIII, 2-6 in spite of its gross contradiction with what he had written on fol. 88 v°.

At XV, 11 where our translation tells us that the body of the man who made away with money bequeathed to the poor was found *en un perruchoi,* corresponding to the Latin (109, i): in *cuiusdam silicis fastigio,* P11 has (fol. 88 v°, 1.10) *en une chaussie* and the Ménestrel (fol. 51 v°, a): *en une sauçoie.* It would seem here that the Ménestrel was translating a Latin text which read *salicis* for *silicis* (his text continues in a way which

---

[35] See Ian Short, "The *Pseudo-Turpin Chronicle:* Some unnoticed Versions and their Sources" *Medium Aevum XXXVIII,* 1969, p. 8.

makes a clump of willows more appropriate than a stony height: *une sauçoie qui duroit .iii. lieues et estoit jouste la mer .iii. granz lieues loing de la cite de Baionne;* for *mer* here, Bern MS 607 has *riviere*); in any case there can be no doubt that the scribe of P11 took his *chaussie* from a text of the Ménestrel.

At XIX, 10 and again at XXXI, 21, where our translation mentions the aumaçor de Cordres, P11 refers to him as *l'amachour Aimont (Eaumont) le roy de Cordes* (fol. 89 v°, 1.13, fol. 95, 1.10). The Ménestrel does not have *aumaçor,* but (in both places) *Aymont (Yaumont) le roy de Cordres* (fol. 53, a, fol. 60, a). The name *Eaumont* is not in the Latin *Turpin;* its use in P11 along with the designation *le roy* shows that in P11 we have here a borrowing from the Ménestrel.[36]

At XXIII, 7 the Johannes translation, conforming to the Latin (123, xi), describes Olivier as *cuens de Genevois, filz Renier le conte.* P11 however makes him *quens de Viane, filz Regnier Genevois* (fol. 91 v°). This closely follows the Ménestrel: *cuens de Viane, fius le conte Raignier de Gennes* (fol. 55 v°, b).

In the Latin Chapter XIII, Agolant goes to Charlemagne's headquarters to discuss terms for a truce and sees assembled at Charles's table representatives of various ecclesiastical orders. He asks Charlemagne to tell him how to recognize each order by its habit. All the vernacular translations of the *Turpin* show some hesitation in rendering the passage describing the vestments which distinguished the secular clergy from the monks and canons regular: *birris unius coloris indutos* (137, viii). Johannes wrote: *vestuz d'une color* (XXIX, 9). In P11 we find *vestus de buriaux a ces robes rondes* (fol. 94) which corresponds to the Ménestrel: *vestuz de cez buriaus qui ont ces robes reondes* (fol. 58 v°, a).

---

[36] The mention of Aimont (Eaumont, Yaumont) in the Ménestrel and in P11 is borrowed from the poetic tradition of the war against Agolant in Spain, still obscurely known to us. In the *Chronique de Baudouin d'Avesnes,* soon after Charlemagne had been crowned Emperor in Rome, news came to him that Agolant, a powerful prince in Africa, had sent his son Yaumont with a large army to Spain. Charlemagne moved against Yaumont and met with him in Aspremont where, after a series of hard battles, Yaumont was finally defeated and slain. It was to avenge his son's death that Agolant later himself led an army into Spain and undertook his campaigns against Charlemagne.

We have caught (p. 33 above) another echo of this tradition in our MS P1, which adds to what the Pseudo-Turpin tells us of the part played against Agolant by Hernaut de Beaulande the note that Hernaut hated Agolant above all his enemies because of the shameful treatment he had suffered at his hands. But we do not know the story which is behind this statement.

During the battle before Saintes, Charlemagne lost his horse and fought on foot: *reclaymant l'ayde Nostre Seignor* (XXI, 17). P11 reads more dramatically here: *et reclama l'aide N.S. en criant aux siens: Moltjoie! Or devant, mes amis!* (fol. 90 v°) which seems to echo the Ménestrel: *et reclama N.S. hautement et rassembla sa gent et reconforta et cria: Montjoie! Or avant, chevalier, de par Jhesu Crist* (fol. 54 v°, a-b).

I may add now two further passages in which P11 reads with the Ménestrel and both are in accord with the Latin text with which Johannes is at variance. In view of what we have just seen of borrowings in P11 from the Menestrel, we may be sure that here too the scribe of P11 was using not a Latin text but the Ménestrel's French *Turpin.*

1. At LI, 18 ff. Johannes has it that Ganelon, upon his return from Saragossa, passed on to the *hauz homes* of the French army the gift of wine and Saracen women sent by Marsile. The result was that the gentlemen got drunk and lay with the women. But the Ménestrel, following the Latin, insists that the gentlemen took the wine and refused the women who were received only by the rank and file.

Latin, 181, xii ff.	:	Maiores vero pugnatores vinum solummodo ab eo acceperunt mulieres vero nullatenus, sed minores acceperunt.
The Ménestrel, fol. 64 v°	:	Li plus grant seigneur sanz faille pristrent volentiers le present du vin, mes des Sarrasines ne voudrent il nules recevoir Mais li meneur de l'ost les retindrent.
P11, fol. 102	:	Les grans seignurs pristrent volentiers le present du vin et des Sarrazines n'oerent cure. Mais le commun prist les mile Sarrazines dont chascun fist sa volonté par ivresce.

The phrase in P11 *pristrent volentiers le present du vin* seems to be the mark of the scribes indebtedness to the Ménestrel.

2. At LII, 14, Johannes tells us that the first Saracen force of twenty thousand men fell upon the Christian rearguard. The Latin text and the Ménestrel assure us that they fell upon them from behind.

Latin, 183, iii-iv	:	Illa vero quae erat viginti coepit post tergum subito percutere nostros.
The Ménestrel, fol. 65 r°, a	:	Cele qui fu faite de .xx. m. assailli nostre gent par derriere.

P11, fol. 102 v°   :   La bataille des .xx. mile payens courut
                          sus par derriere aux .xx. mile Crestiens

Our comparison could lead on into lesser details. For example, P11 and the Ménestrel agree at XV, 4: *grant estourbillon* (for *escrois*); at XVII, 18: *.iiii. marchis des parties de Lombardie* (for *.iiii. m. d'Italie*); at XX, 3: (repostement) *en un breulet;* at XX, 31: *et passerent Gironde, la riviere qui est de coste la cité*, where Johannes omitted the name *Gironde.*

One wonders just what procedure the scribe of P11 was following as he made these borrowings. It would seem that as he copied F he followed closely a copy of the *Chronique des rois,* and took from the latter such details of fact or such elements of style as would heighten the interest of the Johannes text. There is a passage where we can, perhaps, look over his shoulder and see him as he worked. When the scribe of F came in his copying to the chapter in his model describing the episode at Bayonne where a dying man's bequest to the poor was misappropriated by his executor (XIV), he wrote as his chapter heading: *Comment K. repaira en Espaigne et comment li mors s'aparut al sen sergant.* As he went on copying the story he came to the words (1.5): *comenda un suen norri;* the reading is assured by its exact reproduction in A2. The other Johannes manuscripts have *parent,* corresponding to the Latin *cuidam consanguineo suo praecepit* (107, iv-v). In F (fol. 123 v°, b) *norri* is half effaced; written above it in a fifteenth-century cursive is the word *cousin.* In P11 we find exactly the same chapter heading (fol. 88), but at 1.5 we read instead of *norri, sergent,* the scribe having preferred to repeat here the *sergent* of the rubric instead of copying the *norri* of his model. But, in an afterthought, the scribe of P11, without deleting the *sergent* of 1.5, wrote *cousin* in the interlinear space above. The word *cousin* is the word we find here in the *Chronique des rois* (MS 5700, fol. 51, b). Taking care to avoid the danger of discovering what one would like to find, I think the superscript *cousin* in F is in the hand of the scribe of P11. The scribe of P11 was then using F as his model and had at his elbow the *Chronique des rois.* He added *cousin* taken from the *Chronique des rois,* both to his own copy and to F, half obliterating *norri* in F as he made the emendation.

MSS C1, B2, C2, A3 and S form another sub-group. They have in common a number of variants which distinguish them from the rest of the tradition. I list below a sample of these readings giving first the authentic Michel text, represented by P8 unless otherwise shown, with which, I might add, MSS F and A2 agree in most cases and second, the variant text of MSS C1, B2, A3 and S, represented by C1.

1. VII, 7		:	que Herodes li rois ocist. Mes cors gist en Galisce (Galilee P8) qu'on ne set ou
	C1 etc.	:	que H. li r. o. (Mes c. g. en G. *lacking*)
2. X, 15 MS V		:	Osche, ou il soloit nonante nuef tours avoir par nombre, Teragonne (soloit tous jors par nombre .ix. t. a. P8)
	C1 etc.	:	Orce, ou il soloit avoir nonnante nuef tours, Avot, T.
3. X, 32		:	The Latin text is, *ubi maris est angustus concursus* (99, ix). In Groups I, II and III R *angustus concursus* is generally represented by *escrecete* or a similar word.
	C1 etc.	:	les regorz (cf. les tres forz ondes P8; les tresors V; les destrois F, P11; les destors A2)
4. XLVI, 8		:	A Yrie qu'on cuidoit cite
	C1 etc.	:	A Richeleu (Au riche leu B2, C2, A3, S) qui estoit chités,
5. LVI, 6		:	agrevés des plaies et des cols qu'il avoit receus
	C1	:	a. des plaies qu'il avoit recheues et des orbes caus qu'on li avoit donné
	B2	:	a. de cels qu'il vit morir des plaies et des cops qu'il meismes avoit receuz.
	C2, A3, S	:	a. de chiaus qu'il vit mourir des p. qu'il meismes avoit r. et des orbes caus.
6. LXVIII, 5		:	Ostreval
	C1 etc.	:	nostre val
7. LXXI, 4		:	par queles letres les parz et les sillabes se devisent
	C1 etc.	:	par q. l. les sillesbes et les dictions (discretions C1) se d.

These readings are enough to show that MSS C1, B2, C2, A3, and S form a group of their own, stemming from an intermediary distinct from the manuscript which served as immediate source for MSS F and A2.

MS T bears the marks of a special relationship with C1. The two manuscripts have in common the *Troie* of Jean de Flixecourt, the *Chronique* of the Ménestrel de Reims, and the copy of Michel de Harnes' edition of the Johannes *Turpin*. As for the *Turpin,* the readings show that the text in T is a copy of the text in C1. Here are some examples of particular readings common to T and C1 which should serve to establish the point. I quote from T:

1. LXVIII, 13 : et maint autre de Puille
   T, C1 : e molt des autres mors

2. LXVIII, 16 : que je avoie sofferz en Espaigne
   T, C1 add : (Espaigne) *et en Rainchevaus*

3. LXVIII, 21 : Je Torpins . . . remés ensint a Viane, et li rois qui ert auques affebloiez s'en parti atot sa gent et vint a Paris
   T, C1 : remés la que je ne puch de plus prés aprochier Ffranche pour me maladie. Et li rois qui ert afoiblis sse departy de Vianne a toute sa gent qui remese li estoit et vint a Paris

4. LXIX, 11 : ne nus evesques dampnez a Rome ne receuz
   T, C1 : ne nulz evesques dampnez ne ssacrés se par son consel non

5. LXX, 9 : rendoient les deniers
   T, C1 : r. chel argent

6. LXXIV, 5 :
   T, C1 *add* : ou quans grains de fourment il y avoit en un boistiau de blé.

7. LXXV, 16 :
   T, C1 *add after* ame : Chis ars ne ffu mie point. *They continue with the particular readings noted in italics as follows:* Eynsi ffurent peint *et pourtrait* ly .vii. ars *ens u* palais le roy *et tout parfurni et en ordne devizé.*

8. LXXVI, 10
   T, C1 *add after* chaï : tout ensy comme i l'avoit ffait ffaire.

9. LXXVI, 14-15
   T, C1 *omit* : Donc corurent si compaignon, si l'en redrecierent

10. LXXVIII, 19 ff.

T, C1   :   si comme il ffu tesmoignie dou capitle
de l'eglize et de chiax de Viane et de
pluisours anchiens clers qui chertain-
ement la tesmoignerent et sseurent et
par qui il est mis en memore et iert tenus
perpetuelment jusques a le ffin du siecle.

I have noticed no readings which would suggest that T is separated from C1 by a lost intermediary. On the contrary, such a reading as the following: *car il edifie [sa] propre maison* (LXXVIII, 14), where both T and C1 omit *sa* seems to me to be proof of direct and slavish copying. So too is *Galassiens* (*Galatiens* C1), for *Galiciens* at LXXVII, 17.

At this point C1 with T part company with B2, C2, A3 and S. There are variants peculiar to these four manuscripts which prove that they are removed by another intermediary a further stage from the original Michel text. Here are examples of these variants:

1. I, 5   :   (*St. James's body was borne*) desi en
Galisce

     B2 etc.   :   desi en Galilee

2. V, 18   :   qui devotement les departi
     B2 etc.   :   qui debonairement et devoltement les d.

3. XV, 12   :   Iluec avoient la charoigne gitee li deable
     B2 etc.   :   Ilec troverent la ch. que li d. i avoient
gitee

4. XXVI, 15   :   molt m'en complaing
     B2 etc.   :   m. m'en poise et mout m'en complaing

5. XXXV, 15   :   grant planté
     B2 etc. *add*   :   (grant p.) car molt le resoignoit aprochier
de prés.

6. XXXVII, 14   :   *The readings vary here in a passage which
the scribes found difficult. B2 etc. all
have the particular variant:* Es persones
est proprietez et unitez et o la saintee et
o la majeté est unitez aoree.

7. XLIX, 24   :   *Here again in a seemingly difficult pas-
sage B2 etc. read alike and quite distinc-
tively:* Nus ne lisoit devant li qui n'en
eust bone merite.

8. LII, 19   : La fu esprovee la proesce Olivier
   B2 etc.   : la fu e. la force (la force *lacking* C2, A3,
                    S) Rolland (Rollans C2, A3, S). La fu
                    esprovee la force (proeche C2, A3, S)
                    Olivier

9. LII, 24 (A1 L2 P8 V)   : n'en eschapa uns
   B2 etc.   : n'en e. piez

10. LXIII, 7   : beaus niés, braz destre
    B2 etc.   : braz *lacking*

There are many more such cases. In most of them we can see the intervention of a scribe who, without much talent to draw on, sought to make obscure passages clear and to heighten at moments the style of his original. But he succeeds only in passing on a deteriorated text to those who copied him.

First among these were on the one hand the scribe of B2 and on the other the copyist of another lost manuscript which served as source for C2, A3 and S. The variants introduced by the latter scribe and which distinguish these three manuscripts as a group are quite numerous. The following examples show variants common to C2, A3, S and contrasting with the reading in B2 which is, apart from irrelevant variants, correct.

1. Prol., 8
   B2   : a .xii. .c. anz et .vi. de l'incarnacion
   C2 etc.   : et .vi. *lacking*

2. IX, 10
   B2   : Li Sarradin qui ierent repairié a la loi
               crestienne, Torpins li arcevesques de
               Rayns les bautisa
   C2 etc.   : Et Turpins l'a. baptisa les Sarrasins qui
               baptisier se vaurent

3. XXIII, 4
   B2   : Et uns autres Rollanz
   C2 etc.   : Et uns autres Charles (*The* Charles *is
               probably due to the misreading of an
               abbreviation R as K.*)

4. XLIX, 17
   B2   : Mains manjoit de pain
   C2 etc.   : Mout mainjoit de p.

5. LXV, 25
B2   :   a .iiii. plus forz chevaus
C2 etc.   :   . . . fors ronchins

6. LXVI, 2
B2   :   Arle en Aleschans
C2 etc.   :   Arle en Alixandre

7. LXVIII, 14
B2   :   et maint autre baron de Puille
C2 etc.   :   molt d'autre pule (d'autres pules S)

8. LXX, 15
C2 etc.   :   Car desor totes genz doivent estre
                                      seignor *lacking*

9. LXXVI, 6
B2   :   Et li portaus
C2 etc.   :   Et le porte

There are signs that A3 and S are separated from C2 by yet another intermediary from which both manuscripts were copied. I do not think the following concordances between them in readings inferior to those in B2 and C2 can be otherwise explained.

1. XXII, 20
B2, C2   :   .c. .m. et .xiiii. (.xxxiiii. C2) i ot d'omes
                                      estre les escuiers et ceus a pié
A3, S   :   Cent mille et .xxxiiii. homes i ot a
                                      cheval sans chiaus a pié

2. LXV, 13
B2, C2   :   qu'il estoient
A3, S   :   qui la estoient

3. LXXII, 8
B2   :   en la gigue
C2   :   en le gligle (the first *l* expunctuated)
A3, S   :   en l'eglyse

A3 and S are however very close to C2, especially S whose scribe rarely changed his original. He is, indeed, more reliable than the copyist of C2, though his reliability where this source was already so degenerate a copy, is not of much importance to us. A3 on the other hand was more independent and often modified his original, usually in the effort to correct some of the flagrant errors which S reproduces quite composedly.[37] He was however often careless, and omitted many single words and short phrases essential to the meaning, for example *regulers* at LXVI, 17. We are here, indeed, far from Michel's original text.

With the classification of the III M manuscripts our collation of all the manuscripts representing the Johannes tradition is complete. The general conclusion as to their relationship is illustrated in the stemma on p. 84.

We have now the proper context in which to take up the question as to who was Maistres Jehans, named as the translator in the colophon to the *Turpin* in MS V. The colophon in V, a manuscript which I have dated at the end of the thirteenth century (the details are given in the supplement), comes into the Johannes tradition only in MS V (I omit further mention in this regard of MS P9, the copy of V), and there it occurs as an appendage to the supplementary chapters on the aumaçors de Cordres and on the Navarrese which also appear in our tradition only in MS V. These supplementary chapters were borrowed by the scribe of V from another French translation of the *Turpin,* the translation published by Frederick Wulff as "La Chronique dite de Turpin . . . II: Texte contenu dans le ms. B. N. 2137 f. fr." in *Lunds Universitets Ars-Skrift* XVI, 1879-1880, pp. 43-76. Wulff thought his MS 2137 was the unique representative of this French *Turpin,* but it occurs also in Bibl. Nat. French MS 17203. The first question we must answer then is this: does the colophon naming Maistres Jehans belong to the Johannes translation, or to the translation represented by MSS 2137 and 17203 from which it might have been borrowed with the supplementary chapters?

There is a colophon in MSS 2137 and 17203 which reads: *Ci faut et fine l'estoire Charlemainne (Ci fine l'estoire de Charlemainne et de ses gens).* The scribe of V copied this: *Chi faut et finne li estoire Karlemainne;* the phrase *que Maistres Jehans tranlata* is an addition in his text. A comparison of the readings in the

---

[37] For instance:

LXVII, 14

B2	:	El cimetire saint Seurin de Bordiaus fu entierés, Gaifiers
C2, S	:	Et a B. el cimetiere fu saint Severin entierés, Gaifiers
A3	:	Et a B. el c. saint S. fu (enterrez *lacking*) G.

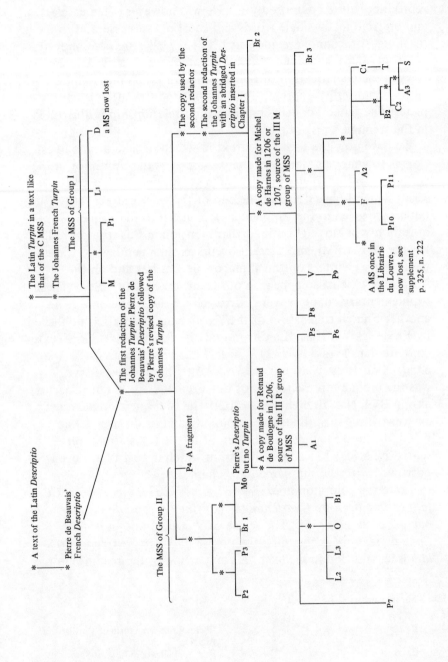

supplementary chapters as we have them in MS V and in MSS 2137 and 17203 shows that the scribe of V did not use either MS 2137 or MS 17203 as his model. Was the phrase *que Maistres Jehans tranlata* in his model and so name not the translator of the Johannes *Turpin* but the translator of that other French *Turpin* to which the scribe of V was having momentary recourse? I think we have only to consider this possibility to reject it. If the ascription was in his model, the scribe of V is far more likely to have left it uncopied than to have used it falsely in his transcription of Johannes. I think we may be sure that the phrase in the colophon must be our scribe's ascription to Maistres Jehans of the translation he was copying. In writing the colophon and thus enlarging it, the scribe of V must have had in mind what he had copied in the prologue, namely, the statement that here was a *Turpin* translated for Michel de Harnes from a Latin manuscript belonging to Count Renaud de Boulogne. The ascription to Jehan, though appearing only in V, may preserve a statement made in the original Michel text by Maistres Jehans who referred to himself in the third person. But it is not likely, if such were the case, that the name Jehans disappeared from all but this one of the many manuscripts which make up our Group III M. So, then, the ascription of the translation to Maistres Jehans is more probably an addition made by the scribe of V informing us out of his own knowledge that Maistres Jehans translated the Latin *Turpin* for Michel de Harnes.

However, we know that Michel's text is no new translation of the Latin *Turpin* but simply a copy of the French *Turpin* made for Renaud. We remember also that the prologue to Renaud's *Turpin* proclaimed that it too was a new translation made from a Latin text procured in Saint-Denis, again a false statement since, as we have seen, Renaud's text is but a copy of the second redaction of the Johannes translation. Looking at the colophon through this web of falsifications, we might fairly conclude that Maistres Jehans was really the scribe who simply copied Renaud de Boulogne's French *Turpin* for Michel de Harnes.

But this assumption is too facile. Contemporary documents show us that in the entourage of Renaud and serving him as chaplain, there was a certain Jehans who by his function can be seen as qualified to be addressed as *Maistres: Liberate et Johanni capellano Comitis Bononiensis quinque marcos* . . . (Close Rolls, I, 518b, anno 15° Johann.; i.e. 1213), and again, with the same title (*ibid.*, I, 518ᵇ), in the seventh year of Henry III, that is 1222.[38]

Is this John the Chaplain, serving in Renaud de Boulogne's household, the Maistres Jehans of the colophon in V? If so, and it seems very plausible that he is, then the colophon is wrong only in attributing to him the authorship of the translation; he was simply the scribe who made for Count Renaud a copy of the second redaction of the Johannes *Turpin.* Plausible, but not sure. If the colophon naming Maistres Jehans had appeared, not in a manuscript of the Michel group but in one of the Renaud group, we might be less hesitant to make this identification. Besides, *Jehans* was a very common name in the Middle Ages and *maistre* a very common title of address. The possibility remains that the colophon may speak truth and preserve an earlier authentic assertion that a Maistres Jehans, other than Renaud's chaplain, was author of the French *Turpin* copied in MS V.

Others have addressed themselves to this problem. Long ago, Demarquette, in his *Précis historique sur la maison de Harnes* (1856), convinced, as anyone who read the two texts would be, that Michel's *Turpin* was the same as Renaud's, expressed the opinion (p. 166) that Maistres Jehans was indeed the translator, that he made the translation for Renaud in 1206 but then passed into the service of Michel de Harnes for whom in 1207 he copied his former work. Demarquette even went so far as to identify Jehans with a cleric who, in 1233, had risen to the position of official in the entourage of the bishop of Arras. A Magister Johannes does indeed appear in a document of that date, the cartulary of Sainte-Marie de la Brayelle, near Annay, which has been preserved in a seventeenth-century copy: Arras, Bibl. Municipale, MS 672 (formerly 606), fol. 33: *Magister Johannes domini attrebatensis clericus et officialis.* "C'est lui, sans doute," writes Demarquette. I fear however that with no more proof than the fact that they both bore this very common name and title, there must remain much doubt as to the identity of this dignitary with a cleric attached to the household of Michel de Harnes about twenty-six years earlier.

Gaston Paris, in his dissertation of 1865 (p. 57), saw through the fictions of the Michel prologue but, with his limited knowledge of the whole manuscript tradition, took Renaud's prologue at its face value and then, without any discussion, simply *quum aliud desideretur,* accepted Johannes as the name of the translator.

---

[38] I am indebted to Mr. Ian Short of the University of London for these references.

The problem indeed could not be embraced in the scope of his labor of that moment. It extends indeed beyond the considerations which we have entertained so far, to the Welsh Charlemagne cycle preserved in the Red Book of Hergest and in the Hengwrt manuscripts. The *Turpin,* Chapters I to XX, forms a part of this compilation, the rest of the *Turpin* forms another. The first part of the *Turpin* in the Welsh cycle is preceded by a Welsh *Pèlerinage de Charlemagne* and followed by a Welsh *Otinel* and a Welsh *Chanson de Roland.* This last leads into the latter part of the *Turpin* which describes the final scenes in Roncevaux and the death of Charlemagne. The Welsh cycle still awaits a competent and thorough study, but the printed texts inform us that, as far as the *Turpin* is concerned, one Madawc ap Selyf translated a Latin text into Welsh for Gruffydd ap Maredudd, prince of Deheubarth. At the end of the *Turpin* as the Hengwrt manuscripts have it, comes a colophon which reads in translation: "This book Madawc ap Selyf translated which John the Scholar wrote" *(yr hwn a yscriuennawd Jeuan yscolheic).* To us now, or to anyone more or less familiar with the Johannes tradition, *Jeuan Yscolheic* must appear to be our Maistres Jehans. This was enough, indeed, for M. de. Mandach to conclude (*La geste,* p. 143 and p. 225) that this was so, and that for the last part of the *Turpin* Madawc's Welsh translation was made from Maistres Jehans's French. Do we then indeed have here another mention of Maistres Jehans of which we must take account in trying to understand the colophon in V?

I do not think so. The fact is that the Welsh *Turpin* to which Jeuan Yscolheic's name is attached is not the Johannes *Turpin.* There is nothing in Madawc's Welsh text to belie his repeated assertion that he translated from a Latin *Turpin.* M. de Mandach's only criterion, beyond the coincidence of the name, is the form *tiester* "indiquant l'Allemagne" (p. 143), which M. de Mandach thinks can only reflect the *Tiescheterre* of the Johannes translation. But it reflects not *Alamania,* or *Germania,* but *terram theutonicam* (ed. Jones, 239, vii) and it occurs in a chapter which is not in Johannes. In the Welsh text, Ch. XXII, which in M. de Mandach's own opinion is based on a Latin *Turpin,* we find the form *Cheisser.* No French text is needed to explain the forms *Tiester* or *Cheisser.* Compare too in the second part of the Welsh *Turpin*, which M. de Mandach argues was taken from the French, the Welsh *Alatlen* with the French *Arles* and the Latin *Arelaten,*

the Welsh *Teodoric* with the French *Tierri* and the Latin
Theodoricus, the Welsh *Ciser* with the French *Cise* and the Latin
Ciserae. But an even more convincing refutation of M. de Man-
dach's too facile conclusion lies in his own pages. He shows on
p. 140 how the Johannes translation makes at one point a change
in the order of events as they are recounted in the Latin text.
How did he fail to see that the order in the Welsh text is that of
the Latin not that of the Johannes translation? So it is through-
out the Chronicle; the French text at times shows, as we have seen,
radical reorganization of the Latin sequences, and the agreement is
always between the Welsh and Latin, not between the Welsh and
French texts.[39] If the Johannes text is not the source of the
Welsh one, can Jeuan Yscolheic be Maistres Jehans? As in the case
of Demarquette's Magister Johannes we must conclude that there
is no identity of persons, only of the name.

The *Turpin* in the Red Book of Hergest ends with an explicit in
Latin: *Explicit istoria domini Sarlim regis francie de actibus in
yspania contra paganos et inimicos IHU. Xpi.* The Hengwrt *Tur-
pin* ends with this same explicit but here translated into Welsh and
followed at once by the colophon quoted above mentioning Jeuan
Yscolheic. Perhaps Jeuan Yscolheic is the Welsh form of a "Johan-
nes Magister" or rather, perhaps, of a "Johannes Scholasticus,"
mentioned in the Latin *Turpin* used by Madawc as the scribe who
wrote the Latin book now lost. But this is a conjecture which
takes us at the moment beyond where we need to go.

There is a Reinallt too mentioned in the Welsh texts, in whom
with even less circumspection, M. de Mandach sees Count Renaud
de Boulogne. At the end of the Welsh *Pèlerinage* and again at the
beginning of the Welsh *Otinel,* the translator of these, be it noted,
French romances into Welsh indulges in a panegyrical apostrophe
to his patron, "Reginald, King of the Isles" *(Reinallt brenhin yr
ynyssed).* This is none other, according to M. de Mandach, than

---

[39] M. de Mandach has been led astray by his wrong assumption also on p. 119 of his *La
geste de Charlemagne.* "Aucun n'a noté," he writes, "que le Cistercien Madawc af
Selif complète le symbole de Nicée arrêté dans son modele sur ces mots 'et ressuscita
au troisième jour' en ajoutant 'et il remonta au ciel a la droite de Dieu.' " It is true
that the phrase "et il remonta. . ." is lacking in Johannes; but Madawc did not "com-
plete Johannes" here; he was translating a Latin text and found the sentence there
complete as he translated it. The Pseudo-Turpin, by the way, seems to have been
following the Athanasian rather than the Nicene creed.

"Renaud de Dammartin, comte de Boulogne *et sire de l'Isle*" (p. 225, but my italics!). I do not know in what document M. de Mandach finds justification for styling Renaud "sire de l'Isle," or "Lille;" I do not understand how he can identify *l'Isle* with the plural *yr ynyssed;* nor do I understand how he can bring Rainallt from his French poems into association with Jeuan Yscolheic and the *Turpin.* Reinallt is in all probability the famous Reginald, King of the Western Isles, so named in the *Chronicon Regum Manniae et Insularum* (see Camden's translation in *Britannia,* 2nd ed., London, 1806, iv. 513, anno 1205), who, I would presume, set on foot the translation of the French poems which entered the Welsh compilation. Jeuan Yscolheic and Reinallt when we first meet them together sound very much like our Maistres Jehan and Count Renaud; but they are quite different persons and have led us away on a false trail.

One might go on and pour into this discussion every Johannes Magister encountered in one's enquiry into the problem of Maistre Jehan's identity. Even within the compass of this date and this locality, there are many of them. But to do so would be to no advantage. Not one of them has more than this common name and title to suggest identification as the author of our translation.

The question may now be put in another form, not who was Jehans but who was the translator. And this makes us turn again to Paul Meyer's suggestion of long ago that it could be Pierre de Beauvais himself.

Paul Meyer's opinion that Pierre de Beauvais was in all probability the author of our translation of the *Turpin* was prompted by his study of this *Turpin* as he found it copied along with the corpus of Pierre's works in our MSS P2 and P3 (*Notices et extraits* XXXIII: 1, 1890, pp. 1 ff.).[40] Both manuscripts contain, as we have seen, the *Descriptio-Turpin* compilation characteristic of our Group II, the French *Descriptio* translated by Pierre, who names himself in the prologue as the translator, followed by our French *Turpin.*

Paul Meyer's first tentative attribution of the translation of the *Turpin* to Pierre is made on pp. 9-10, where he was led to his

---

[40] P3, the Clayette manuscript, was lost when Paul Meyer wrote his article; he used Mouchet's copy made for Lacurne de Sainte-Palaye, preserved at the Bibliothèque Nationale in the Moreau Collection, 1715-1719.

opinion by the fact that he found the *Turpin* among Pierre's works collected in each of these manuscripts. But in the absence of any mention by Pierre of his authorship, it seems more likely that the *Turpin* is there because it belonged as sequel to Pierre's *Descriptio*. Paul Meyer admits a doubt: "(la version de Turpin) peut n'être qu'un renouvellement d'une version un peu plus ancienne, auquel Pierre a ajouté la traduction du voyage de Charlemagne à Jerusalem" (p. 10). In his *De Pseudo-Turpino,* p. 59, Gaston Paris had already expressed the thought that Pierre simply copied as sequel to his *Descriptio* the "anonymous" *Turpin* of 1206. Paul Meyer took the same view in *Romania* XVI, 1887, p. 61; but on pp. 31 ff. of his article in *Notices et extraits* XXXIII: 1, he produces evidence which strengthened his opinion that Pierre was indeed the translator and that later he simply copied his translation as sequel to his *Descriptio.*

Paul Meyer found his first piece of evidence in a passage condemning verse as a vehicle for historiography which occurs in almost identical form both in the prologue to our *Turpin* and in the prologue to Pierre's *Bestiaire,* this latter written shortly before 1217. Meyer quotes the passage from the *Turpin* in Bibl. Nat. French MS 2464: *Et por ce que rime se velt afeitier de moz conqueilliz hors de l'estoire, voust li cuens que cist livres fust sanz rime selonc le latin que Torpins* . . . The passage in the *Bestiaire* is as follows: *Et pour ce que rime se vieut afaitier de moz conqueilliz hors de verité, mist il sanz rime cest livre selon le latin dou livre que Physiologes* . . . This obvious borrowing left Paul Meyer with the question whether the use of the passage in the *Bestiaire* was proof enough that Pierre was the translator of the *Turpin* and used in the *Bestiaire* a passage of his own earlier composition, or whether he was simply plagiarizing another author's work.

A conclusion in favor of the first alternative was prompted by a second piece of evidence (*ibid.,* pp. 43 ff.). In the prologue to another of his works, *Les trois Maries,* Pierre names himself as follows:

> *Pierres qui fist de Charlemenne*
> *Et mist ou moult* (i.e. "monde") *descrire paine* . . .

this second line referring to Pierre's *Mapemonde.* Paul Meyer, with the earlier testimony in mind, thought that the phrase *qui fist de*

Charlemenne could only refer to the French *Turpin* and so read it as Pierre's assertion of authorship of the translation. Thus emboldened, no doubt, he had written on p. 31 of his article: *Chronique du Pseudo-Turpin traduite en prose par Pierre,* and he repeats this on p. 44. Yet it is clear in his argument that some doubt lingered in his mind. Writing later in *HLF* XXXIV, pp. 385-86, he was still not quite sure. However, his ascription of our *Turpin* translation to Pierre has been widely accepted since: by Van den Geyn in his description of Brussels MS 4631 (our Br 3), by Doutrepont à propos of Brussels MS 10437 (our Br 1) in *La littérature française a la cour des ducs de Bourgogne,* p. 19, by Mlle. S. Solente in *Scriptorium* VII, 1953, p. 229, by Guy Mermier in *RF* LXXVIII, 1966 and by Charles J. J. Liebman in *La vie de saint Denis,* p. LVI.[41] O. Jodogne however, becoming more and more aware as he examined the question that he could not be sure of the relationship of the manuscripts involved, preferred to withhold judgment ("A propos d'un manuscrit du *Bestiaire* de Pierre de Beauvais," p. 34). His prudence was justified, for the evidence put forward by Paul Meyer is not conclusive.

Paul Meyer, like Gaston Paris, did not, could not, know the whole manuscript tradition of the French *Turpin* in question. The passage about rhymed history which he quoted from the *Turpin* in MSS 2464 (our P5) and which Pierre borrowed for the introduction to his *Bestiaire,* comes from our second redaction, not from the translation in its original form. The passage in the original translation as this is preserved in our MSS M, P1, L1 reads, apart from irrelevant variants: *Et pour ce que histore traitie par rime samble menchongne, est ceste sans rime mise en rommans selonc le latin tout ensi que Turpins. . .* If Pierre was indeed the translator of the *Turpin,* surely he would have borrowed the phrase he wanted for his *Bestiaire* from his own prologue, not from the one rehandled by our second redactor. Pierre's passage in the *Bestiaire* is then a plagiarism, made without acknowledgement, simply with the liberty which mediaeval authors accepted as legitimate. It is evidence against, not for, his authorship of our translation. As for the phrase *qui fist de Charlemenne* in *Les trois Maries,* Paul Meyer

---

[41] In its description of Bibl. Nat. French MS 17203, the *Catalogue des manuscrits* wrongly ascribes the French *Turpin* in this manuscript to Pierre: "traduite en Français par Pierre."

seems not to have thought of the possibility that Pierre could have been referring to his translation of the *Descriptio.* Pierre makes no statement which would allow us to date his *Descriptio.* But we can see now, from the history of the Johannes *Turpin* as it has been traced above, that it must have been written before 1206 by which year our second redactor made use of it. So the phrase *qui fist de Charlemenne* could indeed refer to Pierre's *Descriptio.* But it is even more likely that it refers to Pierre's *Descriptio-Turpin,* his own *Descriptio* followed by his copy of our original French *Turpin,* the composite history which was reduced and unified by our second redactor in 1206 or shortly before. The vagueness of the reference seems to be Pierre's manner of referring to a work not easy for him to define in a simple title, to the *Descriptio* drawn from a Latin source for which Pierre could cite no author's name to guarantee its authenticity, linked with the famous Turpin's *Historia Karoli Magni,* to have translated which Pierre did not, probably because he could not, make any claim.

Further evidence pointing in the same direction lies in the fact that nowhere in our tradition does Pierre make any explicit claim that he translated the *Turpin.* True, he does not always assert his authorship in the works which he is known to have written, the *Vie de saint Germer* for example. But he usually does so, e.g. in his *Translation and Miracles of St. James,* in his *Descriptio,* in his *Bestiary,* in his *Olympiad,* and in most of his verse translations. But there is no mention of his name in any manuscript of our *Turpin* tradition. We might have expected such a claim, had it been justified, in Pierre's prologue to his *Descriptio,* which he carefully presents to his readers as deserving to be known as well as the familiar *Turpin.* In the *Descriptio-Turpin* as it appears in MSS P2 and P3, lost folios have carried away the beginning of the *Turpin* and with them any prologue which might have enlightened us further on this matter. MS Br 1, which is complete, ends the *Descriptio* and begins the *Turpin* as follows: *Cy fault l'istoire comment Chalemaine fu oultre mer e aprés commence comment il conquist Espaigne si comme Turpins l'arcevesque traita et ouÿ la verite.* Br 1 is a late manuscript and is often unreliable. Its incipit to the *Descriptio* is unique and so is its incipit to the *Turpin.* Yet it is the only complete manuscript we have of Pierre's *Descriptio-Turpin* and so we must note that it does not mention Pierre as translator of the *Turpin*. The silence in our *Turpin* tradition with regard to Pierre is then total. As usual, the *argumentum ex silentio* is difficult to evaluate. However, the story told by the Latin *Turpin* was well-known, our translation at once became very popular; and to whom could it have recommended itself better than to Pierre's well-known patron, Philippe de Dreux, the Count-Bishop of Beauvais, the warrior-bishop who, like the legendary archbishop Turpin, by temperament no less than in obedience to Philip Augustus's insistence, went gaily to war against his king's, and his own, enemies, who in 1182 made the pilgrimage to Compostella and who later joined in the third crusade? Yet of Pierre as translator, of Philippe de Dreux as sponsor, no word. The silence in this case does seem to echo voices which cry that Pierre was not our author.

But let us seek out all the proof that is there for us to find. In a statement which Pierre makes at the beginning of the prologue to his *Descriptio* we read: *Es livres qui parolent des roys de France trovons escrit que par la proiere monseigneur saint Jaque dona Nostre Sires cest don a Charlemaine c'on parleroit de lui tant com le siecle dureroit.* This sentence must be based on one which we find in the *Turpin*. It occurs in the passage where St. James exhorts Charlemagne to liberate Spain and to drive the Saracens from his burial place in Compostella. It is rendered in our translation as follows (VII, 22-23) . . . *et deci au darrien jor iert tis nons enloengiez* (cf. the Latin, 93, v-vi: *et usque ad novissimum diem erit nomen tuum in laude*). I do not think that the phrase in the *Descriptio* could have come from anywhere but the *Turpin*. Pierre however says he found it *es livres qui parolent de France*. This cannot be a reference to the isolated *Turpin*, Latin or French; still less does it suggest a *Turpin* which Pierre had just translated. It could only refer to a Latin *Turpin* already incorporated in the royal chronicles such as the *Historia regum Francorum* which were in process of elaboration at Saint-Denis where Pierre, judging by statements made in his writings, must have been a frequent and respected visitor and where a number of the Latin texts which he translated were made available to him. There, among the compilations of national history written at Saint-Denis and collected in its library, Pierre probably found the Latin *Descriptio* from which he made his translation, followed no doubt by the Latin Turpin, the established sequence[42] which may have given him the idea of putting the French version of both chronicles together.

The sum of all this evidence is against Pierre's authorship of our *Turpin.* But there is a point to be made which might be judged to favor an opposing view. We saw above that, in his translation of the *Descriptio,* Pierre showed dissatisfaction with the Latin author's exposition of his subject matter (p. 24). In a number of places he rearranged the order of the events chronicled in order to give more naturalness to the narrative sequences. We find throughout our French *Turpin* a structural re-organization which resembles what Pierre did with the *Descriptio.* Again, our translator, presenting his French *Turpin* to cultured, lay readers, the *haus hommes* of his prologue, changed the rather drab and unfeeling style of his Latin model into a more lively manner of writing, acquired in part through familiarity with epic poetry, with its dramatic vitality, its realism in detail and its laconic expressiveness. This style, characteristic of our translator, passed on of course through the hands of Pierre and of the second redactor; it forms the subject of our Chapter III. At one point however, we find in Pierre a passage in which he improves on our translator by the application of a similar technique. We shall see in Chapter III, p. 105, that our translator almost rewrote the Pseudo-Turpin's Chapter XVI, *De bello Furre.* Pierre goes further and makes certain eloquent additions to the text he was copying completely conformable to our translator's innovations. The Pseudo-Turpin tells us of the miracle which took place before the battle of Monjardín. The evening before the battle, Charlemagne prayed God to show him which of his men were to die on the morrow. The next morning, the doomed men were seen to bear a cross on their shoulders. Here is the Latin text (147, iv ff.): *Quos ut vidit Karolus mox retrusit illos in oratorio suo ne morerentur in bello.* Our original translation reads (MS M, fol. 106 v°, a): *Quant il vit ce, il les fist aler en un sien oratore et commanda qu'il ne se meussent.* But Pierre writes, and with him our Group III manuscripts (XXXIII, 9 ff.): *Il les comenda devant lui a venir et les conjura sor s'amor qu'il alassent tuit en une chapelle qui dejoste ce liu ert et qu'il l'atendissent ilec tant qu'il fust repairiez de la bataille.* With these

---

[42] Cf. Walpole, *Mouskés,* pp. 366 ff., especially pp. 368 ff.

touches, like our translator elsewhere, Pierre vitalizes the Pseudo-Turpin's insensitive style. He expresses that tenderness in Charlemagne which, in the *Chanson de Roland,* made him for his feudal subjects *nostre emperere magnes* and applies a visual imagination to make that contrived *oratorio suo, un sien oratore,* into the much more real *chapele qui dejoste cel leu ert.* This case of divergence between Pierre and our original French *Turpin* is unique, but it shows in this detail as in the larger matter of structure, a similarity between Pierre's style and that of our translator which must prompt the thought that Pierre and our translator were one. A study of Pierre's style and a comparison with that of our translator is called for. It must include a study of Pierre's linguistic forms in so far as these may be discerned behind the manuscript tradition of his works, his vocabulary, the technique of his translation and the art which underlies his style. This cannot be done here. For the moment I would say that the resemblances in the manner of translation which I have pointed out between Pierre and our translator are real, but that they could have been learned by Pierre from the style of our translator and imitated by him in his translation of the *Descriptio* and in his copy of the *Turpin.* The weight of evidence, I would conclude, is against the ascription to Pierre of our translation.

Is it therefore to be classed among the other anonymous Old French translations of the *Turpin?* Again we turn back to the colophon in MS V with its flat assertion: *que Maistres Jehans tranlata.* We have considered the possibility that the Jehans here referred to may be Renaud's John the Chaplain who, serving Renaud, did not translate a Latin *Turpin* but copied a French one. This identification we have decided is probable but not sure. We have found and set aside in our search for the translator, along with Pierre de Beauvais, a number of possible candidates whose claim to the authorship is only the fact that they bore the name and title *Maistre Jehans.* Having found so many, can we be sure that one more, and this time the winner, has not eluded us? Out of a lingering sense that the scribe of MS V may have meant what he wrote in his colophon and have shown there that he knew more than we do, we must leave open the possibility that a Maistres Jehans, known by tradition to him but lost to us, was indeed the author of our translation which, on his frail but not entirely disproved authority, may still be known as the Johannes *Turpin*. Johannes the translator, if we may call him so, must have worked before 1206, for by the end of that year his translation had passed through the hands of two redactors, the first, Pierre de Beauvais with his *Descriptio-Turpin* combination and the second, an anonymous, who rearranged Pierre's compilation, in the briefer, neater form which is reproduced in our printed text and which, through the copies made for Renaud and Michel, spread far and wide among the feudal courts of northern France and Anglo-Norman England.

Chapter III

Johannes as Translator

The Latin *Turpin* from which Johannes made his translation was a text of the C type as defined by C. M. Jones on p. 22 of his edition. It is represented in his variants by his MS C3, Bibl. Nat. Latin MS 3768 which, he tells us on p. 29, reproduces without exception all the particularities of the group. A. Hamel, in spite of fundamental criticism of Jones's classification of the manuscripts, accepted the C texts as forming a homogeneous group (*Speculum* XIII, 1938, p. 251). M. André de Mandach (*La geste de Charlemagne,* pp. 385 ff.) has traced their descent from the copy, made for Geoffroi du Breuil, of the Codex Compostellanus at an early stage in its development, and on pp. 130 ff. has, a little fancifully, explained its individual character as due to Poitevin influences: southern courtesy and Plantagenet sympathies. The most striking variants which characterize the C manuscripts are interpolations and these show not so much a local coloring of this kind as the influence of French heroic poetry, particularly of the *Chanson de Roland.* The *Pseudo-Turpin* is a claustral book,[1] lacking in human warmth. The interpolations in the C manuscripts, and there are many more than those which appear in Mandach's analysis, show touches of a more poetic style and deeper feeling, insistence on Roland's presence alongside of Charlemagne and, beyond the recital of his feats of arms, an affection for him and something of the

---

[1] Dr. Pius Fischer's argument that the Pseudo-Turpin was a monk is convincing *(op. cit.* pp. 81-82, pp. 96 ff.). Dr. Fischer, himself a Benedictine, has recognized in the Pseudo-Turpin's prose the great number of biblical phrases which seem to come to him naturally as he writes. They come to him not directly from the Bible, but indirectly through the liturgical books and in their slightly altered wording. With these the Pseudo-Turpin had a familiarity only to be explained as that of a monk, so much of whose day throughout the year was spent in reading and reciting the Breviary, the Missal and the Psalter.

tenderness which in the *Chanson* Charlemagne feels toward him.[2] All these variants have passed into our translation. But we do not have the text itself which Johannes used. His French at times reads with the other manuscripts of the Latin tradition against the C group.[3] However, the discrepancies between the Johannes translation and the extant C texts are not important for our present

---

[2] Because the distinctive character of the C group is important in itself and also because it has impressed itself on the Johannes translation and on the English, Welsh and Irish *Turpin* traditions, it is urgent to make clear what are the particular readings which define the group and how we are to understand them. Some of these readings have been listed before as evidence of filiations in the *Turpin* tradition, e.g. Walpole, *Speculum XXII*, 1947, pp. 260-262; Mandach, *La geste*, pp. 131 ff.; Short, *Med. Aevum* XXXVIII, 1969, p. 8. But only a few of the distinctive variants have been used, just enough to serve each scholar's purpose at the time. There are in fact twenty-four important variants peculiar to the group which seem to be deliberate rather than accidental and all of them should be examined if we wish to establish a firm basis for a judgment as to what they imply. Since these readings will certainly serve in the future the purpose of discovering filiations still unperceived, and since we do need to interpret them properly, I list them all here.

1. 119, xiii   C *adds before* resumptis: invocato omnipotentis auxilio et

2. 123, v   C *adds before* armis: manibus et

3. 123, viii   C *adds to the description of Roland after* Karoli: vir magnissimus et summae probitatis

4. 125, xi   C *omits what is said of Ogier:* De hoc canitur in cantilena usque in hodiernum diem, quia innumera fecit prodigia.

5. 127, xix   Novissime vero venit Karolus cum aliis
      C: "   "   "   "   cum Rotholando et c.a.

6. 133, iii   *(Charlemagne to Agolant)*: unde patet quia magis valet lex nostra quam vestra
      C *adds after* vestra: Et quia omnium creatorem non cognoscitis, nec cognoscere vultis, ius vel hereditatem in terra aut in celo habere non debetis, sed prius vestra et possessio erit cum diabolo et cum Mahummet Deo vestro.

7. 133, vii   sed pugnabo ego et gens mea
      C *omits* ego et gens mea

8. 141, xvii   . . . et ex alia Karolus cum innumeris exercitibus suis. Tunc Arnaldus
      C: . . . K. et principes exercituum ex alia parte agmina sua producentes coeperunt tubis eburneis tonitruare et in Domino confitentes alacriter amovebant. Tunc A.

9. 143, iii   clamor omnium
      C: clamor et ululatus omnium

10. 149, xix   *As Roland goes out to meet Fernagu,* C *adds:* Et timebat Karolus valde propter Rotholandum quia adhuc iuvenis erat et tenere diligebat eum. Orabatque ad Dominum ut nepotem suum corroboraret in virtute sua.

11. 151, vi   Rotolandus spata propria evaginata
      C: R. comes spata sua e. quae Durenda apellabat

12. 153, v   Rotolandus vero, ut erat iuvenis alacer
                  C adds after alacer: et nobilis animi

13. 153, xvi   *Fernagu has told Roland that his only vulnerable spot is his navel.*
                  C adds: Quo audito Rotholandus tacuit et quasi non intellexis-
                  set aurem avertit

14. 153, xx   *Fernagu to Roland:* Cuius generis, inquit gigas, es, qui tam forti-
                  ter me expugnas? – Francorum genere oriundus, inquit R.
                  C1 adds after expugnas, C3 after es: Numquam actenus inveni
                  hominem qui me ita fatigare posset

15. 157, xxiii   C omits: Talis enim decet partus Deum

16. 165, xix   *Frightened by the masks and noise, the French squadrons flee:*
                  in fugam omnes conversae sunt.
                  C adds here: Quo viso Karolus super modum miratus est donec
                  cognovit quare ita fieret.

17. 167, xiv   vexillum rubeum   C omits: rubeum

18. 167, xix   Tunc propria spata perticam, quae vexillum sustentabat, abscidit
                  (Karolus) et statim
                  C: Tunc gaudiosam perticam quae v.s., a. et lavarum (C1: labarum)
                  evertit, et statim

19. 167, xxiii   rex Sibiliae occiditur
                  C: r. S. Ebrahim o.

20. 169, vii   Terram Navarrorum et Basclorum Brittannis
                  C: ”   ”   ”   ”   Normannis

21. 177, x   *In the portrait of Charlemagne C omits:* Et erat donis largis-
                  simus, iudiciis rectissimus

22. 205, x   Sansoni assimilatus   C: S. fortitudine a.

23. 209, ix   *Charlemagne came upon the Saracens on the Ebro* iacentes et
                  comedentes. C adds: Tunc irruit super eos ut leo rugiens ad
                  praedam

24. 225, xv   senatores romani ceterasque urbes
                  C: ”   ”   Romam ceterasque u.

The theme on which the C. variants lay particular stress is Roland: his eminence,
the precedence he takes over all other vassals of Charlemagne, his prowess, his high
moral character (Nos. 3, 5, 12, 14), his closeness to Charlemagne and the latter's
affectionate solicitude for him (No. 10). Perhaps the omission of the phrase distin-
guishing Ogier (No. 4) is also due to this purpose of assuring Roland's pre-eminence.
In all this, the influence of the *Chanson de Roland* is obvious. It is apparent too in the
mention of Durendal (No. 11) and probably in No. 18 with its mention of Joyeuse. I
say probably, because the reading in the C manuscripts is not sure. We must take time
to resolve the difficulty if we can, for the reading is most pertinent to our discussion.
Mandach, *op. cit.* p. 31, § 5, quotes from Jones the C variant here as *Tunc Gaudiosa . . .
Karolus perticam abscidit,* but Jones prints, *Tunc gaudiosam perticam . . .,* correctly
reproducing the manuscripts in which a tilde shows above the final *a* of *gaudiosa.*
There is no doubt that the extant C manuscripts read *gaudiosam perticam.* But
what does *gaudiosam* mean? Perhaps "joyous" in the sense of "flaunting," since
the standard on its staff was a symbol of the Saracen's self-confidence. But this is to

strain a little after the sense, especially as *gaudiosam* qualified the staff and not the banner itself. It is more probable that the *gaudiosam* of the extant C manuscripts is a copyist's "emendation" of a model which read *gaudiosa* instead of *propria spata,* that is *Gaudiosa* "Joyeuse." The "emendation" to which a later scribe was led must have been due to his ignorance of the legendary name. It has been passed on by scribes equally unaware or simply servile in their copying, to all the C manuscripts which survive. We may then accept *Gaudiosa* as the genuine but lost C reading. Besides these prominent echoes of the poetic tradition the variants reflect some of the clichés of vernacular poetry: the thunder of the "olifans" in the *tubis eburneis* of No. 8; the synonymic repetition in the *clamor et ululatus* of No. 9, and the simile in No. 24 where Charlemagne falls on the Saracens like a hungry lion on its prey. This famil- iliarty with popular poetry shows a sympathy with the popular mentality and this is evinced also in other ways. The interpolation in No. 13 seems meant to mitigate the extreme and unverisimilar simplicity of Fernagu revealing to his adversary his only vulnerable spot. The one in No. 16 appears due to a similar preoccupation with psychological verisimilitude and the addition in No. 6 drives home to simple minds the Christian Emperor's case against Agolant. To sum up we may say that the C texts have a slightly distinctive character given to them by an interpolator more sensi- tive than the Pseudo-Turpin to the color and tone of the *Chanson de Roland* in par- ticular and of the Carolingian epics in general.

M. de Mandach's interpretation is different. It has led him to define and entitle the Latin C tradition with its vernacular descendants as *La version C – Coeur de Lion des manuscrits turpiniens* (*op. cit.* p. 130 and p. 385). Since this label if accepted is likely to cling, we must see whether it is warranted.

Mandach bases his interpretation on a choice of eleven readings in the C manu- scripts; he sets these forth as §§ 1-11 on pp. 131-132 of *La geste.* We must examine them one by one.

In § 1, à propos of our No. 20, Mandach writes: "Le rédacteur introduit à plusieurs reprises le nom des Normands et celui de l'Angleterre dans le récit. Ainsi ce texte nous apprend que Charlemagne conquit l'Angleterre." For the first part of this statement he refers us to his note 344, but the note is lacking. The Normans are not mentioned in the *Pseudo-Turpin Chronicle* except that in the single passage noted in our No. 20 (not "à plusieurs reprises") the C texts replace *Brittannis* with *Normannis:* in the distribution of territories conquered in Spain, Charlemagne allots the regions of the Basques and Navarrese to the Normans, not to the Bretons. For the second part of his statement, to the effect that the C texts distinctively assert that Charlemagne conquered England, he refers us to Jones' edition 169, vii. There is no such assertion there. Such a statement is indeed made at 89, xi, but by the general tradition of the Latin *Turpin.* The substitution of Normans for Bretons certainly seems to reflect on the part of a scribe the partisan view of a supporter of the Angevin dynasty, and the fact that since 1171 the Bretons had been subjected to Norman suzerainty, but it is going too far to say that this represents an effort to "normannize" the *Turpin.* I must add that the Johannes translation reads *Bretons* so that, as in the case of *gaudio- sam,* we may have to presume that a lost manuscript of the C group read *Brittannis* and that the substitution *Normannis* is proper to the extant C manuscripts but not to the C tradition as a whole.

In § 2, Mandach asserts that the C texts draw a parallel between Charlemagne and Richard Coeur-de-Lion. His reasoning is based on the interpolated simile in our No. 23, whence he deduces that for the interpolator Charlemagne "est un personnage au coeur de lion," in fact another Richard Lion-Heart, and that here again is a sign of the normannization of the *Turpin.* But the simile is a commonplace among the wri- ters of the period. For example, in *Gui de Warewic,* Herault d'Arderne attacks Huencun

　　　　Cum leun qui out juné
　　　　E sa preie ad mult desiré (vv. 1315-1316).

At Lincoln, Guillaume le Maréchal "corut sore a ses enemis" more eagerly than

Lions famillos sor sa preie
(*Histoire de Guillaume le Maréchal*, v. 16612)

and in the *Récits d'un Ménestrel de Reims*, the Count of Saint-Pol, joining battle with the Flemings at Bouvines, *se fiert entr'eus comme lions familleus* (ed. N. de Wailly, Ch. 285). It is simply deforming the evidence to read into this cliché the intention on the part of a reviser to present Charlemagne to us as Charles au Coeur-de-Lion and thus to flatter the Norman Richard by giving him Charlemagne as prototype and namesake.

Mandach's § 3 notes that the genealogy of the English kings which is attached to the *Turpin* in the C manuscripts is brought down in some to include (Mandach's phrase is "met en vedette") Henry II, Richard Lion-Heart and John. But the genealogical list of the English, as of the French, kings, varies in the manuscripts according to the date of the copy and the interest of the copyist. Some manuscripts reproduce an old model exactly, others bring the succession down to their own time. The inclusion of Henry II, Richard I and John in the C manuscripts does not bring any of these kings into special prominence, still less does it mark any copyist as pro-Richard or pro-Henry or pro-John. However §§ 1 and 2 have already decided Mandach on the name befitting the C redactor; here in § 3 he baptizes him le *pro-Richard*. In his list of manuscripts on p. 385, Mandach mentions a lost manuscript of Saint-Martial de Limoges, to which he gives the siglum C.03* It handed down Geoffroi du Breuil's dedicatory letter to the Abbey of Saint-Martial, a letter, writes Mandach, "portant aux nues Richard Coeur-de-Lion." Well, far from lauding Richard to the skies, it does not praise him at all; it simply mentions him as Duke of Limousin and of all Gascony.

In his § 4, Mandach interprets the addition shown in our No. 12 as the impress of that courtesy which was the hall-mark of Eleanor of Aquitaine's court at Poitiers. But we have only to read the whole passage to see that Roland's behavior is explicitly in accordance with military custom honored by Saracen and Christian alike. The adjectival phrase applied by the C redactor to Roland, *nobilis animi,* marks less the infiltration of southern courtesy into the barbarian north than the influence again of epic poetry, in which the epithet *nobilie* is used so often to describe high moral quality, in the *Chanson de Roland* for instance: *Li quens Rollant fu noble guerrier* (v. 2066); (Naimun) *le nobilies vassal* (v. 3442); *E Oliver, sun nobilie cumpaignun* (v. 3690).

The mention of *Gaudiosa* is discussed by Mandach in his § 5. His treatment of the reading is cavalier, but if we accept *Gaudiosa* as authentic the conclusion would follow that the interpolator knew epic poetry, quite probably that he knew above all the *Chanson de Roland*. But it does not follow at all that he knew the *Chanson de Roland* in a written text, still less that this text was the one belonging to Eleanor of Aquitaine.

In § 6 Mandach deals with our No. 8. He sees in the phrase *tubis eburneis tonitruare* an addition prompted by a recollection of Roland's ivory horn and its poetic role in the *Chanson de Roland*. This could be so; but the parallel is not likely. We must note that the scene and the occasion in this *Turpin* passage are totally different from those depicted in vv. 1753 ff. of the *Roland*. It is forcing the evidence again to see an echo of Roland's lonely and desperate call in the trumpetings which sound the onset of the French against Agolant at Pamplona. The *olifans* sound the battle all through mediaeval epic and romance so that all we may legitimately see in this interpolation is the influence on our redactor of vernacular poetry.

In his § 7, cf. our No. 1, Mandach gives us an interpretation which seems impossibly far fetched. In the battle at Saintes, Charlemagne's horse has been killed and Charles, at first a little dazed by his fall, *resumptis viribus . . . peditus interfecit multos illorum* (119, xiii). The C texts add before *resumptis: invocato omnipotentis*

auxilio. "Selon Guillaume de Malmesbury," writes Mandach, "les Normands à
Hastings chantèrent la *cantilena Rollandi,* et aussi un chant invoquant l'aide de
l'Éternel. Or," he continues, "notre Religieux Priorichard insère au début de la
description de la bataille de la prise de Saintes, la mention de l'invocation de l'aide de
Dieu," and Mandach goes on to compare this with the *Aïe Deus* so often uttered in
the *Chanson de Roland.* There is little need to think that the C interpolator had to
borrow his addition here from anybody, and when we think of the different circum-
stances: on the one hand, Charlemagne unhorsed and surrounded by Saracens, on
the other, the Norman army advancing to the attack at Senlac, Mandach's theory of a
borrowing appears wholly imaginative. A similar phrase comes to the Pseudo-Turpin
at 151, ii. This time it is Roland who is in difficulty. Fernagu is carrying him off on
the neck of his horse to Nájera. Then *Rotolandus,* we read, *resumptis viribus suis,* in
Domino confisus, *arripuit eum per mentum.* What appeal could be more natural
under the Pseudo-Turpin's pen in the case both of Charlemagne and of Roland?

Mandach's designation of the C interpolator as le *Religieux Prorichard* in his
§ § 3, 4, 5, 7 has now become formulaic. In No. 8 he explains le *Religieux.* It arises
from the implication which he sees in our No. 6, where the C interpolator makes
Charlemagne repeat in plain and forceful terms why Agolant has no place on earth or
in heaven. But is this necessarily the distinguishing mark of a monk? Could it not
rather be ascribed to a popular preacher? The mark of one who wanted to preach
like the Pseudo-Turpin but to preach more incisively for minds which needed help?
The C interpolator was neither distinctively a *religieux* nor distinctively pro-Richard.
As a designation invented to define what he was, le *Religieux Prorichard* simply will
not do.

In his § 9, Mandach distinguishes his Religieux Prorichard also as a "psychologue."
His conclusion is drawn from the passages presented in our Nos. 10 and 16: the
attribution to Charlemagne made by the C redactor of solicitude for the young
Roland and of surprise as he sees his best troops unaccountably put to flight.
Mandach is quite right in discerning here an effort on the part of the interpolator to
give the Pseudo-Turpin's Charlemagne more life. These touches and those which are
added in our Nos. 8, 9, 13, 22, 23 may not make of him a "psychologue," but they
certainly reveal to us a scribe who brought to the chronicle he was transcribing a
little more human awareness and practical vision.

But not the sense of humor which Mandach ascribes to him in § 11. The passage
in question is presented in our No. 14. Roland and Fernagu are resting after their
first encounters, and are talking together. Fernagu asks Roland who he is and of
what nation: *cuius generis es qui tam fortiter me expugnas?* And here the C inter-
polator adds: *Numquam actenus inveni hominem qui me ita fatigare posset.* In this,
Mandach writes, "il fait dire à Fernagut que Roland est le personnage le plus ennuy-
eux, le plus fatigant qui soit, avec ses disputes théologiques qui n'en finissent pas."
And then Mandach translates the interpolated passage thus: "Jamais n'ai-je trouvé
jusqu'ici," dit-il avec sarcasme, "homme qui puisse fatiguer autant." First of all, this
is a mistranslation. Mandach has neglected to render the *me.* Roland is not a general
bore, but one only for Fernagu. Yet this too is a misrepresentation. Somehow
Mandach has failed to notice, or has forgotten, that the theological discussion
between Fernagu and Roland has not, at the moment of the conversation, taken
place. Fernagu cannot yet have been bored by a tiresomely argumentative Roland.
The sense of the interpolation could not be more plain. The young Roland has up to
then, and in contrast to the other champions sent against Fernagu, fought so well that
Fernagu ungrudgingly admits to him that he has never before met with so strong an
opponent, one who has so worn him down. There is no sarcasm in what he says,
simply the frank admission of his opponent's valor. The phrase follows with perfect
naturalness on the *qui tam fortiter me expugnas.* The added phrase is another touch
showing that the C interpolator was a little closer than the Pseudo-Turpin to the
chivalric mentality of the time.

comparison. Failing the model itself which Johannes used, the comparison will be with the Latin texts of Jones's MSS C1 and C3, Brit. Mus. MS Harley 6358 and Bibl. Nat. Latin MS 3768. The Johannes text which is to be used for our comparative scrutiny will be the text of the second redaction printed below. As basis for an appraisal of Johannes as translator it can be taken as a faithful representative of the Johannes *Turpin* tradition as a whole.[4]

What strikes us at once as we take our comparative view is the modification Johannes made in the Pseudo-Turpin's exposition of his subject matter. Johannes evidently studied the Latin Chronicle before he began to translate it, and found much fault in its organization. He could not change the basic character of the *Turpin*

Let us not then deduce from the evidence of the C texts more than it allows. The C manuscripts represent Geoffroi du Breuil's copy of the Compostella manuscript in its state of ca. 1172. The C manuscripts seem to have flourished and multiplied in the Plantagenet domains, first on the Continent and then across the Channel. There are traces of local patronage in some of them, but the only general character which we may discern in their distinctive readings is the influence of vernacular poetry, especially of the *Chanson de Roland,* and the slight impress of a lay mentality.

[3] For example: at 95, v, C lacks, Johannes has, the phrase *sine contrario* "sanz nul contredit" (IX, 5); at 97, xii and xv C lacks, Johannes has, the names of the towns *Barbagalli, Carbone, Hora Malaguae* "Barbagalle," "Carbone," "Oramalgie" (X, 18); at 169, vii the C texts read *Normannis* for *Britannis,* but Johannes has *Bretons* (XLV, 4); at 177, x C lacks, Johannes has, the phrase: *Et erat donis largissimus, iudiciis rectissimus* "Molt ert larges de doner et droituriers en jugemenz" (XLIX, 30). At 179, ix-x, the extant C manuscripts omit *et qualiter Romae imperatorem fuit et dominicum sepulcrum adiit,* an important passage for us (see above, p. 13). but one obviously omitted by homoioteleuton, the lost words falling between *et qualiter* in 1. ix and *et qualiter* in 1. x. The presence in the extant C manuscripts of the phrase *et qualiter lignum dominicum secum attulit,* a non sequitur in the passage as erroneously preserved, assures us that the full reference to the *Descriptio* legend belonged to C texts now lost. At 105, vi Johannes has in place of *urbem Bitterensium,* "Boorges," though elsewhere "Boorges" is his correct rendering of *Bituricas, bituricensis.* The error is not confined to the Johannes translation (cf. Short, *ZrP* LXXXVI, 1970, p. 528) and is probably to be explained by a reading *Bituricensium* in a Latin manuscript. There are other examples but they are few in number and of small importance; they do show, however, that Johannes used for his translation a Latin C text now lost.

[4] Readers may wish to supplement the study made in this chapter with the comparison which Dr. Fischer (*op. cit.*) made word by word between the Johannes translation as represented by Munich MS Gallicus 52, our MS M, and the Latin Chronicle as represented by the Codex Compostellanus, by Munich MS 11,319 and by Madrid, Biblioteca Nacional, MS 1617. Dr. Fischer shows in his study that he was aware of the difficulties inherent in the fact that his comparison was made between Latin and French texts only distantly and confusedly related to each other.

which is a patchwork made of scattered pieces of Carolingian legend, but he did much in a purposeful and sustained effort to give a more logical order to the events which it relates and thereby a more natural flow to the narrative.

A good example of his creative intervention at this level is afforded at the end of the Chronicle after Charlemagne and Turpin have taken leave of each other at Vienne. The Pseudo-Turpin tells us that Charlemagne went from Vienne to Paris and summoned a council at Saint-Denis. After the council he journeyed to Aix and embellished the city, adorning especially his palace with frescoes of the seven arts which are described in detail. *Post exiguum vero tempus,* the Latin continues in a most abrupt transition, Turpin learned that Charles had died. Then follows the description of the vision which appeared to Turpin in Vienne and revealed to him the circumstances of Charlemagne's death. After this, with another most awkward transition: *Nam et ego ab eo in antea . . . ,* Turpin informs us that when he and the Emperor parted company in Vienne, they had made a mutual promise that whichever of them first felt his end approaching would make arrangements for a messenger to carry the news of his death to the other. A messenger now comes in effect to Turpin confirming the news already conveyed by the vision and adding an account of the portents which had preceded the death of the Emperor.

Johannes thoroughly reorganizes this order of presentation. He brings forward to the moment when Charlemagne and Turpin bade each other farewell at Vienne their promise to inform the survivor of the other's death. The council at Saint-Denis and the embellishment of Aix follow in natural sequence. Then Johannes, rendering the Pseudo-Turpin's own transitional phrase quoted above: *Ne demora gueres apres* (LXXVI, 1) uses it to introduce in logical order the description of the portents which warned of Charlemagne's approaching death. He thus brings the Emperor to his death-bed and there lets him remember his promise and dispatch a messenger to Vienne. Now comes Turpin's vision of Charlemagne's death and in natural and dramatic sequence its confirmation two weeks later by the messenger.

Johannes's re-ordering of these happenings is not only a revealing illustration of his method; it allows us also to see the Latin

Chronicle through his critical eyes. The Pseudo-Turpin, intent on the great fiction by which he makes Charlemagne act under the inspiration of St. James and on the grand finale in which he will make the saint the saviour of the Emperor's soul, is careless in the construction of his plot and patches the details of his inventions together in a visibly labored effort to give them verisimilitude. Johannes, we can see, was of the opinion that this loose method, this almost cynical carelessness, would not do. He was not prompted by a disbelief in the trustworthiness of his author, which would have entailed knowledge and a critical perception beyond the general mentality of his time; he reacted in criticism not of the substance but of the style of his model and in this he must have been mindful above all of the lay audience to whom he addressed his translation, people whose minds were made wary by practical experience. For them he re-ordered the Pseudo-Turpin's exposition as we have seen, removing those explanations of past events intruding like after thoughts to allay doubts which should never have been provoked, creating the verisimilitude so artificially sought after in his model simply by giving to the events narrated, a logical, natural order.

This implicit criticism of his model, and the manner and purpose of the innovations which Johannes applied in his translation, appear constantly throughout his work. A similar restructuring of complex episodes can be seen in Johannes's treatment of the death of Fernagu and the capture of Nadres (cf. 163, vi ff. and XLI, 7 ff), of the scene where Charlemagne and Agolant meet to discuss their differences and Charles surprises Agolant by speaking to him in Arabic (cf. 131, v-xi, XXVI, 9-17), of the episode at Saint-Fagon, where the lances change to trees (109, x), in which Johannes (XVIII, 2 ff.) puts the founding of the abbey after the miracle and after the victory, the effect after the cause. The Latin here reads like a guidebook, the French tells a dramatic tale. Johannes makes a similar transposition of the moral and the miracle at 147, v-vi; cf. XXXIII, 13-21. Here the Pseudo-Turpin tells us of the French victory over Furre at Monjardín, a victory made more memorable by the miracle which occurred on that occasion. On the eve of the battle, Charlemagne prayed God to make known to him those of his knights who were to die on the morrow. In answer to his prayer, a red cross appeared on their shoulders to mark these men.

To save them from death, Charlemagne commanded them to
withdraw into a chapel. Here the Pseudo-Turpin breaks into excla-
mations: how incomprehensible are God's judgments and how
inscrutable are His ways! When Charlemagne returned victorious
from the fight, he found the men in the chapel dead, and the
Pseudo-Turpin develops the moral thus: though the sword of the
persecutor had not slain these men, yet they were not thereby
allowed to lose a martyr's crown. Johannes reorders the exposi-
tion and makes the point more clear. He brings the fragmented
moral into one and places it after the events which embody its les-
son, at the moment when the audience is left wondering why these
strange events came to pass. God moves in a mysterious way, he
says, but his will is not to be gainsaid. The story as Johannes tells
it has a dramatic impact lacking in his model. Johannes is the bet-
ter preacher; he knew his congregation and reached out to it more
surely. He does away with the Pseudo-Turpin's rhetorical excla-
mations: *Quam incomprehensibilia . . . ! Quid plura? O Christi
pugnatorum sanctissima caterva!* replacing the inflated style of the
Latin with more simple and more forceful language: *Ne sont mie
legier a veoir li jugement de Deu. Car por ce se cil ne morurent a la
bataille, ne perdirent il mie la corone de martire, car Deus lor avoit
porveu, et ce que Deus a porveu ne puet estre destorné.* Johannes
is not the slave of his Latin model; he is refashioning the Pseudo-
Turpin's thought and sharpening its expression; his French prose,
freeing itself from the Latin, is finding the qualities of simplicity
and clarity.

It is not only in such major matters that Johannes thus invests
the structure of his model with greater logic and realism, he inter-
venes to the same effect in his treatment of matters of less scope.
He brings the Pseudo-Turpin's broken description of Lucerna Ven-
tosa, Capparra, Adania at 99, xvi and 101, xi into one piece at
XI, 8-15, and does the same with the portrait of Fernagu at 147,
xvii-xix and 149, vii-x in XXXIII, 26-29.

In these illustrative examples Johannes achieves his effect of
verisimilitude by changing little more than the surface of the nar-
ration. But his interventions go deeper than that. As our examin-
ation draws us on into more detail we become aware that he
changes the very tone of the Latin *Turpin* and reveals himself to us
as a sensitive personality much more appealing as a man and as a
writer than the aloof and calculating Pseudo-Turpin.

We saw at the beginning of this chapter that the Latin C manuscripts reflect the interventions of a redactor who enlivened the Pseudo-Turpin's narrative with a few additions brought in from his recollections of the poetic tradition of Charlemagne, one of his concerns being to key up a little the Pseudo-Turpin's flat portrait of Roland. In this, Johannes was at one with him in spirit but goes far beyond him in execution. There are moreover in his translation a few passages which show implicitly a downright condemnation of what the Pseudo-Turpin had done with the familiar and beloved themes. In Chapter XI of the Chronicle, Charlemagne has gone back to France to gather an army, strong enough to defeat Agolant, and the Pseudo-Turpin tells us how the Emperor made every effort to win the support of all sorts and conditions of his subjects. These, he then adds (121, xxi): *ego Turpinus . . . a peccatis cunctis relaxabam,* and goes on to list the names of the most famous among the leaders, beginning (123, ii): *Ego Turpinus archiepiscopus remensis, qui dignis monitis Christi fidelem populum ad debellandum fortem et animatum, et a peccatis absolutum reddebam, et Sarracenos propriis manibus et armis saepe expugnabam,* and continuing: *Rotholandus dux exercituum.* Johannes translates faithfully the passage (121, xxi ff.) which describes Turpin's performance of his archiepiscopal functions among the troops and the statement in which Turpin says that he also fought at their side in battle, but he refuses to place Turpin first in the list of *heroes bellatores. Ici sunt li non,* he writes (XXII, 22), *des plus hauz homes qui furent avec lo roi a icest erre. Rollant, guierres des oz . . .* The Pseudo-Turpin's indelicacy had no place in the chivalric company to which Johannes was addressing himself.

Chivalric company; this is the clue to Johannes's profound transformation of the Pseudo-Turpin's Latin chronicle. In his hands it was to become not only true as history but true to life, a history of Charlemagne *le bon roi,* a history *ou li bon fet sunt* for *touz hauz homes* to listen to and cherish that they might profit from its examples and learn *coment l'en se doit avoir en Deu et contenir el siegle honoreement.* It was with this practical conception of his subject in mind and with this practical audience in view that Johannes in his translation modified the form and changed the spirit of his Latin model. The following analysis of two representative passages will show how thorough his purpose and his method were.

Our first example is drawn from the account of the duel between Roland and Fernagu, Chapter XVII in the Latin *Turpin*. Roland and Fernagu have both been unhorsed in their first encounter. They mount again and resume the fight as follows:

(151, v ff.) Ilico Rotholandus comes spata sua evaginata quae Durenda appelabatur, gigantem occidere putans, equum eius solo ictu per medium trucidavit. Cumque Ferracutus peditus esset, spatamque evaginatam manu tenens, ei minans intulisset, R. spata sua in brachio quo spatam suam gigas tenebat, illum percussit, et minime eum laedit, sed tamen spatam eius a manu praecipitavit. Tunc F., gladio amisso, percutere putans pugno clauso R., equum eius in fronte percussit, et statim equus corruens obiit. Deinde sine gladiis pedites usque ad nonam pugnis et lapidibus debellarunt. Die vero advesperascente impetravit trebas F. a R. usque ad crastinum. Tunc disposuerunt inter se, ut die crastina in bello sine equis et lanceis ambo pariter convenirent. Et concessa pugna ex utraque parte, unusquisque ad hospicium suum reversus est. Die autem altera summo diliculo separatim venerunt pedites in campo belli, sicut dispositum fuerat. F. tamen secum detulit gladium, sed nichil ei valuit, quia R. baculum quoddam retortum et longum secum attulit, cum quo tota die illum percussit, et minime eum laesit. Percussit etiam eum magnis et rotundis lapidibus qui in campo habundanter erant, usque ad meridiem, illo saepe consenciente, et eum nullo modo laedere potuit.

(XXXIV, 25 ff.) Rollanz trest Durendal, si le feri si q'a cel col li trencha son cheval par mi. Fernaguz fu a pié et tint s'espee. Adonc le feri si Rollanz el braz dom il tenoit l'espee qu'ele li chai de la main. Mes il nel bleça gueres. Qant li paiens ot s'espee perdue, il corut R. sore et le cuida ferir del poing, si feri son cheval el front si qu'il l'abati mort desoz lui. R. ot perdu son cheval. Il se combatirent a pié desi vers none, et qant vint vers la vespre, F. demanda trives desi a l'endemain, et l'endemain revenissent sanz cheval el champ ensemble si com il erent. R. li otroia par tel covenant qu'il li donast congié d'aporter un baston tel com il voudroit, et li paiens li otroia. Par le creant de l'un et de l'aulre s'en ala chascun a sa herberge. L'endemain, si com covent estoit, revindrent matin a pié a la bataille. R. ot aporté un baston lonc et tort et nouel. Maintenant assemblerent et furent ensint tote jor c'onques R. del baston ne le bleça; mais molt sovent li gita pieres dom el champ avoit a grant plenté. Ensi se combatirent desi au midi c'onques R. ne le pot blecier.

According to the Latin C text, Roland draws Durendal and slays Fernagu's horse. He then deals the pagan such a blow on the arm as to make him drop his sword. Fernagu retaliates by slaying Roland's horse with a blow of his fist. Then they fight on *sine gladiis* and on foot until evening. The Latin text does not say why Roland does not use his sword, though we may presume that he saw to it that Fernagu's weapon remained on the ground. Johannes omits the phrase *sine gladiis*. When it becomes too dark to fight, the two champions agree on conditions for resuming the duel next day. According to the Latin text they will return to the

field *sine equis et lanceis.* Why *sine lanceis?* The combatants have
not used lances so far. Johannes omits *sine lanceis.* When they
come together on the next day, the Latin continues: *F. tamen
secum detulit spatam* and adds that the sword proved useless *quia*
Roland came armed with a club. Although these acts are not liter-
ally inconsistent with the terms of the pact, *sine equis et lanceis,*
the Pseudo-Turpin's sentence is evasive: did he mean to suggest by
his *tamen* that Fernagu broke his promise, and does his *quia* veil
the fact that Roland broke his too? We might not make so much of
this were it not for the fact that Johannes found the passage unac-
ceptable and replaced it with his own version of the terms. The
agreement was, he writes, that the two antagonists were to return
next day to the field *sanz cheval si com il erent* and adds that
Roland obtained permission from Fernagu to bring a club. So on
the morrow they came back to the encounter on foot, Roland
bearing a club. Johannes says nothing about Fernagu bringing a
sword; in truth Fernagu had not lost it so that when he bore it
with him he was in fact returning *si com il erent.*

In both the Latin and French accounts the champions now fight
on indecisively until noon when Fernagu takes his siesta and then
engages with Roland in their discussion of the articles of the Chris-
tian faith. When the battle is renewed, Fernagu fights with his
sword and Roland with his club. But then, in the final moments of
the conflict, the Latin text has it that Roland wrests Fernagu's
own sword from him *(Rotholandus misit manum ad mucronem
eius)* and with it pierces Fernagu through the navel. Johannes how-
ever says that Roland dealt the final stroke with Durendal.

What we see here is Johannes's pervading criticism of his
model's carelessness with regard to details and of the resulting
shoddiness of his structure and of his style.[5] His implied criticism
seems to be most severe in his treatment of the passage which

---

[5] I think we can dismiss the possibility that Johannes was drawing on his knowledge
of other versions of the legend of Fernagu. There were indeed many versions of the
legend abroad. We may come close to its original form and appreciate its ramifica-
tions by reading what Jean d'Outremeuse does with it in his *Myrcur des Histors* now
pleasantly available in Andre Goose's edition, pp. 146-155. There is this point of
similarity between Johannes and the story in Jean d'Outremeuse, namely, that
Roland slew Fernagu with Durendal. But the dissimilarities are manifold, and it is not
likely that Johannes had to go to another source than his own knowledge and con-
viction that no other weapon could have appropriately done this service to the cause
of France and Christendom.

describes the conditions on which Roland and Fernagu agree to
renew their duel on the second day. Johannes makes these condi-
tions fit the fact that both champions had lost only their horses,
and he does away with the equivocal passage in which the Pseudo-
Turpin suggests that Fernagu broke the pact by bringing a sword
but attributing no such faithlessness to Roland who brought a
club. He makes the terms clear and consistent, and honored by
Saracen and Christian alike. His translation shows that educated
opinion in the early thirteenth century was awed but not over-
awed by the authority of authors. The Latin narrative, serving its
propagandistic purpose at times by tawdry means of invention and
style, is full of prevarications which suggest in their author a clois-
tered mind so concentrated on the effect sought after as to be
blind to the moral and intellectual susceptibilities which his liber-
ties might offend. The scribes who passed on the Latin tradition
seem not to have been affected by this aspect of his style. But our
translation shows that there was in the lay world of action more
than in the contemplative life of the cloister, a sense of reality, a
code of honor and a moral tone which the Pseudo-Turpin had been
too obtuse to discern or too cynical to respect.[6]

Our second example comes from the Latin Chapter XXI with
which the Roncevaux episode begins. It opens with the account
of Ganelon's treacherous mission to Saragossa. In the French
translation as in the Latin text (L, 7 ff.; 179, xxii ff.), Charlemagne
sends Ganelon to Saragossa with orders to Marsile and Baligant to
be baptized or send him tribute. From this point on the Latin
sequence is as follows: . . . *aut tributum ei mitterent. Tunc mis-
erunt ei* . . . "Thereupon Marsile and Baligant sent" to Charlemagne
a convoy bearing gold and silver, another one bearing choice wines
and a thousand *Sarracenas formosas.* To Ganelon also they pro-
ferred rich gifts, but *fraudulenter,* as a bribe to betray the French
and bring them to destruction. Ganelon succumbed to the tempta-
tion and took the money. With the treacherous pact agreed upon
he returned to Pamplona, handed over to Charlemagne his charge
of gold and silver and assured him of the Saracens' total submis-
sion. When he offered the gifts of wine and women to the army,

---

[6] I am reminded of what the humble but busy Mouskés says in one of his few pithy
lines — a proverb indeed, but he has made it his own:

Bien est ki dit s'il est ki fait.

the barons took only the wine, the women went to the rank and
file. Charlemagne, in full trust and following Ganelon's advice, set
up the rearguard under Roland and Oliver and made ready to lead
the main body of his army back over the Pyrenees. But because
certain of the French, drunk with the wine, had lain with the Sara-
cen women, they incurred death. *Quid plura?* — and there follows
the account of the destruction of the rearguard.

Here again we can see with Johannes the loose structure and
shifty style of the Latin narrative, and, above all, its failure to
come alive. The Pseudo-Turpin gives no dramatic order or inten-
sity to the details of the episode. He makes little effort to create
character. There is no outward or inward conflict; the action pro-
ceeds disjointedly with little of the vitality which comes from the
natural flow of cause and effect. It is not that the Pseudo-Turpin
did not know the poetic drama into which legend had transformed
the event of Aug. 15th, 778; he tells us that Charlemagne disposed
his rearguard in accordance with Ganelon's advice. It is that in
writing his version of the story he was motivated not by artistic
but by propagandistic purposes. He was less interested in the story
than in the effect he wanted to produce. The plot to betray is not
creatively woven out of the characters and situation. Without
advice from Ganelon, Marsile responds at once to Charlemagne's
demand by gestures intended to seduce him and debauch his army.
This prepares the moral that will follow: the death of the rear-
guard is the punishment of sin. We lose sight of Ganelon's crimin-
ality. For his part, Ganelon yields at once to cupidity: *Qui con-
concessit et pecuniam accepit;* the Pseudo-Turpin tells us no more.
He makes but a patchwork of the fictions which he borrows or
invents, and is as careless of consistency as of coherence. So he
tells us at 181, xii that the gentle men of the French army only got
drunk, the ungentle men committed adultery, but at 1. xxi he says
that the drunken men lay with the women and so brought death
upon themselves. This enmeshes him in further difficulty; we see
him adding patch after patch, afterthought to afterthought, as he
seeks to make plausible the speciously contrived details of his tale.
He has just told us that Marsile had sent a thousand Saracen
women as a present to the French army. The thought must have
come to him that the gift of a thousand women for an army of
which the rearguard alone counted twenty thousand men might

not in its numerical insufficiency have justified the slaughter to
come. So at 181, xxi, where he describes how those who sinned
with the women incurred death, he adds that not only the thou-
sand Saracen women were involved but also Christian women:
quas secum multi de Gallia adduxerant. And this after all he has
recounted of the French victories in Spain! Johannes set about
the Pseudo-Turpin's story with visible zest. He had obviously read
it through and thought it over before beginning to translate it and
decided that it needed thorough revision if it was to gain the vital
substance which it lacked. Here in summary is his version.

Ganelon, charged with his embassy to Marsile and Baligant,
s'atorna et erra tant qu'il vint a Saragosse. To look at him, you
would have thought he was a true knight; but the heart within
belied this appearance. On the evening of Ganelon's arrival, Mar-
sile received him with much honor, then drew him aside and
offered him rich gifts if he would rid him of Charlemagne. Then
and there Ganelon, like many before him, succumbed to greed and
gave his promise to betray, so passing from salvation to perdition.
The night passed in the formulation of the plan. Next day, Marsile
gave Ganelon the promised bribe and made ready the convoys of
tribute, wine and women, these last for the *chevaliers de l'ost* since
Marsile in his cunning knew that the men would be induced by the
wine to lie with the women for which crime God would punish
them with death. Ganelon took leave of Marsile and made his way
back to Pamplona. He came before Charlemagne and delivered his
message: "Marsile sends you greetings. He will follow you to
France, will be baptized where you please and will hold his king-
dom in fief of you in full friendship and loyalty. What is more, he
sends you this rich tribute." Charlemagne, Johannes adds point-
edly, was pleased with the promise of baptism. Ganelon sent to
the men of high rank the wine and the women; most of them got
drunk and lay with the women, for a drunken man loses his wits
and all self-control. Charlemagne began his preparations to return
to France . . .

Johannes has not only, with very deliberate touches, restored to
the story the drama of which the Pseudo-Turpin had emptied it; he
has also given it a logical, natural structure and rid it of its impu-
dent inconsistencies. His translation here is a work less of inven-
tion than of restoration. He has filled the Pseudo-Turpin's vacant

account with the reality which belonged to the legend of
Roncevaux but which the Pseudo-Turpin, laboring with less art
than doctrinal purpose, ignored. Johannes wrote with understand-
ing of the mentality and taste of his lay audience which saw in
Charlemagne and the peers embodiments of their own experience
and ideals, active participants as they were in crusading warfare
and political life. The realistic touches which he added belonged
to the world which they knew: character and conflict, physical
and psychological detail, the drama of good and evil at odds within
men and between them. He knew that his public was not averse to
a moralizing tone; it was preached to in church, in art, in literature.
But he did not accept for it the Pseudo-Turpin's gross style of
sermonizing: his equivocal and sycophantic attribution of the
minor sin of drunkenness to the nobles and the major one of adul-
tery to the commoners; his subsequent inconsistencies in declaring
that the drunken, which included the noblemen, were the adulter-
ers, and that they lay with Christian as well as Saracen women;
that it was by this sin that they brought upon themselves a deserved
death. The Pseudo-Turpin wrote without intellectual scruples,
neglecting in his literary role the morals he preached as a monk.
Not so Johannes, who, by his treatment of the Latin text, shows
that he expected critical attention from the gentlemen to whom
he addressed his translation, that he respected their intelligence,
their taste and their code of behavior and that for himself as his-
torian he took the motto by which they lived as men of action:
vivre sans honors est morirs.

Johannes, to the best of his ability, not only wanted the truth,
he wanted it plain. He seems to have known in his early day the
precept which Acis had to learn in a later one: "Vous voulez dire,
Acis, qu'il pleut. Que ne disiez-vous, il pleut?" The Pseudo-
Turpin, true to type, sought to add authority to his chronicle by
writing it in a rhetorical style. Johannes, in this as in so much else
a world apart from him, wrote simply and plainly as a man of good
sense addressing men and women of good sense in those salons of
the thirteenth century, the *chambres* in the baronial courts where
lords and ladies, squires and demoiselles, gathered to hear him. His
translation, as contrasted with his Latin model, is characterized by
taste. He relaxes the strained and artificial tone of the Latin chron-
icle by moderating its rhetoric, by smoothing its transitions, by

eliminating needless repetitions and over-emphases, by relieving
it of its excess of biblical and liturgical reminiscences. The
Pseudo-Turpin, having listed the names of the captains of Charle-
magne's host, bursts forth (127, ii): *Isti praefati sunt viri fam-
osi, heroes bellatores, potentum cosmi potentiores, fortibus
fortiores, Christi proceres, christianam fidem in mundo propal-
antes.* Johannes reduces this to: *Cil qui ci sunt nomé erent
poissant et de grant renon, et essauçant la loi crestiene* (XXIV,
18). A little later, Charlemagne and Agolant meet to parley.
Tunc, writes the Pseudo-Turpin (129, xvii), *dixit Karolus Aig-
olando: "Tu es Aigolandus qui terram meam a me fraudulenter
abstulisti. Tellurem hispanicam et gasconicam brachio invincibili
potentiae Dei adquisivi, christianis legibus subiugavi, omnesque
reges eius meo imperio everti. Tu autem Dei Christianos, me ad
Galliam remeante, peremisti, meas urbes et castella destruxisti,
totamque terram igne et gladio vastasti, unde multum conqueror
in praesenti.* This too Johannes disowned. He was addressing
the aristocratic subjects of Philip Augustus who, like them, was
not given to oratory in negotiation, *heroes bellatores* indeed but
who, *es chambres des dames,* talked of themselves in other terms.
They would not think that Agolant's counter attack had been
undertaken *fraudulenter;* Johannes omits the word.[7] Repelled
by the Pseudo-Turpin's false eloquence, he wrote quite simply
(XXVI, 11): *Tu es Agolanz qui ma terre que j'avoie conquise a
l'onor de Deu et convertie a crestiene loi, m'as destruite et deser-
tee, et les cités et les chasteaus gastez et les Crestiens ocis demen-
tres que g'ere en France repairiez. Si saches que molt m'en
complaing.* Elsewhere, by rejecting the pompous apostrophes
and exclamations of his model, he brings its forced tone down
to one that is more natural and so more convincing: *O Chris-
tiane!* (143, xiv), *O Christi pugnatorum sanctissima caterva!*
(147, x), *O quam felix et florida erit in celesti regno victoris
anima!* (113, xiv), *O magnum et admirabile ingenium!* (167, vi).
Here and everywhere Johannes decisively eliminates the Pseudo-
Turpin's fatuous insistence on the obvious. Johannes talked with

---

[7]   One of the Pseudo-Turpin's propagandistic devices is to blacken the character of the
Saracens. Just as here he uses his gratuitous *fraudulenter* so at 183, iv he makes the
Saracens attack the French from behind *(post tergum).* Johannes does not translate
fraudulenter (XXVI, 13) or *post tergum* (LII, 14).

his audience, not at them; he knew what they knew and where nothing needed to be said he had the grace to be silent. He does not make these omissions mechanically. Where the dying Roland holds Durendal before him and addresses to it his cry of anguish, and when Charlemagne utters his lament over Roland's corpse, Johannes keeps the apostrophe as a figure appropriate in these cases, charged with genuine emotion.

Another feature of the Pseudo-Turpin's style which Johannes evidently found distasteful is the frequent injection into the narrative of his own personality. The Pseudo-Turpin does this as an aside to his audience, seeking to evoke an emotional response which he must have thought the events would not of themselves communicate. As he is describing how after Roncevaux the French prepare the bodies of their slain companions for transport back to France, he breaks in (211, v ff.): *Si videres cum multi corpora multorum per ventrem findebant . . . corde compunctus plorares.* This is like his intervention quoted above: *O magnum et admirable ingenium!* There, "see how clever!," here "see how sad!" Johannes's treatment of his model in both instances shows his revulsion at the Pseudo-Turpin's melodramatic style, spurious for him and egregiously out of taste in that it presupposes a grossly insensitive and unperceptive audience. He does away with the Pseudo-Turpin's subjective intervention and translates with the simply declarative: *li un les ovroient et gitoient fors les entrailles, et cil qui n'avoient les chiers oignemenz les appareilloient de sel* (LXV, 30). In this as in other ways, Johannes in his French prose is carrying on a stylistic tradition of vernacular poetry. Like the jongleurs of the best epoch he lets events speak for themselves. Where the Pseudo-Turpin is striving after effect, Johannes's translation is laconic and virile. In the scene where Roland drags's himself to the marble stone intending to shatter Durendal upon it, the Pseudo-Turpin writes (189, xi): *Habebat ipse adhuc quandam spatam suam secum, opere pulcherrimam, acumine incomparabilem, nimia claritate resplendentem, nomine Durenda;* Johannes translates (LVI, 10): *Il avoit encor s'espee qui si ert bele et bone, qu'en apeloit Durendart.* And a little further on where the Pseudo-Turpin lets Roland praise Durendal in a long string of turgid superlatives, Johannes quietens his tone with: *Ha! bele espee luisant . . .* In the vision which brings to Archbishop Turpin the news of

Charlemagne's death, he sees according to the Pseudo-Turpin (229, xi): *tetrorum agmina innumerabilia militum.* This becomes in Johannes: *une compaignie de malignes esperiz;* and where a Latin cliché tells us that the French, victorious over Agolant, *usque ad bases in sanguine natabant* (143, viii), Johannes declines responsibility for the hyperbole: *Desi as chevilles estoient li vein-queor el sanc, ce dit l'estoire* (XXXI, 21).

The passages, long or short, thus omitted or reduced by Johannes are very munerous, but there is no need to go further in our treatment of them. They all reflect the conceptions and purposes which emerge from the illustrations which we have so far considered. These conceptions and purposes appear with similar consistency in the additions which Johannes makes to his model. Just as his critical judgment of the Pseudo-Turpin's style and his own orientation towards a lay audience induced him to eliminate elements which he judged offensive to the intelligence and taste of his public, so a similar acumen and concern led him to add touches to aid its understanding and to elicit its deeper responses.

We have seen above (p. 104) how Johannes, towards the end of the Chronicle, re-ordered the events leading to Charlemagne's death as these were presented by the Pseudo-Turpin. Among his many changes here he placed the premonitory signs of Charlemagne's approaching death before this came about. But he is not content with re-arranging the parts; he fits them in their new order into the context and makes them cohere. In an extraordinary *non sequitur* the Pseudo-Turpin, having described the last of the portents, Charlemagne's fall from his horse, and told us that his attendants ran to pick him up, continues (235, xi): *Nunc igitur illum esse participem in corona martirum praefatorum credimus.* Johannes has transposed this episode to his Chapter LXXVI where, instead of telling us blandly that Charles fell off his horse and is now a saint, he adds the touches which keep the moments of the evolving drama before our mind's eye: *Donc corurent si compaignon si l'en redrecierent, mes n'ot adonc mie de mal. Aprés ce affebloia molt li rois et amaladi tant q'au chief de .iii. anz aprocha au lit de la mort* (LXXVI, 14 ff.).

The Pseudo-Turpin moralizes at the drop of a hat, and Johannes moralizes with him, but with more tact. He sometimes found it necessary to gloss phrases which, though part of the every day language of clerics, he thought might be less readily intelligible to laymen. At 113, xiv, after the miracle of the sprouting lances, the Pseudo-Turpin makes the point that the Christian who arms himself against vice will find his lance blossoming on judgment day. Johannes thought it wise to explain the metaphor and adds (XVIII, 16): *La lance, c'est l'ame de celui qui bien se combat contre les vices en terre.* In the Latin Chapter XIII, where Agolant rebukes Charlemagne for his unchristian treatment of the poor, the Pseudo-Turpin draws his resounding moral from Matthew XXI, 42 as follows (139, xxi): *. . . ite in ignem aeternum. Quia esurivi et non dedisti michi manducare. Et cetera.* Johannes ekes out the too casual allusion: *. . . departez de moi el perdurable feu d'enfer. Car je oi fain et soif et froit, vos ne me regardastes* (XXX, 8). In another passage, Johannes's gloss not only explains a problem but comes to grips with it more honestly than does the Pseudo-Turpin. It occurs in the Latin Chapter XVII, where Roland is explaining the mysteries of the Christian faith to Fernagu. They have come in the course of their discussion to the question of Christ's death, which Fernagu does not understand because he knows God cannot die. The Pseudo-Turpin's answer, put in Roland's mouth, is (159, vii): *Si natus est ut homo, igitur mortuus est ut homo. Quia omnis qui nascitur, moritur.* And he leaves it at that. But Johannes seems to have realized that this was a question of special interest to an audience which no doubt included many who had known the Saracens at first hand and were aware of the fundamental opposition between Islam and Christianity on this matter of the double nature of Christ, a question of which, moreover, the explanation came more nearly within their reach than that of the Trinity or of the Virgin Birth. And so he adds a further clarification to the Pseudo-Turpin's bald comment (XXXVIII, 15): *Se Deus reçut com hom mort en la croiz. Mort, di je, que l'umaine char en la croiz dormi et la deïtez veilloit qui tot gardoit en soi.*

There were other matters too in which Johannes judged that a layman's knowledge might fall short. When he came to the place named *Petronum* (95, v), the spot to which St. James's body had been miraculously borne and to which Charlemagne marched to mark the western limit of his conquests, he adds: (et vint au Perron) *qui sor la mer gist.* It is a timely and unobtrusive gloss. Similarly unobtrusive, no less timely and worked into the very

warm and woof of his narrative are the phrases which Johannes
adds to smooth the Pseudo-Turpin's negligent transitions. In
Chapter VIII, Agolant proposes to Charlemagne that they decide
the battle by opposing a given number of men from each army,
twenty, sixty, a hundred and so on, or simply *unum contra unum*
(109, xviii). And then the Pseudo-Turpin begins his next sentence:
Interea missi sunt a Karolo centum milites contra centum. Johan-
nes found *interea* inadequate as a connective and wrote: *ou .i.
contre .i. Ensint fu otroié d'une part et d'autre. Lors envoia
Charles* (XV, 22). He emends a similarly careless passage at 119, i.
Agolant has come out of Saintes to meet the French army on the
plain before the city and has agreed with Charlemagne that Saintes
shall belong to the victor: *ut illius esset urbs qui vinceret alium.*
From this the Pseudo-Turpin passes to the story of the lances
which took root, beginning with this phrase: *Sero vero ante diem
belli.* There is no concatenation; *vero* is a perfectly superfluous
cliché used with the pretense of supplying a connective. Johannes
drops it and makes the transition as follows (XXI, 4): *que la cité
fust celui qui veintroit l'autre. Ensint fu creanté d'une part et
d'autre. Le soir devant le jor de la bataille . . .* These two exam-
ples represent what is in fact Johannes's almost total rejection of
the Pseudo-Turpin's adverbial connectives. In the Latin, not only
interea and *vero - vero* above all, with which the hurrying Pseudo-
Turpin stumbles from one occasion to another again and again on
almost every page — but also *igitur, inde, quidem, etiam, enim,
statim, ilico statim, namque, itaque, tunc* have been emptied of
almost all meaning and are used interchangeably by the Pseudo-
Turpin to link one happening to the next. The weakening in them
of the sense of time, place or cause deprives the transition which
they are used to provide of almost all logic and so of naturalness.
The Pseudo-Turpin seems to have written his chronicle with the
assurance that his Latin would be the canon of its authenticity.
We see him here, as we have seen him in matters of broader scope,
neglecting under this persuasion, even in the smallest details of
style, to endow his fictions with that resemblance to life and truth
which makes acknowledged fiction art and without which the
truths themselves of history would leave critical minds incredulous.
For the most part, Johannes simply leaves out the meaningless
cliché: *Est igitur in maris margine lapis antiquus* (103, iv) — *Sor*

la rive de cele mer est une pierre anciene (XII, 12); *Erat enim illorum exercitus quatuor milibus* (119, xi) – *Quatre mile i ot de cels* (XXI, 15); *Et statim ad hanc vocem occurentes, Sarraceni rapuerunt eum* (163, vii) – *Li Sarrazin acorurent* (XLI, 10). Sometimes he replaces it with a more meaningful word or phrase: *Ilico statim Christiani una cum Sarracenis . . . in oppidum ingrediuntur* (163, x) – *Mes nostre Crestien . . .* (XLI, 11); *Statim nostros tanto bello fatigatos . . . alia triginta milia Sarracenorum aggrediuntur* (183, xii) – *Quant Marsiles vit ce, il lor corut sore . . .* (LIII, 1).

In a case like the following we see quite plainly how lacking the Pseudo-Turpin was in the narrator's art and how much better a teller of stories Johannes was as detail by detail he supplies the touches of reality which give the warmth of life to the Pseudo-Turpin's cold abstractions. Agolant has sent messengers to Charlemagne inviting him to come with a small escort to talk with him in Agen, but with the hidden intent of getting to know his enemy the better to overcome him in battle. Charlemagne saw through the trick: *Sed Karolus haec animadvertens cum duobus milibus fortiorum . . . prope urbem Agenni venit* (115, ix) "But Charles seeing through this came to Agen." The *sed* goes perfectly well with *animadvertens* but as an adversative not at all well with *venit;* it is a very inadequate connective unable to carry the complex movement of incident and thought. The Pseudo-Turpin is too hurried; he is like the ungifted musician who plays notes but no music, leaving mind and feeling inert. Johannes brings him to life: *Mes Charles s'en apensa molt bien porquoi il le feisoit. Qant il ot oï les messages il li manda qu'il iroit a lui et qu'il feroit a sa volenté. Qant li message s'en furent parti, Charles en vint . . .* Charles not only sees through the message, he sees through the messengers as they deliver it, sends these deceptors home deceived and makes ready to follow up the adventure with everyone on the French side, including Johannes's audience, informed and admiring.

It is the same drive towards clarity and realism which makes Johannes render many of the Pseudo-Turpin's abstract terms with concrete ones: *martirio coronantur* "reçurent il corone el ciel par martire;" *martirii palman . . . accepturi erant* "qui devoient morir;" *gavisus est* "si en out mout grant joie;" *nimis doleo* "molt en sera m'ame dolente;" *defunctis translatis* "Les morz et les navrez fist Charles prendre et porter;" *cunctos* "nous tous;" *vulgo dicuntur* "sunt nomees par tes nons que vous ores ci;" *factus est clamor* "Dont oïssiez si grant noise;" to use proper instead of common names: *ingressus urbem* "s'en entra en Cordres;" *urbs et castrum capitur* "fu Nazres prise;" *viri bellatores de septem urbibus* "Sarrazin de set citez;" and sometimes to use a noun for a pronoun: *Quod illi videntes* "Qant ce virent li Sarrazin."

Johannes emendation of his model in these seemingly slight details can be seen then as an essential element in his general transformation of its style: the Pseudo-Turpin tends through his obtuseness to destroy the life of the stories he was retelling, Johannes by his stylistic revisions restores it to them. We need to stress one more aspect of this process to see how thorough his revision was. The Pseudo-Turpin, borrowing from all sides and inventing as he made a synthesis of his borrowings, sometimes dropped a thread of his complex plot and so let elements in his chronicle fall into incoherence. We see an example of this lack of command in the story of Roland's sword and horn. The Latin and Johannes versions tell us in full agreement how Roland failed to break Durendal on the stone (193, ii; LVII, 8) and how Roland then sounded his horn, hoping to bring back the French army to see to his proper burial and to keep his sword and horn from falling into enemy hands (193, x; LVII, 15). And so he lies down to die and is found by Baudouin who does what he can to comfort him. The Latin carries on the story thus: Baudouin, seeing that he could do no more for Roland, mounted Roland's horse and went off to rejoin Charlemagne and the main body of the French army (195, x). Later (203, xxi) he rode into their camp on Roland's horse and told of all that had happened. When Charlemagne had led the sorrowing army back to Roncevaux and accomplished his vengeance on the Saracens and Ganelon, he brought Roland to Blaye and buried him in Saint-Romain: *mucronemque ipsius ad caput et tubam eburneam ad pedes . . . suspendit* (213, xiv). But the Pseudo-Turpin had left the sword and horn with the dying Roland as Baudouin rode away from him. Johannes picks up this loose thread. Baudouin, he writes (LVIII, 9), *monta sor le cheval Rollant,* et prist son cor et s'espee, *si se mist a la voie vers l'ost,* and later, when Charles saw to it that Roland's body was laid on a litter and carried back to France, Johannes adds: *s'espee et son cor avec lui* (LXVI, 15).

Johannes is constantly attentive to such lapses on the part of the Pseudo-Turpin. The latter, at 217, xx, makes much of Turpin's infirmity as he remains in Vienne and says farewell to Charlemagne; *et ibi vulnerum cicatricibus verberisque et percussionibus multisque alapis quas in Ispania sustuli, angustiatus remansi.* To any attentive listener, this statement would have come as a surprise, for though the earlier part of the Chronicle has told us that Turpin fought well, it has not mentioned his wounds. Johannes prepares us earlier for what is to come. When, after Roncevaux, Charles pursues the Saracens and annihilates the remnants of their army on the Ebro, Johannes, mindful of what is to follow later, adds (LXV, 10): *Ilec ot Torpins tant cous et tantes bleceures qu'il en fu aprés pires del cors et moins en vesqui.* At 209, xv, the Pseudo-Turpin tells how Thierry fought Pinabel in the judiciary combat to decide the question of Ganelon's guilt. At 217, xiii, the Pseudo-Turpin, in complete contradiction with himself, lists Thierry among those who died at Roncevaux and were buried in the Aliscans. Johannes omits Thierry from this list.

The falseness of the Pseudo-Turpin's fictions, which are not to his honor however he may have thought them justified as a means to serve his political purpose, remained his secret throughout the Middle Ages. Johannes was his dupe and thereby had a different conception of his subject. He believed it. For him, the Pseudo-Turpin's *Historia Karoli Magni et Rotholandi* embodied the historical details of Charlemagne's campaigns in Spain and the vision of his greatness. He did not make his translation in order to disseminate among clerics a piece of clerical propaganda but to share with the cultured laymen of Western Europe, especially of north and north-eastern France, the truth about the exploits and character of a beloved and admired hero, Charlemagne. Taught by the jongleurs, the feudal gentry and their households shared with him this vision, but, as we may judge by all the signs of the times, they wanted the poetic image to be confirmed by the writers of trustworthy history. Johannes was alive to their need and thoroughly sympathetic with them. He was an educated man, no doubt a secular cleric. He knew the awakened interest in history of these cultured people and he knew them as active participants in the great events of their time. He knew too that, as makers of history, they would demand of historiography that it should be true, and the great truth which they could all discern was trueness to life. Historians of contemporary events like Robert de Clari and Henri de Valenciennes who had taken part in the actions which they narrate and who were endowed with the gift of writing, came naturally by the qualities which made their histories actual. But those who like Johannes accepted the more scholarly task of translating the Latin chronicles of past events were handicapped. The truth of these chronicles was implicit in their Latin form; their life lay in the style of the author. In the task which Johannes set himself he was more handicapped than most of his kind, for the *Turpin* was a wholly artificial construction. The Pseudo-Turpin's world was a given world, and his characters more like automata which it set in motion than men of action making their lives and renewing the conditions in which they lived. His style was equally wooden, to which the flourishes of rhetoric and pious ejaculation could not impart a life which was essentially lacking. What Johannes did was to think out for himself the Pseudo-Turpin's story in the French which was the natural vehicle for the operations of his mind as in understanding sympathy he assumed the mentality of the people to whom he addressed his translation. Writing for them he achieved at once the vitalization of the Pseudo-Turpin's chronicle and the emancipation of French prose as he drew it from its Latin shell. His translation deserves in these ways to be considered as an original work. In contrast to the Latin chronicle it seems already classical in structure and style — *simplex dumtaxat et unum.* Johannes's pragmatic principle seems to have been so to tell the story as to let men see it happening, to hold their gaze and through their eyes to reach their minds and hearts. He met, as the story of the manuscript tradition of his translation shows, with immediate and lasting success, but his humble work has been overshadowed by the more arresting chronicles of contemporaneous events. Yet he stands alone among the many translators of the *Pseudo-Turpin Chronicle* in his creative effort. As one of the first practitioners in France of vernacular historiography, without benefit of theoretical tradition and without advantage of example, he created the prose form of historical writing which was to persist after him through the turmoil of debate concerning the questions of form and purpose which, à propos of Charlemagne and Archbishop Turpin, he sought to solve, *si que la verité fust apres els en memoire.*

The Text

Preliminary Note

Chapters I and II will have shown which text of the Johannes translation it is most fitting to publish here. The translation in its original form is already available in Auracher's edition of Munich MS Gallicus 52, our M, whose edition may be supplemented with Dr. Pius Fischer's commentary, and in Dr. Rudolf Schmitt's edition of Brit. Mus. MS Harley 273, our L1. The first redaction, Pierre de Beauvais's *Descriptio-Turpin* compilation, has not been published as a whole, but Pierre's translation and adaptation of the *Descriptio* as it is made to serve here as prelude to the *Turpin* can be read in my edition based on Bibl. Nat. French MS 834, our P2. The most interesting text to publish now is that of the second redaction in which a reduced *Descriptio* has been grafted into Chapter I of the Johannes *Turpin,* and which proved to be by far the most popular form in this or among all the Old French translations of the *Pseudo-Turpin Chronicle.* More than a hundred years ago, in 1856, A. Demarquette, without in any way studying its place in the manuscript tradition, published the text of this redaction as it is found in Bibl. Nat. French MS 1444, our P8; but, like Auracher and Schmitt, he made no critical edition, simply reproducing the text of P8. It remains now only to decide how best to present the text of the second redaction.

The second redaction survives, as we have seen, in the Renaud and Michel groups of manuscripts and in MS Br 2. The eight manuscripts in the Renaud group stem from a copy, made by Renaud's scribe, from a copy of the original manuscript of the second redaction. Michel's scribe had access to Renaud's model, and his copy proliferated in the fourteen manuscripts of the Michel group. Our comparison of the Renaud with the Michel manuscripts has shown that each group in its immediate source represents a stage in the deterioration of the original. This process has naturally been carried further within the distinct groups. Of the two groups, III R is the more homogeneous. The manuscripts of the III M group, more numerous, seem to have multiplied more rapidly and more freely. MS Br 2 has at times a decisive role to play between groups III R and III M since its text, though at some remove, derives independently of them from the original of the second redaction. But it is late, rejuvenated in its vocabulary, phrasing, and syntax, and, adapted as its text is for inclusion in a historical compilation, it shows many omissions, so that it is only upon occasion that it can be called in when groups III R and III M are in conflict. Certainly it cannot serve as basis for an edition; nor is any manuscript of the III M group fit to play this role. P8, V and Br 3 are seemingly independent representatives of Michel's copy; but their readings show that lost intermediaries lie behind them. The scribe of V was faithful but uncomprehending, and evidently used a faulty model; he was unable to decipher some passages and was willing to write meaningless words and phrases as he copied. The scribe of P8 was rather ignorant too but constantly innovative in a trite and often silly fashion. Br 3 is at moments correct where the other manuscripts are faulty, but again it is a late manuscript and has undergone much change in what must have been a long process of transmission. The other manuscripts of Michel's text all represent another copy of Michel's text, independent of P8, V and Br 3, but it would be neither an easy nor a fruitful task to restore by a collation of their readings the hypothetical source from which they all spring. For the purpose of establishing a critical text of the second redaction, the Michel group of manuscripts is best represented by P8 and V. For group III R the choice of a reduced number of representatives is delicate. P6, as a late copy of P5, can be ignored. P7, late and adapted for inclusion in a larger history, is also too modified a copy to be representative. The other manuscripts which make up the group all belong to the thirteenth century. MSS L2, L3, O and B1 have a common source which must have been a good text. I have shown above why I think that it was Anglo-Norman, but I also think that it was a copy of a continental model for there is no sign in the tradition that the copy made for Renaud was an Anglo-Norman copy. B1 and O may be eliminated in this process of simplification, B1 because of the markedly individual interventions of its scribe, O because of its many errors and divergences caused by the lack of understanding and nonchalance of its scribe. L2 and L3 are very close to each other, and seem to be faithful and careful transcriptions of their common source. I give the preference to L2, the older of the two manuscripts, copied and to some extent corrected by the scribe with much attention. A1 is more innovative than L2, but offers a text reproduced with more rigor than that of B1 or O. P5, written in Francien of 1225-1250, offers a studiously careful and intelligent copy. It lacks all but three lines of the last chapter; it lacks also Chapter XXVIII which the scribe seems to have skipped unwittingly, it has a few folios in which torn corners have carried away parts of the text, and it shows occasional interventions by the scribe, surely a monk, who sought here and there to emphasize an appeal to thought or feeling, and to clarify the syntax where it seemed to him unclear. In spite of its mutilations, P5 has the quality to serve as basic text. As representative of the Renaud group it needs the control of A1 and L2, and, as representative of the second redaction, of P8 and V of the Michel group and of the independent copy Br 2, where the text of this last manuscript is conservative enough to be relevant to the collation. Our second redaction is of course one form of the translation of the Latin *Turpin,* and so, in cases of textual difficulty, we may have recourse to the Latin text, to the text of the original translation as this is preserved in MSS M P1 L1, and to the text of the first redaction as this is preserved in MSS P2 P3 Br 1. But we must not use this resource under the persuasion that these earlier forms of the tradition are by definition more authoritative. The text we are seeking to establish is one in which the Johannes *Turpin* has passed through Pierre's revision and in which Pierre's *Descriptio* has undergone a drastic process of reduction and adaptation at the hands of the second redactor. We must work up from the manuscript tradition of the second redaction, not down from the sources which the second redactor used.

Our text of the second redaction is therefore the text of P5, emended where necessary according to the evidence of the controlling manuscripts, A1 L2 P8 V and Br 2. The ever-recurring question arises as to how far the process of emendation should be carried. There is much past theory and practice to guide us, but the factors which must determine our editorial method are inherent

in the character of the manuscript tradition with which we are
dealing. The text is in prose and so lacks the conserving discipline
of meter and rhyme. In spelling, forms and syntax, the scribes of
P5 and of our controlling manuscripts vary so in habit that there
can be no question of attempting to reconstruct from them the
outward form of the original text of the second redaction. In their
readings too the manuscripts show a similar diversity; no matter
with what care one applies quantitative and qualitative criteria in
the assessment of their authenticity, the attempt to establish a
critical text results only in an artificial and unreal creation. It is
better to let the original text be represented by P5 than to attempt
its mechanical reconstruction. We may do this with confidence,
for in his linguistic forms, his syntax and his style, the scribe of
P5 is consistently his own informed and conscientious self, con-
cerned to render his model faithfully and, in retouching it here and
there, concerned only to clarify its possible ambiguities or to
emphasize a momentary appeal. His text, written almost in pure
Francien, is reliable in form and content; left to itself it would
bring to modern readers the Johannes *Turpin* as Frenchmen of the
mid-thirteenth century knew and enjoyed it.

But what about those retouches in grammar and style? Are
they merely of aesthetic import or do they constitute distortions
of the sense of the model? Moreover, there is no doubt that the
scribe used a faulty model and that he committed errors of his
own. Here there is need for editorial intervention. The omissions
in P5, caused by the scribe's lapses or by the later mutilation of his
manuscript, must be made good. One would think that P6, the
copy of P5, could provide the natural remedy for these deficien-
cies; but its text is too modernized and free to serve this purpose.
To fill in the gaps left in P5 I draw on the text of A1, leaving it in
all the contrasting color of its Burgundian forms. Where the evi-
dence of the controlling manuscripts, considered in themselves and
in the whole context of the Johannes manuscript tradition, shows
P5 to be in error, I emend its text in accordance with their indica-
tions. But the question here is what is error, and we can only take
it to be the destruction or alteration of the sense of the chronicle
as the evidence of the tradition allows us to see it. There is no
way of avoiding some arbitrariness in the understanding and treat-
ment of such cases, especially when we find ourselves on that

borderline of sense and sensibility where stylistic change may seem to involve a change of meaning. To mitigate this, and to keep the reader always in a position to judge for himself, I have listed the rejected readings of P5 apart at the foot of each page of the text and listed all the variant readings of the controlling manuscripts in a second series which is to be found in the supplement. In the first series, the rejected reading of P5 is followed by a square bracket after which come the sigla of the controlling manuscripts which provide the adopted reading. When the reading in a controlling manuscript agrees with the rejected reading of P5, the siglum of that manuscript is placed inside the square bracket. When the controlling manuscripts are not in agreement as to the adopted reading, their particular readings will all be found listed in the second series of variants. Difficult cases are treated in the *Notes to the Text*. The result is a bulky critical apparatus; but the virtue of the method can only be safeguarded by its thorough application, and no critical reader would, I think, be willing to dispense with the complete lists of variants. Moveover, it is in such a critical apparatus that the quality of the individual scribes which I have adumbrated in my description of the manuscripts given in Section I of the supplement will show more clearly to the interested reader, who will find there too patterns of change and error which will reveal something of the life of a prose text as it underwent the process of mediaeval publication.[1]

I note in the right hand margin the foliation in MS P5 as it corresponds to the printed text. In the matter of orthography I present the text of P5 with little change. I have applied the rules of modern punctuation. I have distinguished *j* from *i* and *v* from *u*, and have used the diaeresis to distinguish *aï* from *ai, oï, oÿ* from *oi, oy, aü* from *au*. In the case of *ei, eu* where, in a prose text of the mid-thirteenth century, the disyllabic pronunciation must remain doubtful, I use no diacritic. The scribe's abbreviations offer little difficulty. *Par,* preposition or prefix, is written in abbreviation as *p* with a bar through the lower shaft; *por* is always written in full. *p* with a bar above it is sometimes used for *pr* but sometimes also for *pre* as in *p̄ndre (prendre), p̄s (pres)*. This gives

---

[1] For example, the preference in A1 for *lors* instead of *donc*, for *jusqu'a* instead of *desi a*, for *que* causal instead of *car*, for *autant* instead of *altretant*, and for *ce, ces* instead of *cel, ceus*. P8 usually omits *messire, monseigneur* before the names of saints.

cause for hesitation in cases like $\overline{p}ist$, $\overline{p}issent$, but *preist* is also written in full (fol. 68, 1.11) so I expand to *preist, preissent* which, perhaps a little arbitrarily, is in accordance with the form which the scribe gives elsewhere to the imperf. subj. of sigmatic verbs, e.g. *feist, feissent, deissent.* A supralinear vowel stands for *r* plus the vowel; thus ent^ex is for *entreus*, $t°is$ is for *trois.* The adverb *comme* is almost always written ꝯ , more rarely $c\overline{o}$. Occasionally however the scribe writes it in full as *com* (fol. 61, 1.2 up, fol. 108 v°, 1.3), more rarely still as *come* (fol. 100, 1.8); somewhat arbitrarily I expand to *com.* The scribe also uses ꝯ for the prefix: ꝯ *batons,* ꝯ *plaing,* ꝯ *giė,* ꝯ *quist* and he also writes ꝯ *ques* for *qu'onques,* ꝯ *ta* for *conta* and sometimes ꝯ *me* for *come.* The sign obviously represented for him both *com* and *con.* Since he writes *combatoit, combateor* in full I expand to *com* before labials, to *con* before other consonants. But this too remains somewhat arbitrary since the scribe's treatment of preconsonantal nasals is inconsistent, witness *menbre (< membra), menbra (< memoravit),* and *enporta - emporta, emplorant - en plusors.* I expand $n\overline{o}$ to *non (< $n\overline{o}men$)* which is sometimes so written in full. The scribe abbreviates *Charles* to *Charl;* he uses this abbreviated form both as nominative and accusative. He also writes *K.,* especially towards the middle and later part of the Chronicle, and, much more rarely, *Klm.,* again as nominative and accusative. As we may see in the description of P5 given in the supplement, the scribe, though he observes the rules of declension with some care throughout the Chronicle, very often uses the accusative of proper names for the nominative. Yet, he does at times write *Charles* in full (fol. 93, 1.14) and, (fol. 68 v°, 1.2) *li bons rois Charlemaines.* I therefore expand *Charl* and *K.* to *Charles* in the nominative and to *Charle* in the accusative, *Klm* to *Charlemaines, Charlemaigne* in the same way, thus giving a rather arbitrary appearance of regularity to these forms. Among the numerical abbreviations I resolve only .m. which the scribe writes frequently as *mile.* The chapter divisions are those of P5 ; I have numbered the chapters and used the heading *Prologue* for convenience of reference. Each chapter is marked in the manuscript by beginning on a new line with a large and ornamented initial. Chapter LXXIII begins with the description of Dialectic, but contains also the descriptions of Rhetoric and Geometry whereas Grammar, Music, Arithmetic and Astrology have each a chapter to themselves. However, Rhetoric and Geometry are each preceded within the line by the sign for a new paragraph; it is the usual Greek π elaborated by the mediaeval scribes. It would seem that the scribe was concerned here to save space. I keep these three arts within a single chapter but observe the scribe's distinctions by beginning Rhetoric and Geometry each on a new line.

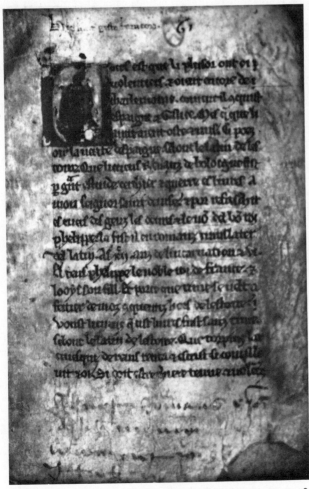

Paris, Bibliothèque Nationale, French MS 2464, fol. 61 r°.

PROLOGUE

Voirs est que li plusor ont oï volentiers et oient encore (61)
de Charlemaine, coment il conquist Espaigne et Galice. Mes
que que li autre aient osté et mis, ci poez oïr la verité
d'Espaigne selonc le latin de l'estoire que li cuens Renauz
5   de Boloigne fist par grant estuide cerchier et querre es
livres a monseignor Saint Denise. Et por refreschir es
cuers des genz les oevres et le non del bon roi, la fist il
en romanz translater del latin as .xii. c. anz de l'incar-
nation et .vi., el tens Phelippe le noble roi de France et
10   Looÿs son fill. Et por ce que rime se velt afeitier de moz
conqueilliz hors de l'estoire, voust li cuens que cist livres
fust sanz rime selonc le latin de l'estoire que Torpins
l'arcevesque de Reins traita et escrist si com il le vit et
oï. Si doit estre chiere tenue et volentiers / oïe de toz (v°)
15   hauz homes. Car por ce sunt les bones vertuz el siegle
auques defaillies et li cuer des seignorages affeblioé,
que l'en n'ot mes si volentiers com en soloit les oevres
des enciens, ne les estoires ou li bon fet sunt qui en-
seignent coment l'en se doit avoir en Deu et contenir
20   el siegle honoreement. Car vivre sanz honor est morirs.
Huimés comencerai coment et par quele maniere et par
quele achoison Charles mut a aler en Espaigne et Torpins
avec lui, qui tot mist en escrit si com vos orroiz
que la verité fust aprés els en memoire.

I

Hic incipit
hystoria
Karoli
Magni

Voirs est que li glorieus apostres misires saint
Jaques o les autres deciples Nostre Seignor qui divers
leus del monde cerchierent, prehecha primes en Galice,
et puis l'ocist Herodes li rois, et fu ses cors portez
5   de la terre de Jerusalem par mer / desi en Galice. (62)
Icele meismes Galice prehecherent li apostre. Mes li
Galicien leisserent puis lor foi par lor pechié desi

---

7 roi Phelippe] A1 L2 P8 V – 13 recita et escrist] A1 L2 P8 V

130

au tens lo roi Charle. Cestui Charle fist Galafres
chevalier en son palés a Tolete quant il fu de France
10   essilliez. Et puis se combati Charles por s'amor a
Braiman, un fort roi de paiens, et ocist en bataille.
Aprés conquist mainte terre. Cist Charles fu empereres
de Rome, rois de France et ot Engleterre, Danemarche
et Tiescheterre, Baiviere, Loherroine, Borgoigne, Lom-
15   bardie, Bretaigne et plusors autres terres de l'une
mer desi a l'autre.

II

En cest grant pooir que Charles ert si cremuz
et si renomez par les batailles dont il avoit eue la
victoire, en Sessoigne et en autres terres, fu assise Jeru-
salem de paiens et li païs environ essilliez et
5   li Crestien enchaitivé, si que li patriarches qui avoit
non / Jahan s'en issi de la terre et plusor autre prudome.   (v°)
Il en vint en Costentinoble a l'empereor qui avoit non
Costantins, et ses filz Leo. Il li mostra complaignenment
l'essill de la terre. Li empereres fu molt
10   dolenz et entra en pensee coment il porroit la terre
rescorre. Donc li aparut uns angles, si li mostra un bel
home molt grant tot armé sor son cheval. Ses escuz estoit
tous vermaus et ses heaumes et li ponz de s'espee, et la
lance qu'il tenoit ert blanche trestote, dont la pointe
15   del fer gitoit flambe sovent. Li angles dist a Cos-
tentin: "Charles, rois de France, empereres de Romme,
en qui semblance tu voiz ce bel chevalier, t'aidera de
la voie ou tu penses." Il s'esveilla adonc plains de
joie, et ne demora gueres qu'il fist fere letres a la
20   forme de sa vision et les envoia a Charle et / li   (63)
patriarches les soes escrites de sa main.

III

Cil furent quatre message, dui Crestien bon clerc
et dui Hebreu. Li uns des clers ot non Jahanz de Naples,
hom de bone vie et de grant simplesce, li autres David
de Jerusalem, justes hom et religieus. Li uns des

II, 12 Ses armes erent totes vermeilles et ses escuz autressi (aut-
ressi *lacking* A1, ensement L2) et ses hiaumes A1 L2] P8 V

5　Hebreus ot non Ysaac, li autres, Samuel, sages et dis-
crez de lor loi. Il tindrent tant lor jornees qu'il
vindrent la ou Charles ert, si le saluerent de par le patriarche
et li baillierent les letres. Charles les prist et les lut. El
lire comença a plorer molt durement por la pitié de la terre.
10　Lors manda par tote France et comenda qu'il s'apareillassent
d'aler en ost aprés lui, et qui n'i iroit, il seroit sers, et il et
si oir, a toz jorz. Il assembla donc molt tres grant
ost, puis erra tant qu'il vint en Costantinoble. Li empereres
le re/çut molt honoreement atot son pooir et atot son empire, (v
15　et li patriarches a grant joie et a grant sollempnité. Puis
esploita tant par la volenté de Deu qu'il delivra tote
la terre et le sepulcre Nostre Seignor. Aprés s'en vint
en Costantinoble. Li empereres, qui molt le desirroit
a tenir a honor por la grant bonté qui estoit coneue en
20　lui, fist amener lions et bestes de diverses manieres,
et chiens et oiseaus, et dras de soie, or et argent, et
pierres precieuses, si li pria qu'il en preist a sa volenté.

IV

Charles n'en vost riens prendre por ce qu'aucuns
n'i notast covoitise. Ainz li proia qu'il li donast de
la croiz ou Nostre Sires avoit soffert torment por nos
et des reliques de son crucefiement. Li empereres li
5　otroia benignement. Il fist lors assembler arcevesques
et evesques et abez et chanoines. Puis eslurent .xii. des
plus prudomes et / des plus sainz homes por ateindre　　(c
si haut saintuaire com il requeroit. Cil alerent avant
et li dui empereor aprés, et toz li pueples aprés par
10　grant humilité el leu ou il cuidoient que la sainte
corone fust et li clou. En ce qu'il ovrirent le saint
leu tuit confés de lor pechiez et assouz, de la chasse
ou li saintuaires iert si tres grant odors en issi qu'il
sembla a toz que paradis fust aoverz. Et de cele odor
15　furent sané .ccc. malades et un. Donc mist hors la sainte
corone uns evesques de Grece qui avoit non Daniel. Iluec
pria Charles que Deus i demostrast tel miracle que tuit
cil qui le verroient fussent certain que c'iert des espines
dont Nostre Sires fu coronez en la croiz.

IV, 12 assouz et de] *see variants*

V

Lors descendi une rosee del ciel qui si arrosa
les espines dont il fu coronez, qui erent seches de lonc tens,
qu'eles de / vindrent totes verz et comencerent a florir ausi   (v°)
come la verge Aaron fist. Ilec fu l'odors si granz et la
5   clartez qu'il ne cuidoient mie estre el siegle mes en
paradis. Charles fist metre en un sac fet de cuir de
bugle les espines molt saintement, et une partie de la
sainte croiz, et un des clous, et le suaire Nostre
Seignor, et la fesse dont il fu liez en son berçuel, et
10 le braz saint Symeon, et la chemise Nostre Dame Sainte
Marie. Et qant il ot si grant saintuaire receu, dom
iluec et en autres leus sunt avenu maint miracle apert,
puis s'en parti au congié de l'empereor et de toz et
s'en vint a Es la Chapele atot si haut saintuaire qu'il
15 meismes portoit dignement. Ilec fu cist grant saintuaires
a grant honor et en grant reverence de plusors des pueples
qui de partot i acoroient por les granz miracles que Deus i
feisoit desi au tens Charle le Chauf, qui devotement les
departi en France ou eles sont en plusors leus./

VI

Emprés les granz poines et les granz travaus   (65)
que Charles avoit eu en Costantinoble et en Jerusalem
et en plusors autres terres loing et pres, se torna a
repos et proposa qu'il n'ostoieroit mes. En son pro-
5 posement, esgarda une nuit vers le ciel et vit un chemin
d'estoiles en semblance de feu qui començoit de la mer
de Frise et tendoit par Tiescheterre et par Ytaile entre
France et Aquitaine, droit trespassant par Gascoigne et
par Bascle et par Navarre et par Espaigne desi en Galice
10 ou li cors monseignor saint Jaque gisoit, qu'en ne savoit
adonc ou il iert. Cel chemin d'estoiles esgarda Charles
par plusors nuiz et comença a porpenser que ce pooit estre
et senefier.

V, 2 fresches] A1 L2 P8 – si qu'eles] A1 L2 P8 V –
   17 que Nostre Sires i f.] A1 L2 P8 V

VII

De appar-
itione
Sancti
Jacobi

En cele meismes pensee s'aparut a lui par nuit
un berz plus beaus que l'en ne porroit dire et si li
dist: "Que fes tu, filz?" Et il respondi: "Qui es tu,
sires?" "Je sui," dist il, "Jaques li apostres, norriçons
5   Deu, filz Zebedee, freres / saint Jahan l'evangeliste,   (v
que Nostre Sires deigna eslire par sa grace a prehechier
les pueples sor la mer de Galilee, que Herodes li rois
ocist. Mis cors gist en Galice qu'en ne set ou il est,
apriens de Sarrazins ledement. Si me merveil molt porquoi
10   tu n'as ma terre delivree des paiens, qui tantes terres as
conquises. Por ce te faz je savoir car si com
Deus t'a fet plus puissant de toz rois terriens, autressi
t'eslist il a delivrer mon sarqueu qu'il t'aparoil corone
el ciel. La voie des estoiles que tu voiz senefie que tu
15   iras en Galice atot grant ost et feras voie a visiter
mon sarqueu. Et aprés toi toz li pueples qui est de l'une
mer deci a l'autre i iront requerant pardon de lor mesfez
et racontant les loenges de Deu et les vertuz de lui;
des le tens de ta vie jusqu'a la fin de cest siegle i
20   iront si com je te di. Or va plus tost que tu porras,
car je serai tis aidierres partot et por tes travals
te ferai avoir corone en ciel, et deci au darrien jor iert
tis nons enlo/engiez." Ensifaitierement s'aparut li   (6
beneoiz apostres par trois foiz a Charle. Qant Charles
25   oï tel chose, il aüna par la promesse de l'apostre granz
oz, puis erra tant qu'il entra en Espaigne atote s'ost.

VIII

De obsidione
de Pampeluna

La premiere cité que Charles assist ce
fu Pampelune, et si i sist trois mois que
prendre ne la pot, car ele ert garnie de tres
forz murs. Adonc fist Charles sa proiere a Deu et
5   dist: "Deus Jhesu Crist, por cui foi je ving en ceste
contree, done moi prendre ceste cité en l'enor de ton
non. Et tu, sire saint Jaques, se ce est voirs que tu
appareus a moi, done la moi prendre." Adonc par Deu et
par la proiere monseignor saint Jaque chaïrent li mur

VII, 11 ce le (le *added above the line*) te] L2 P8 V; *see note* —
    13 t'aparoit el ciel] A1 — 17 i *lacking* L2 V] A1 P8 — 19 i
    lacking V] A1

10   de la cité. Les Sarrazins qui baptisier se vostrent fist
garder a vie et cels qui le refuserent fist ocirre. Et
qant iteus miracles et teus merveilles orent veu li Sarra-
zins, partot la ou Charles aloit, l'enclinoient et enveoient
contre lui le treu et li / rendoient les citez.   (v°)

IX

Ensi s'atriva tote la terre par cel miracle. La
paiene gent se merveilloit trop qant ele veoit la gent
françoise si bien vestue et si noble de cors et de face.
Honoreement et pessiblement les recevoient, lor armes
5   gitoient jus. D'ilec ala Charles sanz nul contredit
au sarqueu monseignor saint Jaque et vint au Perron qui
sor la mer gist. Si ficha en la mer sa lance, graces
rendant a Deu et a monseignor saint Jaque qui desi la
l'avoit mené, et dist q'avant ne pooit il aler. Li
10   Galicien, qui puis la predication monseignor saint Jaque
et ses deciples erent repairié a la loi paienime, par
les mains Torpin l'arcevesque furent baptisié. Cil qui
recevoir ne le voustrent, furent li un livré a mort, li autre
enchaitivé par le regne des Crestiens. D'ilec ala Charles
15   par tote Espaigne de l'une mer desi a l'autre.

X

Les citez et les graindres viles que Charles / con-   (67)
quist donc en Galice sunt nomees par teus nons com vos
orrez ci selonc le latin de l'estoire: Usime, Lamesche,
Dumje, Columbre, Luche, Aureliane, Urie, Tude, Mindone,
5   Bracara, mere des citez, Vimarane, Granie, Compostele,
qui a cel tens ert petite. De celes d'Espaigne sunt ci
li non en ordre: Auchale, Godelfaiar, Thalamanche, Ubete,
Uline, Canailes, Madrite, Machede, Talavere, qui n'est mie
planteive, Medinacele, une cité haute, Berlange, Osine,
10   Segunce, Segobe qui est granz, Salamanche, Sepunilege, Tolete,
Kalatrave, Badaioth, Turgel, Godiane, Emerite, Alcemore,
Palance, Luiserne, Ventose qui est en Val Vert, Capaire,
Asturge, Ovete, Legion, Karrion, Burs, Nazres, Calaguirie,

VIII, 11 garder la vile] A1 L2
IX, 11 deciples qui puis erent] A1 L2 − 12 qui renoier ne le v.]
   L2 P8 V − 13 li un *lacking*] A1 L2 P8 V
X, 10 Segobe *lacking* A1 L2] P8 V

Urance, Lestoile, Kalatraus, Miracle, Sarragoce, qui est
15   apelee Cesarraguste, Pampelune, Baione, Jasche, Osche, ou
il soloit avoir .lxxxxix. tors par nombre, Terragone, Leride,
Tortose, uns chasteaus forz, / Aurelie, uns autres,   (v
Barbagalle, chasteaus ausi, Carbone, uns autres chasteaus,
Algate, qui est citez, Adanie, Arpalide, Esqualone, Ora-
20   malgie, Orraburrianie, Oracotante, Bargete, Petrose, ou
l'en fet le tres bon argent, Valance, Demite, Sative,
Granade, Sebile, Cordube, Abule, Acinte, ou li cors saint
Torquace gist, deciple monseignor saint Jaque. Uns
arbres d'olive croist sor la tombe verdoianz et charchiez
25   de meur fruit par chascun an au jor de sa feste en mi mai.
Si conquist une autre cité qui a non Biserte. Li chevalier
de la sunt tres fort et sunt apelé Arrabite. Si conquist
Bogie, ou il a roi, et Agabie, une ille, et Coatha une cité
en Barbastre, et Meloÿde et Vice, Formentere et Alcocors
30   et Almarie, Moneque, Gilbadaire, Cartage, Septe, qui est es
destroiz d'Espaigne ou la mer est perrilleuse por l'estreceté
que la mers a ilec, et Gesit et Astaruch.

XI

Tote la terre des Espaignous fu el pooir /   (6
Charle: la terre Alandaluf, la terre de Portigal,
la terre des Parz, la terre de Castele, cele des Mors,
cele des Navars, cele des Alavars, cele des Bicaios
5   et des Bascles, et cele des Palacres. Totes cez citez et
cez greignors viles qui ci sunt nomees, et cez illes,
conquist Charles, les unes par miracle les autres par
bataille, fors Luiserne qui est en Val Vert qu'il ne pot
prendre desi au darreain qu'il vint la, et si l'asist et
10   fu entor .iiii. mois. Adonc fist sa proiere a Deu et a
monseignor saint Jaque qu'il la preist et errament chaïrent
li mur et est deserte desi au jor d'ui. Uns estans de noire
eue crut en mi la vile ou il a granz poissons qui sunt noir.
Cele cité maudist Charles et trois autres, Ventose,
15   Capaire, Adamie, et por ce ne furent puis abitees. Autre
prince et autre roi conquistrent en Espaigne aprés Charle
et devant. Clodoveus, qui fu li premiers rois de France

XI, 3 des Porz] A1 L2 P8 V − 5 et cele des Palacres *lacking*] A1
L2 P8 V − 17 qui fu li premiers rois des C.] *see note.*

crestiens en conquist, Clotaires, Dagoberz, Pepins, Charles
Marteaus, Charles li Chaus, / Looÿs. Icist conquistrent   (v°)
20   partie de la terre et partie en leisserent, mes li bons rois
Charlemaines conquist tote Espaigne en son tens a l'onor de Deu.

XII

Les ydres et les mahomeries que Charles trova en Es-
paigne destruist totes fors une ymage qui est en la
terre de l'Andaluf. Cele ymage si est apelee Salancadis.
Cadis, c'est li leus ou ele est; Salan, c'est Deus en
5   langue arrabioise. Li Sarrazin dient que cele ymage qui
la siet fist Mahometh a sa vie en son non, et une legion
de deables enseela anz par nigromance qui sostient par
tel force cele ymage que de nullui ne puet estre depeciee.
S'aucuns Crestiens l'aproche, errament il perist, et
10 s'aucuns Sarrazins i va por orer, sains et aligres s'en depart,
et se par aventure s'asiet aucuns oiseaus sus, et errament
il muert. Sor la rive de cele mer est une pierre enciene,
entalliee d'uevre sarrazine, asise / sor terre, desos lee   (69)
et quarree, desus estroite, et haute tant com uns corbeaus
15 porroit voler haut. Sor cele pierre est cele ymage fete d'arain
en la semblance d'un home sor ses piez dreciee, sa face tornee
vers midi, une grant clef en sa main destre. Si com Sarrazin
dient, cele clef charra de sa main en l'an c'uns rois nestra
en France qui tote Espaigne metra a crestiene loi es
20 darreanetez del siegle, et si tost com Sarrazin verront la
clef chaoite, il repondront lor avoirs si s'en fuiront hors
de la terre.

XIII

De l'or et de l'argent que li roi et li prince
d'Espaigne donerent Charlemagne, fist il l'eglise de
monseignor Saint Jaque en la demorance qu'il fist adonques
en la terre par trois anz, si i mist evesques et chanoines de
5   l'ordre de saint Ysidoire le Confessor et si establi; d'esche-
les, de vestemenz et de livres et de toz autres aornemenz les
aorna. Del remenant fist l'eglise de Nostre Dame / Sainte   (v°)

XII, 13 dehors leé] *see note*
XIII, 5 d'escheles *lacking* A1 L2: desqueles] see above p. 59, p. 63.

Marie qui est a Es la Chapele, et l'iglise de monseignor Saint
Jaque en cele meismes vile, et l'iglise de monseignor Saint
10   Jaque a Boorges, et cele qui est a Tholose, et cele qui est en
Gascoigne entre la cité qui a non Aus et Saint Jahan de Sorges
en la voie de monseignor saint Jaque. Et si fist cele
eglise qui est entre Paris et Monmartre et autres abaïes
par le regne. Charles repaira adonc d'Espaigne vers France.
15   Et qant il fu repairiez, uns paiens rois d'Aufrique qui
avoit non Agolanz vint en Espaigne atot granz oz, et prist
les citez et les chasteaus, et ocist toz cels que li rois
avoit leissiez en Espaigne a garder la terre. Qant Charles
oï ce, il rala en Espaigne atot grant ost et Miles
20   d'Aiglant avec lui.

XIV

Si com li ost Charle fu herbergiez en son retor a
Baione, une cité de Bascles, uns chevaliers qui avoit
non Romars amaladi, et por la dote de mort dont il
ert / pres, se confessa et receut corpus domini. Aprés   (7(
5   comenda un suen parent qu'il vendist son cheval et de-
partist por s'ame les deniers et a clers et a povres.
Il fu morz. Cil vendi le cheval .c. sols, si les despendi
en boivre et en mangier et en vesteures. Mes por ce
que la vengence del Vrai Jugeur est prochaine au mal
10   feisant, s'aparut li morz a lui au chief de .xxx. jorz et
si li dist: "Por ce que le mien te comendai a doner en
aumones por m'ame, saches que Deus m'a deslié de toz mes
pechiez, et por ce que m'aumosne retenis, .xxx. jorz m'en as
fet estre en poine. Si te di que en cel leu dont je sui
15   issuz, enterras tu demain et je serai saus en paradis."

XV

Quant li morz ot ce dit, il se departi d'iluec, et
cil toz esperiz s'esveilla. El demain matin conta
par l'ost ce qu'il avoit oï. Si com il parloient entr'eus
de si grant merveille, este vos sodainement un escrois
5   sor lui en l'air ausi comme un ruiement de lions ou de

XIV, 3 Romains] A1 L2 P8 − 7 Il fu morz *lacking*] A1 L2 P8 V −
9 vengence Nostre Seignor] L2 (*with which* L3 O B1, *and* P2 P3
Br 1 *in Group II, agree; cf. the Latin (107, vii):* divini iudicis)

leus ou de veaus. / En cele hore fu raviz toz vis en-   (v°)
tr'eus toz en l'air. Quatre jorz le quistrent par monz
et par vaus chevalier et sergent, mes ne le porent
trover. Doze jorz aprés ce que ce fu avenu, erroit l'ost
10   par la terre de Navarre et de l'Avaire. La troverent
le cors tot froit en un perruchoi a trois liues de mer et
a quatre jornees de Baione. Iluec avoient la charoig[ne]
gitee li deable et l'ame en enfer ravie. Par cest es-
semple sachent cil qui les aumonnes des mors retienent qu'il
15   se dampnent perpetuelment. Aprés ce comença Charles atote
s'ost a querre Agolant par Espaigne, et tant le sui
qu'il le trova en une terre qui est apelee la terre De
Chans sor la rive qui a non Cee, en uns prez dont li
leus est beaus et honniz. Si com les oz s'entr'aprochierent,
20   Agolant manda au roi Charle bataille, s'il voloit .xx.
contre .xx., ou .lx. contre .lx., ou .c. contre .c., ou mile
contre mile, ou .ii. contre .ii., ou .i. contre .i.
Ensint fu otroié d'une part et d'autre. /   (71)

XVI

Lors envoia Charles .c. Crestiens a la bataille
et Agolant .c. Sarrazins, et toz les ocistrent iluec
li .c. Crestien. Aprés envoia Agolanz autres .c. contre
.c., et tuit refurent li Sarrazin ocis. Aprés en ren-
5   voia .cc. contre .cc., et de rechief furent ocis li Sarrazin.
Ilec a la parfin en envoia Agolant .ii. mile contre
.ii. mile. Iluec fu ocis une partie des paiens et
l'autre torna en fuie. Ensint fu entr'eus la bataille par
.ii. jorz. Au tierz jor gita sort Agolant et conut bien en
10   son sort et vit que se il se combatoit gent a gent que molt i
perdroit Charles des suens. Il manda la bataille a l'endemain.
Ele fu acraantee d'ambedeus les oz. Adonc li un de nos Crestiens
le soir devant le jor de la bataille appareillierent lor
armes molt ententivement et fichierent en terre lor lances
15   droites devant lor herberges es prez de joste l'eue.

XV, 12 la charoig] A1 P8 V; *see note* − 14 sachiez cil] A1 L2
     P8 − des mors *lacking*] P8 V − 18 Cenen en] Cee L3 O; *cf.*
     Ceee B1 ; Chee P8
XVI, 12 li (un de nos *lacking*) Crestien] A1 L2 P8

XVII

    L'endemain matin, cil qui en cele batail [le] / durent   (v°
morir troverent lor lances reprises et charchiees d'es-
corces, et de fueilles ploines et de verdor. Molt se mer-
veillerent de si grant merveille. Il les trancherent
5   emprés terre, et les racines qui remestrent en la terre
engendrerent d'eles meismes grant arbroie autreteles come
longues perches qui encor perent en cel leu. Merveilleuse
chose fu, et grant joies, et grant profiz as ames,
et granz destruiemenz as cors. Il assemblerent et d'une
10   part et d'autre. Cel jor i ot ocis .xl. mile Crestiens,
et li dus Miles d'Angiers, pere Rollant, fu ocis ilec
avec cels cui les lances florirent, et li chevaus Charle
fu ocis ilec, et Charles fu a pié atot .x. mile Crestiens
entre les Sarrazins. Il trest s'espee qui avoit non
15   Joieuse de cui il ocist adonques molt de paiens. Einsi
furent deci au vespre, et a l'avesprer s'en tornerent d'ambedeus
parz a lor herberges. L'endemain vindrent secorre / Charle   (7
quatre marchis d'Itaile atot .iiii. mile homes.

XVIII

    Qant Agolant sot ce, il se parti d'iluec et s'en
ala es contrees de Legion. Charles establi une abaïe
la ou la bataille fu, et molt riche eglise en l'onor de
monseignor saint Fagon de cui li cors gist ilueques.
5   Encore i est grant la vile et planteive qu'en apele
Saint Fagon. D'ilueques repaira Charles vers France.
En la compaignie de cels cui les lances florirent a
molt a entendre de salu. Si com les genz Charle ap-
pareillierent lor armes a la bataille, autressi devons
10   nos appareillier noz armes, ce sunt bones vertus, contre
vices. Cil qui met foi contre mauveise error, charité
contre haine, largesce contre avarice, humilité contre
orgueill, chasteé contre luxure, oroison assiduel contre
temptacion de deable, silence contre tençon, obedience
15   contre charnel corage, sa lance ert florie au jor del

XVII, 1 batail (*comes at the end of a line; cf.* charoig XV, 12 –
    5 les tronçons] A1 L2 P8 V; *see note* – 6 granz arbres] A1 L2
    P8 – 8 est et fu] A1 L2 V – 11 i fu] A1 L2 P8 V - 12 les *lack-*
    ing A1] P8 V L3 – i fu] A1 L2 P8 V – 16 vespre (et a l'avesprer
    lacking) qu'il s'en retornerent] P8 *(see variants)*

joïse. La lance, c'est l'ame de celui / qui bien se   (v°)
combat contre les vices en terre. Car si com li comba-
teor Charle morurent por Deu en bataille, ausint devomes
nos morir es vices et es covoitises et vivre es saintes
20   vertuz el monde que nos puissons deservir el ciel florie
corone.

XIX

Agolant, qui tret se fu arrieres molt dolenz,
aüna de genz tres grant planté, Sarrazins et Mors,
Moabites, Ethiopiens, Aufricans et Persans, et ot
avec lui .ix. rois et un aumaçor dont ci sunt li non tot
5   selonc le latin de l'estoire: Thezepins i fu, li rois
d'Arrabe, Burabeaus li rois d'Alixandre, Avices li rois de
Bougie, Osbins li rois d'Agabe, Facins li rois de
Barbarie, Aylis li rois de Marroc, Alphinors li rois de
Maiorgues, Maiomon li rois de Meque, Ebraÿns li rois
10   de Sebile, et l'aumaçor de Cordres. Atotes ses genz
s'en vint Agolant en Gascoigne et prist Agiens
par force. D'iluec manda a Charle qu'il venist parler
a lui a poi de / chevaliers. Il li donroit or et argent   (73)
et autres richesces .ix. somiers charchiez s'il voloit
15   estre a s'amor. Por ce le disoit qu'il le voloit veoir
et conoistre et qu'il le peust en bataille ocirre. Mes
Charles s'en apensa molt bien porquoi il le feisoit. Qant
il ot oï les messages, il li manda qu'il iroit a lui et qu'il
feroit a sa volenté.

XX

Qant li message s'en furent parti, Charles en
vint atot .ii. mile chevaliers a quatre liues d'Agiens.
Ilec les leissa repostement et s'en vint atot .lx. desi
a un mont qui pres est de la cité qu'en l'en puet bien
5   veoir. Ilec fist li rois cels remenoir et chanja sa
vesteure; sanz lance, son escu torné detriés son dos si
com costume est de messages de guerre, s'en vint a la cité,
avec lui un sol chevalier. Adonc s'en issirent plusors

XVIII, 17 si com *lacking; the omission is probably due to the
following* li com-] P8 — 19 cointises] A1 L2 P8 V
XX, 7 et s'en vint] A1 L2 P8 V

contr'els et enquistrent qu'il queroient. "Nos
10 somes," distrent il, "message Charle qui nos envoie a
Agolant vostre roi." Adonc les / menerent devant Agolant.   (v°)
Il li distrent: "Charles nos envoie a toi, car il vient
atot .lx. chevaliers si com tu comendas et velt fere a
ta volenté se tu li tiens ce que tu li as promis. Si
15 vien a lui atot .lx. des tuens et parole a lui!"
Adonc dist Agolant qu'il repairassent a Charle et li deissent
qu'il l'atendist. Ne Agolant ne cuidoit mie que ce fust Charles
qui parloit a lui. Mes Charles le conut adonc et enquist de
quel part ert la cité plus legiere a prendre. Il vit les
20 rois qui erent en la cité, puis s'en repaira as .lx. chevaliers
qu'il avoit leissiez lez le mont. Avec cels s'en repeira as
.ii. mile. Agolant le sui tost atot .vii. mile homes
com cil qui le voloit ocirre s'il peust. Mes Charles s'ert
aperceuz de sa felonie, si ne le vost mie atendre. Ainz s'en
25 ala et s'en repaira en France. Lors assembla molt grant ost,
puis s'en vint arrieres a Agiens. Adonc asist la cité et si i
sist / .vi. mois. Au setime mois fist drecier perrieres et   (74
mangoneaus as murs et chasteaus de fust et autres enginz a
prendre la vile. Adonc s'en issi Agolant une nuit, et li roi
30 et li plus haut home, par un[s] faus trous qu'il orent fez
es murs et passerent l'eue qui cort joste la cité. El demain
entra Charles en la vile a grant joie. Adonc i ot ocis .x.
mile paiens. D'ilec vint Agolant a Saintes qui adonc ert
de paiene loi.

XXI

Ilec demora Agolanz. Charles le sui et li manda
qu'il li rendist la cité. Il ne li vost rendre. Ainz s'en
issi a bataille contre lui par tel covenant que la cité
fust celui qui veintroit l'autre. Ensint fu creanté
5 d'une part et d'autre. Le soir devant le jor de la
bataille, drecierent les uns de noz Crestiens lor lances
en terre es prez qui sunt entre le chastel qu'en apele
Tailleborc et la cité sur l'eue qui a non Charante. El
demain troverent lor lances / reprises et foillues cil qui   (v°

XX, 29 Qant ce vit Ag. il s'en issi par nuit] A1 L2 P8 V – 30 qui
   erent fez] A1 L2 P8
XXI, 8 (sur l'eue *lacking*) qui avoit non] A1 L2 P8 V

10   en la bataille devoient mort recevoir, si come devant avint
a Saint Fagon. Il tranchierent lor lances pres de terre,
esjoïssanz de si grant miracle. Il assemblerent et
ferirent premiers en la bataille. Molt i ocistrent des
paiens et en la fin reçurent il corone par martire.

15   Quatre mile i ot de cels qui troverent lor lances reprises.
Ilec reperdi Charles son cheval et fu entre sa gent a pié
reclamant l'aÿde Nostre Seignor Jhesu Crist. Cil ne porent
soffrir la bataille, ainz s'en entrerent en la cité. Charles
l'asist de totes parz fors devers l'eue. Cele nuit s'en

20   issi Agolanz et ses oz par l'eue. Qant Charles sot ce, il
l'en sui et ocist lo roi d'Agabe et lo roi de Bogie et
molt autres paiens bien entor quatre mile.

XXII

    Agolanz ala tant qu'il passa les porz d'Aspre et
vint a Pampelune. Adonc manda a Charle qu'il l'atendroit
par / non de bataille. Qant Charles oï ce, il repaira   (75)
en France et de tote sa cure fist a lui venir granz oz

5   et de loing et de pres. Il manda et commenda par tote
France que tuit cil qui serf erent de lor chars par les
mauveses costumes des seignors, fussent franc permenablement,
et il et lor ligniee, cele qui ert presente et a venir.
Ensint le fist de toz cels qui en Espaigne avec lui iroient.

10   Toz cels qu'il trova en prison mist hors. Les povres et
les nuz vesti. Cels de male volenté apeisa ensemble. Les
debotez de lor heritages remist en lor honors. Les sages
d'armes et les escuiers ordena de l'ordre de chevalerie et
cels qu'il avoit deseritez de s'amor de tot en tot a s'amor

15   converti. Car autrement ne le doit fere rois qui bien velt
tenir terre. Les privez et les estranges acompaigna a lui
a cel erre, et je, Torpins, arcevesques de Rains, les
asoloie de toz lor pechiez par l'auctorité de Deu, et a
mes propres mains / me combatoie et rendoie le pueple   (v°)

20   fort et ferm en bon corage vers paiens. .c. mile et .xxxiiii.
i ot d'omes combatanz estre les escuiers et cels a pié
dont il n'iert nombres. Ici sunt li non des plus hauz
homes qui furent avec lo roi a icest erre:

XXIII

Rollant, guierres des oz, cuens del Mans, sire de
Blaives, niés Charle, filz le duc Milon d'Angiers, nez
de Bertain la seror Charle. Cil i fu, hom de grant corage
et de soveraine proesce atot .iiii. mile homes. Uns
5   autres Rollanz i fu de cui home se doit tere. Olivier,
guierres des oz, chevaliers tres aigres, sages en bataille,
poissanz de braz et d'espee, cuens de Genevois, filz
Renier le conte. Cil i fu atot .iii. mile homes. Estouz
li cuens de Langres atot .iii. mile, Arestanz li rois
10 de Bretaigne atot .vii. mile. Uns autres rois ert en
Bretaigne au tens cestui de cui on ne doit mention fere.
Angelier li dus d'Aquitaine i fu atot .iiii. mile homes.
Cil erent sage d'armes et plus d'ars et de saietes. Au
tens Angelier ert uns autres dus en Aquitaine a Poitiers
15 la cité de cui ne fait ore a dire. Cil Angeliers ert par
lignage / Gascoinz, et ert dus de la cité d'Aquitaine qui   (76
ert entre Limoges et Boorges et Poitiers, que Cesar Auguste
fist primes en cele contree, si la noma Aquitaine. A
cele cité sozmist Limoges et Boorges et Poitiers et Saintes et
20 Angolesme, atotes les contrees de chascune, dont toz li païs
fu et est apelez Aquitaine.

XXIV

Cele cité, aprés la mort Angelier, veve de son
seignor, torna a gast por ce que si citeain morurent
tuit en Roncesvaus, ne puis n'i ot autres habiteors.
Gaifier li rois de Bordeaus vint au roi atot .iii.
5 mile homes. Geliers i vint, et Gelins, et Salemons
qui fu compainz Estouz de Langres, Baudoin li freres Rollant,
Gondelbuef li rois de Frise atot .vii. mile homes,
Hoieaus li cuens de Nantes atot .ii. mile homes,
Hernaut de Bellande atot .ii. mile homes, Naimes li dus de
10 Baiviere atot .x. mile homes, Ogier li dus de Danemarche
atot .x. mile homes, Costentins / li prevoz de Rome atot   (v°
.xx. mile, Renaut d'Aubespine, Gautier de Termes,

XXIII, 4 Uns et autres] A1 L2 V – 10 uns autres rois . . . fere
lacking] A1 L2 P8 V – 13 Au tens . . . a dire *lacking*] A1
L2 P8 V – 21 et est *lacking*] A1 L2
XXIV, 5 Selins A1] L2 (*with* L3 B1 O) P8 (Galins) V – 11 Costans
A1 L2] P8 V Br 2

Guielin, Garin li dus de Loherroine atot .iiii. mile
homes, Begues, Aubri li Borgoignon, Berarz de Nubles,
15 Guionarz, Estormiz, Tierri, Yvorins, Berangier, Hates, et
Guenes qui puis fu traitres. L'oz de la propre terre
Charle fu de .xl. mile, estre cels a pié dont nombre
n'iert. Cil qui ci sunt nomé erent poissant et de grant
renon et essauçant la loi crestiene. Car si com Nostre
20 Sires Jhesu Crist atot ses .xii. apostres et ses deciples
conquist le monde, tot ausis Charles li rois de France,
empereres de Rome, conquist Espaigne a l'onor de Deu.

XXV

Es landes de Bordeaus s'aünerent adonc les oz
et covroient tote la terre en lonc et en lé .ii. jornees.
De .xii. liues loing pooit en oïr la noise et la fremor.
Adonc passa Hernaut de Beaulande primes les porz d'Aspre a-
5   totes ses genz et vint a Pampelune. / Et aprés vint Estouz   (77)
li cuens de Lengres atote s'ost. Aprés vint Aristans li
rois et Angeliers atote lor ost. Aprés vint Gondelbuef
atote s'ost. Aprés vint li rois Ogiers et Constantin de Rome
atote lor ost. Au darrien vint Charles et Rollant atote
10 lor ost, et covroient tote la terre de l'aigue de Rune
desi au mont qui est a .iiii. liues de la cité en la voie de
monseignor Saint Jaque. Vint jors demorerent a passer les porz.
Adonc manda Charles a Agolant qui ert en la vile qu'il li
rendist ou qu'il issist a bataille contre lui. Agolant vit
15 qu'il ne porroit mie la cité tenir contre lui, si vost mielz
issir a bataille fors que morir leidement dedenz. Donc
manda a Charle qu'il li donast trives tant que ses oz
fussent issues et appareilliees de bataille et tant qu'il
eust parlé a lui boche a boche.

XXVI

Molt desirroit Agolant a veoir Charlemagne.
Ensint furent donees les trives. Agolanz s'en issi

XXIV, 21 ausis rois Charles, de France rois, empereres] L2 P8 V
XXV, 2 .xii. jornees] A1 L2 P8 V − 3 poïst en] A1 P8 V Br 2 − oïr
      lacking] A1 L2 P8 V − 6 li cuens . . . Aristans *lacking*] A1 L2
      P8 V − 12 Trente jors] A1 L2 P8 V; *see note* − 13 qu'il l'aten-
      dist ou] A1 L2 P8 V − 18 fussent conrees et ap.] A1 L2 P8 V

et ses oz. Il se rangierent joste la cité, et Agolanz
s'en vint atot .xl. de ses / plus hauz homes au tref   (v
5   Charle qui ert a une liue de la cité. L'ost Agolant
et l'ost Charle erent en un beau leu joste la vile
qui avoit de lonc et de lé bien .vi. liues, si que la voie
monseignor Saint Jaque departoit l'une ost de l'autre.
Agolanz fu venuz au tref Charle. Donc li dist Charles en
10   langue sarrazinoise qu'il avoit apris a Tholete qant il
i demora en enfance: "Tu es Agolanz qui ma terre que
j'avoie conquise a l'onor de Deu et convertie a crestiene
loi, m'as destruite et desertee, et les cités et les chasteaus
gastez, et les Crestiens ocis dementres que g'ere en France re-
15   pairiez, si saches que molt m'en complaing." Quant Agoulans
oï le sarrasinois qu'il parla, si s'en esmervilla molt et esjoï.
Il respondi donques a Charlemagne: "Je te pri que tu me
dies porquoi tu quiers ceste terre, qant tis peres ne tis
aives ne tis tresaives ne l'ot, n'escheue ne t'est
20   en heritage." "Por ce," dist Charlemagne, "que Nostre Sire
Jhesu Criz, crierres del ciel et de la terre, eslut nostre
gent crestiene et establi a estre dame desor totes les genz
del monde, et je, en / tant com je poi, ai convertie la   (7
gent paienime a nostre loi."

XXVII

"N'est mie digne chose," dist Agolant, "que la
nostre gent soit sozgiete a la vostre. Car nostre loi
valt mielz que la vostre. Nos avons," dist Agolant,
"Mahommet qui fu messages Deu cui comendement nos tenons,
5   et li deu que nos aorons et par qui nos vivons et regnons,
nos manifestent et demostrent les choses qui sunt a avenir
par le comendement Mahommet." "Agolant," dist Charles, "tu
foloies. Nos creons en Deu qui nos fist, et tenons ses
comendemenz, et vos creez et aorez le deable en voz ymages.
10   Noz ames vont en la perdurable vie de paradis après la mort
par la foi que nos tenons, et les voz ames vont en la perpetuel
mort d'enfer par la loi que vos tenez. Ce demostre que nostre
lois valt mielz que la vostre, et por ce que vos ne creez ne

XXVI, 11 Es tu ce Ag.?] A1 L2 V — 13 cités et les *lacking*] A1
L2 P8 V — 15 Quant Agoulans . . . et esjoï *lacking* A1 L2]
P8 V Br 2 — 17 Agolanz respondi] A1 L2
XXVII, 9 et voz ymages A1 L2] P8 V (*so too* P2 P3 Br 1; Br 2:
a voz)

ne volez croire le criator de tote criature, n'avez vos
15   droit el ciel / n'en terre. Por ce te di je que tu reçoi-   (v°)
ves baptesme, et tu et ta gent, ou tu vien a bataille contre
moi que tu muires de la male mort." "Ja ce n'aviegne," dist
Agolant, "que je reçoive baptesme ne que je renoi Mahommet
mon deu. Mes je me combatrai a toi et a ta gent, ou a tanz
20   qanz s'il te siet, par tel covenant que, se nostre lois valt
mielz que la vostre, que nos veincons, et se la vostre valt
mielz que la nostre, que vos veinquoiz, et soit deci au darrien
jor reprochié as veincuz, et as veinqueors perdurable loenge.
Ensorquetot je recevrai baptesme se j'en puis eschaper vis.
25   Ensint le te creant je," dist Agolant.

XXVIII

D'une part et d'autre fu outroié la bataille.
Erranment furent esleu .xx. Crestien et vint Sarrazin
ou champ de la bataille par la covenance de lor loi.
Et il vindrent ensamble et furent lues li .xx. paiens
5   *ocis. Aprés en furent envoié .xl. contre .xl. et de re-*
chief furent li paien ocis. Aprés en furent envoié .c.
contre cent ne nus des paiens n'en eschapa. De rechief
envoierent cent cuntre cent par esgart et par atiremant des
.ii. olz, et por ce que li .c. Crestien furent povrement armé
10   *de foi, il foïrent et furent tuit ocis. Cist donent essample*
es bons homes qui se doivent combatre contre les vices, qu'en
nule meniere ne doivent foïr. Quar si com cil furent
mort qui foïrent, ausi moront cil laidemant qui retornent
as vices. Per l'esgart des .ii. olz revindrent por recovrer
15   *la loi .ii. cenz contre .ii. cenz ou champ, et furent ocis*
li .ii. cent Sarrazin. Aprés en vindrent mil contre mil,
ne nuns des paiens n'eschapa. Donc fu trieve donee d'une
part et d'autre, et vint Agolanz au roi Charle affermanz que
la loi crestienne valoit muez que la lour. Lors covenança a
20   *Karle que l'andemain recevroit baptoisme, il et ses genz. Par*
tel covenant repaira es suens et dist as rois et as hauz
homes qu'il se baptizeroit. Li un le refuserent et li autre
l'outroiarent.

XXVIII *The whole chapter is lacking in* P5, *with no sign that the*
scribe noticed the omission. The text printed is taken from A1
except for rejected readings which follow. 4 furent lors] P8 V
Br 2 – 7 .c. contre cent (ne nus . . . cent cuntre cent *lacking*]
L2 P8 V – 16 mil contre .ii. mil] L2 P8 V – 22 Li un le
refuserent *lacking* L2] P8 V Br 2

XXIX

El demain vers tierce, si com la trive estoit
donee de venir et d'aler, vint Agolant au tref Charle por
baptisier, lui et sa gent. Il trova Charle seant au
mangier, et vit molt de tables mises entor lui et molt
5   de seanz, les uns evesques, les autres abez, les autres
moines noirs, les autres chanoi/nes blans, les autres   (7⁹
chevaliers, les autres prestres et clers del siegle.
Agolant demanda a Charle de chascun ordre quel gent
c'estoit. "Cels," dist Charle, "que tu voiz la vestuz
10   d'une color, ce sunt evesque et prestre de nostre loi qui
nos esponent les escritures et assolent de noz pechiez.
Et cil que tu voiz de noir habit sont abé et moine, et
cels que tu voiz vestuz de blanc habit, sunt chanoine
reguler qui por nos prient et chantent messes et matines."
15   Entre cez choses esgarda Agolant d'autre part et vit lonc
.xii. povres seant a terre, povrement vestuz, sanz nape et sanz
table, pou pain et poi a boivre devant els. Agolant demanda
quel gent c'estoient. Charles li dist: "Ce sunt message
Nostre Seignor Jhesu Crist que nos peissons chascun jor el
20   non des .xii. apostres." Adonc li dist Agolant, "Cil qui
environ toi sient sunt richement peu et vestu et abevré, et
cil qui sunt message ton Seignor en qui tu croiz muerent de
fain la a val et sieent si vilment et si povrement./   (v°
Mauveisement aime son Seignor qui si vilment et si leidement
25   reçoit son message; grant vergoigne et grant honte li fet.
Ta loi que tu diz estre bone, demostres tu estre fause, et je
refus le baptesme dorenavant, car je ne voi mie en toi droites
oeuvres selonc le baptesme." Maintenant s'en repaira a l'ost
et manda a Charle a l'endemain bataille.

XXX

Qant Charles vit qu'il refusa baptesme por les
povres, molt en fu dolenz. Despuis les reçut tote sa
vie a table et a nape honoreement. Ci devons nos prendre

XXIX, 7 prestres, les autres clers] A1 L2 V – 12 Et cil . . . moine
lacking] A1 L2 P8 V – 15 lonc *lacking*] P8 V Br 2; *cf.* L3 B1:
loinz – 17 pain et autres viandes] A1 L2 P8 V – 23 fain et de
soif] A1 L2 P8 V – 26 demostre estre] A1 L2 P8 V; *see
variants and note.*

garde que grant corpe aquiert cil qui les povres Deu n'honore.
5 Se Charles perdi un roi a baptizier et sa gent por les
povres, qu'iert il de cels au darreain jor qui les povres
auront traitié laidement? Coment orront il la voiz Damedeu
disant: "Vos maleoit, departez de moi el perdurable feu
d'enfer. Qant je oi fain et soif et froit, vos ne me
10 regardastes." Ci de/vons nos entendre que la lois Damedeu   (80)
et sa foiz valt poi en Crestien sanz bones oevres. Car
l'escriture dit: "Si com li cors est morz sanz l'ame,
autressi est en l'ome foiz morte sanz bone oevre." Si
com li paiens refusa le baptesme, si devons nos criembre
15 que Deus nos refust au jor del joïse por ce qu'il ne
trueve mie en nos droites oevres de baptesme.

XXXI

El demain furent assemblé d'une part et d'autre
et vindrent el champ par la covenance de la loi. L'oz
Charle fu de .c. mile et .xxxiiii. et l'ost Agolant de
.c. mile. Li Crestien firent .iiii. batailles et li paien
5 .v. La bataille des paiens qui primes assembla fu tantost
veincue et la seconde aprés veincue. Qant ce virent
paien, il s'aünerent ensemble, et Agolanz en mi els, et
nostre Crestien les aceinstrent de totes parz. D'une
part vint Hernauz de Beaulande atote s'es/chiele,   (v°)
10 d'autre vint Estout de Langres atot la soe, et puis li
rois Gondelbuef atote sa gent, et aprés li rois Ogiers
et Costantins li prevoz de Rome atote lor eschieles.
Au darrien vint Charles et si autre baron, et se fierent
en els, et comencerent a soner cors et boisines. Donc oïssiez
15 si grant noise et si grant fereïz q'ainc nus n'oï greignor.
Hernauz de Beaulande ala tant ferant a destre et a senestre
qu'il vint a Agolant et l'ocist ilec de s'espee en mi els
par la puissance de Deu. Adonc leverent grant li cri et li
plor des paiens qu'il ocioient de totes parz. Si grant
20 occisions ot iluec qu'a peines en eschapa nus fors lo roi
de Sebile et l'aumaçor de Cordres a petit de gent. Desi as
chevilles estoient li veinqueor el sanc, ce dit l'estoire.

XXX, 4 povres deshonore] A1 L2 — 14 nos entendre et devons
    criembre] A1 L2 P8 V
XXXI, 7 s'armerent] A1 L2 P8 V — 13 autre *lacking*] A1 L2 P8 V —
    15 et si grant cri] A1 L2 — 20 ot iluec de paiens que poi en
    eschapa fors] A1 L2 V — 22 as chevaus] A1 L2 P8 V

XXXII

Toz cels que Charles trova en la cité fist
ocirre. Por ce que Charles veinqui Agolant senefie
que la lois crestiene est sor totes autres lois. Se
Crestien tenoient bien foi en cuer / et en oevre, il   (81)
5   seroient eslevé sor les angles. Car totes choses sunt
poissanz a bien creant, ce dit Deus. Charlemagne aüna ses
oz esjoïssanz de si grant victoire, et herberja soi et ses
genz al Pont d'Arge en la voie monseignor Saint Jaque. Cele
nuit retornerent les uns de noz Crestiens el champ de la
10   bataille par la covoitise de l'avoir as morz, que li rois
ne le sot. Si com il se furent chargié de l'or et de
l'argent et des autres avoirs et il s'en cuiderent repairier,
li aumaçor de Cordres qui de la bataille ert eschapez, lor
corut sore des montaignes ou il erent repoz, si les ocist toz.
15   Bien estoient entor mile. Cist essemples nos mostre car autressi
com cil qui veinquirent lor anemis et il retornerent par
covoitise as morz, par qu'il furent ocis de lor anemis, tot
ausi chascun de nos qui son pechié veint et il en prent peni-
tence, il ne doit mie retorner / au pechié que si anemi   (v°)
20   ne l'ocient, ce sunt li deable. Si com cil qui as des-
pueilles retornerent perdirent la presente vie et de lede mort
morurent, autressint li religieus home qui lessent le siegle,
s'il retornent puis as terrienes choses, il perdent la celestiel
vie et vont en la perpetuel mort d'enfer.

XXXIII

Al tierz jor aprés fu nonchié Charle c'uns princes
de Navarre qui avoit non Forrez venoit contre lui a bataille.
Qant Charles sot ce, il vint a Monjardin contre lui. Cil li
quist la bataille a l'endemain. Charles la craanta. Le
5   soir devant fist Charles oroison a Deu requerant qu'il
li demostrast cels qui devoient morir des suens en cele
bataille. El demain qant l'ost Charle fu armee, il vit
une croiz vermeille sor l'espaule de chascun qui devoit
morir, et qant il vit ce, si fu molt dolenz por la pitié de
10   tanz prudomes. Il les comenda devant lui a venir et les
conjura sor s'amor qu'il alassent tuit en une chapele qui
dejoste cel leu / ert et qu'il l'atendissent ilec tant   (82)

XXXII, 6 ce dit an] A1 L2 P8 V — 21 et *lacking*] A1 L2 V

qu'il fust repairiez de la bataille. Il i alerent, et
Charle vint a la bataille et ocist Forré et .iii. mile
15   Navars. Il repaira, et qant il fu repairiez, il en vint
a la chapele et trova toz cels morz qu'il avoit ilueques
leissiez, et furent .c. et .l. Ne sunt mie legier a veoir
li jugement de Deu. Car por ce se cil ne morurent a la
bataille, ne perdirent il mie la corone de martire, car
20   Deus lor avoit porveu, et ce que Deus a porveu ne puet
estre destorné. Le Montjardin et tote la terre des Navars
prist Charles en sa seisine. En aprés pou de tans fu dit
a Charle qu'a Nadres ert venuz uns paiens des contrees
de Sire qui avoit non Fernagu, del lignage Golias. Si
25   l'i avoit envoié li amiraus de Babiloine atot .xx. mile
Turs combatre a Charle. Cil paiens ert par nature si durs
qu'il ne cremoit nule arme. La force de .xl. homes avoit,
et d'estature .xii. cotes, et de façon .i. cote, et de nés
.i. espan, et de braz .ii. cotes, si doi / de .ii. espanz.   (v°)

XXXIV

Charlemaine vint contre Fernagu a Nadres. Si tost
com cil sot sa venue, il s'en issi de Nadres toz seus et
requist bataille a .i. sol. Adonc i fu envoiez par la
volenté Charle Ogier li Denois. Si tost com il fu el
5   champ, Fernagu l'embraça et l'emporta tot armé voiant
tote l'ost el chastel soz son destre braz. Aprés li fu
envoiez Renaut d'Aubespine, et il l'enporta autressint.
Aprés revint Fernagu el champ et requist la bataille
contre .ii. Li rois i envoia Costantin de Rome et Oël
10   le conte de Nantes. Fernaguz les emporta endeus toz
armez, l'un a destre, l'autre a senestre. Aprés i
envoia Charles .xx. chevaliers, et il les enporta toz .xx.,
primes .ii. et puis .ii. Qant Charles vit ce, molt s'en
merveilla ne puis n'en i osa nul envoier. Donc vint Rollant
15   au roi et li demanda congié de combatre au paien. Li rois
ne li vost doner. Tant li pria Rollanz et dist qu'il ne
li pot veer. Mes molt li otroia a enviz, car juenes ert

XXXIII, 23 a Navarre] P8; *see note* — 25 mile *lacking*] L2 P8 V —
27 .xx. homes A1 L2] P8 V Br 2 — 29 braz .iii. cotes] A1 L2
P8 V
XXXIV, 16 qu'il le li otroia] A1 L2 P8 V; *see too variants;* L3 B1
O *read:* qu'il ne li pot veer

et si l'amoit molt. Rollanz / s'arma, et qant il fu armez   (8
et il ot oï le servise Deu, il en vint el champ.
20   Fernagu le prist en son venir a une sole main si com
il avoit fet les autres, et le leva sor le col de son
cheval devant lui. Si com il l'enportoit, Rollanz le
prist par le menton et le torna si fort arriere qu'endui
chaïrent. Arrament se releverent et monterent es chevaus.
25   Rollanz trest Durendal, si le feri si q'a cel col li
trencha son cheval par mi. Fernaguz fu a pié et tint
s'espee. Adonc le feri si Rollanz el braz dom il tenoit
l'espee qu'ele li chaï de la main, mes il nel bleça
gueres.

XXXV

Qant li paiens ot s'espee perdue, il corut Rollant
sore et le cuida ferir del poing, si feri son cheval el
front si qu'il l'abati mort desoz lui. Rollanz ot perdu
son cheval. Il se combatirent a pié desi vers none, et qant
5   vint vers la vespre, Fernagu demanda trives desi a l'endemain,
et l'endemain revenissent sanz cheval el champ ensemble si com
il erent. Rollanz li otroia / par tel covenant qu'il li   (vᶜ
donast congié d'aporter un baston tel com il voudroit, et li
paiens li otroia. Par le creant de l'un et de l'autre
10   s'en ala chascun a sa herberge. L'endemain, si com covent
estoit, revindrent matin a pié a la bataille. Rollanz ot
aporté un baston lonc et tort et nouel. Maintenant assemblerent
et furent ensint tote jor c'onques Rollanz del baston ne le
bleça, mais molt sovent li gita pieres dom el champ avoit a
15   grant plenté. Ensi se combatirent desi au midi c'onques
Rollanz ne le pot blecier. Donc quist Fernaguz a Rollant
trives tant qu'il eust dormi, car molt ert pesanz de someill.
Rollanz li dona, et cil comença a dormir. Rollanz, qui juenes
ert et de grant corage, li aporta une pierre a son chevez que
20   cil dormist plus volentiers. Adonc se tenoient les genz si
en lor loi que nus n'enfreinsist trives qui donees les eust,
fust paiens ou Crestiens.

XXXIV, 26 et trest] A1 L2 P8 V
XXXV, 6 (sans cheval *lacking*) el champ] A1 L2 P8 V – 11 a pié
lacking V] A1 L2 P8 V – 14 et molt] A1 L2 P8 V – 16 prist
A1 L2] P8 V; requist Br 2

XXXVI

Qant Fernaguz fu refez de dormir, si s'esveilla.
Rollanz, qui sist delez lui, li demanda coment il ert si
durs qu'il ne cremoit nule / arme. Li paiens li dist: (84)
"Je ne puis estre navrez fors par le nombrill, mes je
5   l'ai si garni que je ne crieng arme par la." Qant Rollanz
oï ce, il se tot et torna l'orille d'autre part ausi com s'il
ne l'eust mie entendu. Fernagu esgarda adonc Rollant si li
dist: "Coment as tu nom?" "Rollanz," dist il, "sui apelez."
"De quel gent," dist Fernaguz, "ies tu qui si fort te combaz a
10   moi? Ainz mes ne trovai home qui si me poïst lasser."
"Nez sui," dist Rollanz," de France, niés Charle." "De
quel loi," dist Fernagu, "sunt François?" "De crestiene loi,"
dist Rollanz, "somes, et feisomes les comendemenz Nostre Seignor
Jhesu Crist, et en tant com nos poons nos combatons por sa foi."

XXXVII

Qant Fernaguz oï le non de Crist, il demanda:
"Qui est cil Criz en cui tu croiz?" "C'est," dist
Rollanz, "li filz Deu Nostre Pere, qui nasqui de la Virge
Marie, et soffri mort en croiz, et fu mis el sepulcre,
5   et au tierz jor resuscita." "Nos creons," dist Fernaguz,
"que li crierres del ciel et de la terre est uns deus,
ne nului n'engendra ne plus qu'il fu de nelui engendrez,
et / donc est il uns Deus, non trebles." "Voirté diz," (v°)
dist Rollanz, "c'uns est il, mes la ou tu diz qu'il n'est
10   trebles, la cloches tu en foi. Se tu croiz el Pere, tu
croiz el Fill et el Saint Esperit, car c'est uns
Deus menanz en trois persones. Totes les trois persones
sunt perdurables en soi et ivels. Teus com li Peres est,
teus est li Filz et li Sainz Esperiz. Es persones est
15   proprietez, et unitez en l'essence, et en majesté est
oeltez aoree. En treble persone aorent angle .i. Deu
es cieus." "Or me mostre," dist Fernagu, "coment trois sunt
un." "Je le te mosterrai," dist Rollanz, "par humaines creatures.
Si com en la harpe dementiers qu'ele sone a trois choses, li fuz
20   et les cordes et li sons, et c'est une harpe, ausi sunt en Deu

trois persones, li Peres et li Filz et li Sainz Esperiz, et si
est uns Deus. Ou soloil sont .iii. choses, la blanchors, la
resplandors et la chalors, et si est uns solaz. L'amandre a
trois choses, l'escorce dehors, le test et le noel, et si est
25 une amandre, ausi sont en Deu .iii. persones, et s'est uns Deus.
En la roe del char a trois choses, li moiel et li rai et les
gentes, et s'est une roe. En toi meismes sunt trois choses, li
cors et li menbre et l'ame, et si es uns hom; ausi est en Deu
unitez et trinitez." "Or entent je," dist Fernaguz, "qu'il est
30 uns en trois persones, mes je ne sai coment il fu hom qui Deus
ert." "Cil," dist Rollanz, "qui fist ciel et terre et tot
cria de noient, il pot bien fere nestre son fill sanz humaine
semence." "De ce/ me merveill je molt," dist Fernaguz,   (85
"coment sanz humaine semence, si com tu diz, nasqui de la
35 Virge Marie."

XXXVIII

"Deus," dist Rollanz, "qui Adan sanz semence
d'autrui forma, il fist nestre son saint Fill sanz
semence d'autrui de la Virge Marie, car a Deu covenoit
tel enfantement." "Molt me merveill," dist Fernaguz,
5 "coment la Virge enfanta sanz atochement d'ome." "Cil
Deus," dist Rollanz, "qui fet nestre la mosche de la
feve, et de l'aubre le vermoissel, et poissons et es et
serpenz sanz atochement de masle, il pot bien fere legiere-
ment que la Virge eust a fill Deu et home sanz atoche-
10 ment de nului." "Bien puet estre," dist Fernaguz,
"qu'il nasqui, mes s'il fu Deus, il ne pot en la croiz
morir, car Deus ne morut onques." "Bien as dit," dist
Rollanz, "qu'il nasqui com hom, et puis qu'il nasqui com hom
donc morut il com hom. Car tote chose qui nest muert.
15 Se Deus reçut com hom mort en la croiz. Mort, di je,
que l'umaine char en la croiz dormi, et la deïtez veilloit
qui tot gardoit en soi." "G'entent bien," dist Fernaguz,
"qu'il morut com hom, mes je ne puis veoir coment il
resuscita, / car puis que hom est morz ne voi je qu'il   (v°
20 reviegne en vie."

XXXVII, 21 li Peres et li Filz . . . iii persones (1.25) *lacking*] A1 L2
P8 V; *the text printed is from A* 1 − 30 uns Deus] A1 L2 V
XXXVIII, 7 ramoisel] A1 L2 P8 V − et es *lacking* P8 V] A1 L2 −
10 de masle] A1 L2 V − 17 en soi *lacking*] A1 L2 P8 V

XXXIX

"Fernaguz," dist Rollanz, "saches que tuit cil
qui erent et furent des le comencement del monde desi
a la fin del siegle, resusciteront au jor del juïse et
recevront lor loiers selonc ce que chascun aura fet de
5   bien et de mal. Deus qui le petit arbre fet croistre
en haut et le grain del froment morir et puis revivre
et porter fruit, il nos fera resusciter toz en noz propres
chars au jor del joïse. Esgarde le lion qant nature
velt ovrer en lui; il giete trois pieces de char et
10   par son alener les forme en lionceaus et i fet vie
entrer en trois jorz. Ne te doiz mie merveillier se
li filz Deu resuscita. Helyas et Helyseus resusciterent
plusors morz. Plus legierement pot resusciter Deus qui
devant sa passion resuscita plusors morz. Lui ne puet
15   tenir morz, car ele fuit devant lui, et a sa voiz resusciteront
tuit li mort." "Assez voi ore," dist Fernagus, "ce que tu diz.
Mes coment il monta es ciels ne puis je veoir." /   (86)

XL

"Cil," dist Rollanz, "qui descendi des ciels
legierement i pot bien monter, et qui par lui resuscita
legierement par lui monta es ciels. Par plusors essemples
le *puez v*eoir. Esgarde la roe del molin. Tant tors *con*
5   *ele fait* amont, autretant en fet ele aval. *Tant con*
*li s*oleuz monte, autretant descent *il. Tu meismes* se
tu par aventure eres montez sor *un mont,* la dont tu meus
porroies en *repairier et re*monter a mont. Li soleuz
leva ier *en oriant,* et hersoir se coucha en occident.
10   De la ou *il leva* ier leva il hui." "Or nos
ralons combatre," dist Fernagu, "par tel covent que
se ceste foiz est veraie que tu afermes, que je soie
veincuz, et se ele est fause, que je te veinque, et
au veincu soit reprochié toz jorz et a celui qui
15   veintra soit loange et honors permenablement." "Ensint
l'otroi je," dist Rollanz. D'une part et d'autre fu
acraanté. Il se drecerent adont. Si com Rollanz vint

XL *Part of fol. 86 and part of fol. 87 of P5 have been torn away;*
the readings, printed in italics, are from A1. – 11 alons] A1
L2 P8 V

vers lui, li paiens gita un cop de s'espee, mes Rollanz
sailli a senestre, si reçut le cop sor son baston. Li
20 paiens li trancha par mi le baston. Errament co/rut (v
Rollant sore, si le prist as mains et le gita legierement
a terre soz lui. Rollanz vit qu'en nule maniere ne s'en
povoit estordre. Il garda adonc vers le ciel *et fist
oroison* a Deu et dist:

XLI

"*Deus, ce* voiz tu que por nul oneur terrien ne me
combat se por ta foi non. Sire, es*claire* ton non
por toi non por ton serf." E*rranment après* cele proiere
par la volenté de *Deu torna* le paien desoz lui, si li
5 apoia Du*rendal* sor le nombrill, et enpoint si durement qu'ele
li cola tote el cors. Donc comença li paiens a apeler son
deu: "Mahommet, Mahommet, secor moi, car je muir." Par
tel maniere fu li paiens ocis, et Rollanz s'en vint a nostre
ost tot sains, merci rendant a Deu de si grant victoire.
10 Li Sarrazin acorurent a leur mort et le comencierent a porter
vers lo chastel. Mes nostre Crestien saillirent qui mielz
mielz, si se mistrent avec cels qui portoient le cors et
entrerent mesleement en la vile. Ensi fu prise Nadres et
cil delivré que Fernaguz en avoit porté. / (8

XLII

Aprés pou de tens fu dit a Charle que li rois
Hebraÿm et l'aumaçors de Cordres, qui de bataille
erent eschapé, estoient a Cordres et atendoient iluec
Charle a bataille. Si estoient en lor aÿde venu
5 Sarrazin de .vii. citez qui ci sunt nomees: Sebile,
Granade, Sative, Denive, Abule, Hayces, Hubede. Charles
mut a tant de gent com il avoit et s'en vint a Cordres.
Si com il aprocha de la cité, li paien vindrent contre
lui a trois liues de la vile, et estoient li Sarrazin entor
10 .x. mile et li nostre .vi. mile. Adonc fist Charles trois

XL, 21 si le prist as mains *lacking* A1 L2] P8 V Br 2
XLI, 1 por rien nule ne] L2 P8 V – 2 non essaucier] A1 L2 P8 V –
  10 Li S. ac. de Nadres tantost et l'emporterent vers] *see variants
  and note* – 12 mistrent el chastel avec] A1 L2 P8 V
XLII, 5 Sebile *put last*] A1 L2 P8 V – 6 Charles vint P8] A1 L2 V –
  10 li nostre .viii. mile] A1 L2 P8 V

eschieles. La premiere fu de chevaliers, et la
seconde de gent a pié, et la tierce refist de chevaliers.
Li paien firent autressi trois batailles. La premiere
eschiele fu de gent a pié qui avoient unes barbeoires
15   a merveilles hideuses et cornues, totes semblanz a
deables, et tenoient tuit en lor mains tym*bres.*

XLIII

Si tost com la *premiere* bataille *Charle* qui de chevaliers
iert essembla primes a lour / eschiele qui tele estoit con   (v°)
vos avez oï, il comencerent donc tuit ensemble a ferir
lor tymbres. Si tost com li cheval a la nostre gent oïrent
5   le grant fereïz des tymbres et il virent les barbeoires
si laides et si espoëntables, il comencerent a foïr autressint
come tuit desvé, si que cil qui sus seoient ne les porent
tenir. Qant la seconde bataille de noz Crestiens vit la
premiere fuir, qui ert de si bons chevaliers, il fuirent
10   autressint avec els arrieres. Qant Charles vit ce, il se
merveilla molt desi la qu'il sot porquoi ce fu. Li Sarrazin
les suirent molt joianz le petit pas desi a .i. mont qui
estoit a deus liues de la cité. A cel mont s'aünerent noz
genz et firent chastel d'els meismes. Qant ce virent li
15   Sarrazin, il se trestrent arrieres, et nostre Crestien drecierent
lor tentes et demorerent ilec desi a l'endemain. *Qant ce vint*
au matin, Charles comenda *que tuit li cheval de* l'ost eussent
covers les eulz de dras et les oreilles esto/pees qu'il   (88)
ne poïssent veoir lor ledes feitures ne lor timpanes oïr.

XLIV

Qant il orent coverz les ielz de lor chevaus
et les oreilles estopees, si come li rois l'ot comendé,
il vindrent tuit armé et rengié a la bataille, et assemblerent
a lor genz qui erent issuz hors de la vile. Molt ocistrent
5   li nostre des lor, et furent ensi des la matinee desi a midi.
Adonc s'aünerent li Sarrazin, et ot en mi els un char
que .ix. buef traoient, et une enseigne desore. Lor

XLII, 10 Charles (trois esch. *lacking*) la premiere esch. de ch.] A1
     L2 P8 V – 14 noires barbeoires] A1 L2 P8 V
XLIII, 1 *judging by P6, P5 read here:* com li chevals (cf. 1.4) et la
     premiere b. qui de ch. estoit, assembla primes a lor *see variants*
XLIV, 3 rengié vers les Sarrazins qui] A1 L2 P8 V – 7 .xii. bues]
     A1 L2 P8 V

costume si ert tele que nus ne partoit de bataille
tant com lor enseigne ert droite. Qant Charles vit ce, il se
10 feri en els avironez de la vertu de Deu, et ses genz aprés
lui, et tant ala ferant a destre et a senestre qu'il
vint au char et trancha de Joieuse s'espee la perche qui
sostenoit l'enseigne et abati tot en un mont. Adonc s'en-
foïrent li Sarrazin de totes parz, et li cri et li huz leverent
15 granz sor els. Iluec fu ocis Hebraÿm li rois de Sebile atot
.viii. mile / Sarrazins. Li aumaçors s'en entra en   (v
Cordres atot deu mile. El demain rendi la cité a Charle
par si qu'il recevroit baptesme et que de lui tendroit la
cité d'iluec en avant et seroit a son comendement.

XLV

Qant Charles ot conquise Espaigne, il devisa et
departi totes les terres a cels qui voldrent remenoir,
si con vos orroiz ci selonc l'estoire del latin.
La terre des Navars et des Bascles dona as Bretons, la
5 terre de Castele as François, cele de Nadres et
Sarragoce as Greus et as Lombarz qui erent en son ost, la
terre d'Arragone as Poitevins, la terre de l'Andaluf as
Tiois, la terre de Portigal as Danois et as Flamans.
La terre de Galice ne voudrent François habiter
10 por ce que trop estoit aspre. Nul n'osa puis entrer
en Espaigne contre Charle. Qant Charles ot ensi leissié
ses genz en Espaigne et les terres departies, il s'en /   (8
vint a monseignor Saint Jaque en Galice, et edefia
les Crestiens qu'il trova en la terre et fist riches,
15 et cels qui estoient torné a la loi paienime, les uns
fist ocirre, les autres envoia par France en essill.

XLVI

Par les citez de Galice establi Charles evesques
et prestres et aüna a Compostele un molt grant concile
d'evesques et de princes et d'autres persones hautes.
En cel concile establi il por l'amor de monseignor

XLIV, 14 de totes parz *lacking*] A1 L2 P8 V – 15 li rois H. et li
   rois de S.] A1 L2 P8 V
XLV, 8 et as Flamens la terre de Galice. N'i voudrent] A1 L2 Br 2 –
   14 des Crestiens L2] P8 V; *see note*
XLVI, 3 des e. et des p.] A1 L2 P8 V

5   saint Jaque que tuit li evesque et li prince et li
roi crestien d'Espaigne, et tuit li Galicien, cil qui
erent present et a venir, fussent obeïssant a l'arcevesque
de monseignor Saint Jaque. A Yrie que l'on cuidoit a cité
ne mist mie Charles evesque por ce qu'il ne la tint mie a

10   cité, ainz la comenda estre subjete a Compostele. Et je,
Torpins, arcevesques de Reins, dediai en cel concile atot .ix.
evesques l'eglise de monseignor Saint Jaque et son
autel par le comendement Charle, es kalendes de juig. Tote /   (v°)
la terre enterinement sozmist Charles a Compostele, et

15   comenda que chascune meison d'Espaigne et de Galice donast
par chascun an a l'iglise de monseignor Saint Jaque .iiii.
deniers, et fussent frans de toz autres servises.

XLVII

En icel meismes concile establi Charles et comenda
que cele eglise fust apelee toz jorz mes siege d'apostre,
por ce que li beneoiz apostres messire saint Jaques i
gist, et que li conciles de toz les evesques d'Espaigne

5   fussent iluec tenu, et les croces donees et les corones
des rois par la main l'arcevesque de Compostele. Et se
foiz estoit amenuisiee en autres leus par les pechiez des
pueples ne li comendement Damedeu defailli, ilec fussent
reconcilié par le conseill l'arcevesque. Par droit

10   doit estre foiz iluec reconciliee et establie, car si
con par monseignor saint Jahan l'Evangeliste, frere
monseignor saint Jaque, vint foiz avant en Ephese
et fu iluec establi siege / d'apostre, ausint par
monseignor saint Jaque fu foiz establie et siege

15   d'apostre en Galice.

XLVIII

Cist dui siege, Ephese qui est a la destre partie
d'orient et Compostele qui est a la senestre partie
d'occident, si sient en la devise del monde. Car il
avoient requis a Deu que li uns seïst a destre en son

5   regne et li autres a senestre, et il i sunt en terre

XLVI, 6 roi *lacking* L2] A1 P8 V – 8 A Rite] A1 L2 P8 V – que
    l'on c. a cité *lacking*] A1 L2 P8 V – 11 .ii. evesques] A1 P8 V
XLVII, 4 Espaigne et de Galice] A1 L2 P8 V

et en ciel. Troi principal siege sunt devant toz les
autres del monde, Rome, Compostele, Ephese, si con
Nostre Sires establi devant toz les autres apostres
Perron, Jahan, et Jaque, a cui il revela ses segrez, si
10   come li evangile mostrent. Ausint sunt cist troi siege
par cez trois devant toz les autres en reverence;
Rome, por ce que misires sainz Peres, li princes des
apostres, i preescha et l'arosa de son precieus
sanc; Compostele, por ce que messires saint Jaques,
15   qui fu entre les autres de greignor digneté, la /   (vº‧
saintefia de sa sainte sepulture et encore i fet
aperz miracles et fera des qu'en la fin del siegle;
Ephese, por ce que misires sainz Jahanz l'esclaira primes
et prehecha son evangile: "In principio erat verbum,"
20   et fu iluec sa propre sepolture. S'aucun jugement ne pue[en] t
estre determinez en autres leus par le monde, en cez trois
sieges doivent estre traitié et defeni.

XLIX

Ensint con vos avez oï fu Espaigne et Galice
conquise par la vertu de monseignor saint Jaque et
par l'aïde de Charle. Or fet ci bon oïr queus
Charles estoit, si com la verité del latin de l'estoire
5   le devise. Charles li rois ert noirs de cheveus et
roges de face, et de cors beaus et nobles; cruels
d'esgardeure; por voir avoit .viii. piez de longor a son
pié qui ert granz. Amples ert de reins, gros de braz et
de cuisses, et forz de toz menbres. Sages ert molt
10   en parole, chevaliers tres aigres. Sa / face ert   (9▌
d'espan et demi, sa barbe d'un espan, sis nés de demi
espan; son front si estoit d'un pié. Ielz avoit semblanz
a ielz de lion, estancelanz com escharbocles; si sorcill
si estoient de demi espan. Grant peor avoit cil cui
15   il regardoit par ire. Li ceinz dont il ert ceinz
avoit .viii. espanz de lonc sanz ce qui pendoit de-
hors la bocle. Moins manjoit de pain et plus de char.
S'en li aportoit un mouton, un quartier en manjoit,

XLVIII, 10 trois leus] A1 L2 V − 17 miracles Nostre Sires por
    l'amor de lui] A1 L2 P8 V
XLIX, 7 (por voir *lacking*) .viii. piez avoit] A1 L2 P8 V − 10 tres
    sages] A1 L2 P8 V − 17 Pou manjoit] A1 L2 P8 V

S'en li aportoit char de porc, une espaule en manjoit,
20 ou .ii. gelines, ou une oe, o un poon, o une grue, o
un lievre. Poi bevoit de vin et toz jorz tempré d'eue.
Molt se delitoit en fere lire devant lui les estoires,
et les anciennes gestes, et les livres de saint Augustin,
ne nus ne lisoit devant lui l'espace d'une hore ou demi ore
25 qu'il n'en receust la merite. De si grant / force   (v°)
estoit c'un chevalier tranchoit par mi, et lui et son
cheval, de s'espee Joieuse ..iiii. fers de cheval estendoit
legierement. Un chevalier armé levoit tot droit sor sa
paume de terre desi a son chief isnelement a un sol braz.
30 Molt ert larges de doner et droituriers en jugemenz. A
quatre festes en l'an portoit corone, a Noël et a Pasques
et a Pentecoste et a feste monseignor saint Jaque, devant
lui une espee trete selonc l'emperial costume. Chascune nuit
veilloient entor son lit a lui garder .vi. .xx. homes bien
35 ortodoxe, c'est a dire bien sages et vaillanz, .xl. la
premiere hore de la nuit, .x. a son chief et .x. a ses piez,
.x. a destre et .x. a senestre, et chascuns une espee nue
en sa main destre et en la senestre une chandoile ardant.
La seconde hore de la nuit venoient autre .xl., et cil
40 s'en partoient. La tierce hore de la nuit veilloient li
autre .xl. desi au jor.

L

Puis que Charles li renomez ot conquise tote /   (92)
Espaigne a l'ennor de Deu et de monseignor saint Jaque,
il repaira atotes sez oz a Pampelune. Adonc repairoient
a Sarragoce dui Sarrazin, Marsiles et Baliganz ses
5 freres. Li amirauz de Babiloine les avoit envoiez de
Perse, et erent sozgiet a Charle et partot le servoient,
mes c'estoit faintement. Charles lor manda par Ganelon
qu'il venissent reçoivre baptesme ou il li envoiassent
treü. Guanes s'en torna et erra tant qu'il vint a Sarragoce.
10 Il sembla bien prudome, mes li cuers se despareilla molt
du semblant. Marsiles l'onora molt cele nuit, et qant vint

XLIX, 23 autres gestes] A1 P8 V — 24 hore et demi jor L2] *cf.*
    Br 2: heure ne demye *and see variants* — 25 n'en retenist la
    moitié] A1 L2 P8 V
L, 6 et erent envoié a lui car il erent sozgiet a lui et partot] A1 L2
    P8 V—9 et (et *lacking* L2) errament qu'il L2] A1 P8 V — 10
    cuers ne s'apareille de molt au s.] P8 V Br 2

aprés mangier, Marsiles l'apela a conseill si li dist par
molt atraianz paroles que se il le metoit en eise de
Charle, il li donroit .xx. somiers charchiez d'or et
15   d'argent ne jamés ne li faudroit por rien, ainz seroit
a sa volenté suens a toz jorz mes, et il et sis pooirs.
Iluec fu deceuz Ganes par la covoitise de l'or et de
l'argent, dont maint home / ont esté deceu et sunt   (v
encore et mené de vie a la perpetuel mort d'enfer.
20   Iluec afferma Guanes et devisa qu'il diroit a Charle
que Marsile le sivroit en France por soi baptisier, et
que Marsiles enbuscheroit sa gent es porz d'Aspre si qu'au
passer les desconfiroit.

LI

Ensint fu la nuit afermé et devisé entr'els.
L'endemain dona Marsires a Ganelon .xx. somiers chargiez
d'or et d'argent et d'autres richesces, et .xxx. en envoia
a Charlemaine, et .xl. somiers chargiez del plus dolz
5   vin et del meillor c'onques nus hom beust, et mile
Sarrazines de grant beauté envoia as chevaliers de
l'ost. Molt se porpensa Marsiles de grant boisdie, car
por ce le fist qu'il geussent as Sarrazines par la force
del vin qui teus ert, et que par cel pechié les leissast
10   Deus mort encorre. Guanes se parti de Marsile et s'en
repaira a Pampelune. Il vint devant Charle, si li dist
teles paroles com vos orroiz ci: "Marsires vos salue, si est
toz prez de vos sivre / en France, et recevra baptesme la   (9
ou vos plera et tendra de vos plainement tote la terre.
15   Si sachiez qu'il s'apareille de venir aprés vos com cil
qui velt estre del tot a vostre amor et a vostre volenté.
Aveques ce il vos envoie .xxx. somiers chargiez d'avoir."
Charles ot grant joie des noveles del baptesme. Guanes
envoia par l'ost as hauz homes les .xl. somiers de vin et
20   les mile Sarrazines. Cele nuit furent yvre par l'ost li
plusor et jurent as Sarrazines par ivresce, car tant con
li hom est ivres est il destornez de reison et de tote
mesure.

LI, 1 afermee et devisee entr'els la traïson dont grant dolors avint
    en France] A1 L2 P8 V – 10 mort *lacking*] A1 L2 P8 V – 17
    chargiez d'or et d'argent et d'autres richesces] A1 L2 P8 V

LII

Charles appareilla son erre de venir s'en en
France par le conseill Guenes. Puis comenda Rollant
son neveu et Olivier l'arieregarde fere atot .xx. mile
des plus hauz homes de l'ost endementres qu'il passeroit
5   les porz d'Aspre. Ansint fu atorné. Au quart jor
passa Charles les porz d'Aspre atot .xx. mile Crestiens,
et Guenes avec lui, et Torpins / l'arcevesque,   (v°)
et li autre firent l'arieregarde si com vos avez oï.
Marsires et Baliganz, qui ses freres ert, issirent atot .l.
10   mile Sarrazins des bois et des montaignes ou il s'erent
repost par .ii. jorz et par .ii. nuiz, si com entre
Marsires et Guenes l'avoient devisé. Marsile fist
.ii. eschieles, l'une de .xx. mile, l'autre de .xxx. mile.
La bataille des .xx. mile corut sore a noz .xx. mile
15   Crestiens qui l'arieregarde feisoient. Il guanchirent
sor els et se combatirent des la matinee desi a tierce.
Ausi com li leus qui de fain est enragiez devore les
berbiz la ou il les trueve, tot ausi les ocioit Rollant
de totes parz. La fu esprovee la proesce Olivier, car
20   onques un sol cors d'ome ne reçut tant cous ne tant en un
jor n'en dona, et qui poïst avoir mis en escrit toz cels
qu'il ocist ileques, il n'en fust mie creuz. Ensint les
ocistrent li nostre c'onques n'en eschapa de toz les paiens
un seus.

LIII

Qant Marsires vit ce, il lor corut sore / atote   (94)
s'eschiele qui estoit de .xxx. mile homes. Li nostre,
qui furent las et agrevé de la bataille qu'il
avoient devant sofferte, ne les porent soffrir. Li
5   paien les aloient de totes parz ociant. Li un furent
de lances tuit depecié, li autre d'espees tuit decolé,
li autre detranchié de haches et li autre ocis de dars
et de saietes, li autre de perches et de maces et li
autre furent de couteaus escorchié et li autre ars
10   en feu, li autre pendu a arbres. Iluec fu ocis Oliviers
de totes armes feruz et escorchiez des le col desi

LII, 4 passerent] A1 L2 — 14 noz (.xx. mile *lacking*) C.] A1 L2
    P8 V — 17 enr. d'ocirre] A1 L2 P8
LIII, 7 autre de tranchanz haches] A1 L2 P8 — ocis d'ars] A1 L2 P8

as ongles des piez. Ensint furent iluec ocis de divers
tormenz c'onques n'en eschapa fors Rollanz et Baudoins
et Tierris. Cil dui se tapirent es boschages et Rollant
15   les aloit porsivant de loing, dolent de la mort de tant
prudomes. Adonc se trestrent li paien arrieres une liue
loing molt joiant de la mort des noz.

LIV

Ci fet bon entendre et savoir, si con l'estoire dit
selonc le latin, / por quoi Nostre Sires leissa els ilec   (*
ocirre qui n'avoient mie geu as Sarrasines. Por ce ne vost
Nostre Sires qu'il repairassent en lor païs que par aventure
5   ne pechassent plus griément. Si lor vost rendre por lor
travauz corone es ciels; et cels qui jurent as femes soffri
il mort encorre por esfacier lor pechiez par martire
d'espee. Ci puet en veoir cler que Nostre Sires est
si pius qu'il velt bien guerredoner les travaus de cels
10   qui en la fin reconoissent son non, et regehissent lor pechiez
par confession. Car ja soit ce que cil eussent fet fornicacion,
si furent il ocis por Deu en la fin. Ci esclaire la letre
del latin de l'estoire que molt est despite chose compaignie
de feme a cels qui vont en bataille n'en ost. Car maint
15   prince terrien en ont esté mort et traï. Daires et Antoines,
qui menerent jadis lor femes avec els en bataille, en furent
ambedui mort. Alixandres ocist Daire par fame, et Otoviens
Antoine, / et por ce n'est reisons ne droiture de feme   (S
avoir en ost n'en herberges, la ou luxure doit estre
20   chastiee, car grant enpeeschement est au cors et a l'ame.
Et cil qui fornication firent par ivrece senefient les
prestres et les religieus homes qui ne se doivent en nule
maniere enivrer ne gesir a feme. Car s'il le funt, il sunt
ocis de lor anemis, c'est des deables, et emb[r]acent la
25   perpetuel mort d'enfer.

LV

Si com Rollanz aprés la bataille retornoit sels
vers les paiens et il estoit encores auques loing

LIV, 6 as Sarrazines reçurent mort et Nostre Sires le vost por esf.]
A1 L2 P8; *cf. variants* — 10 lor non] A1 L2 P8 V — 13 molt de
compaignie de feme est petite chose] Br 2; *see above*, p. 57 —
22 qu'il] A1 L2 P8 V

d'els, il trova un paien molt noir el bois repost,
toz las de la bataille. Il le prist et le lia forment
5   a quatre forz arz a un arbre. Puis se parti de lui
et s'en monta sor un mont por lor gent veoir. Il vit
qu'il en i avoit molt. Si retorna arrieres vers la
voie de Roncesvaus ou li fuiant aloient qui covoitoient
a passer les porz por els guarir. Adonc sona Rollanz
10   son cor et rasembla a lui par l'oïe del cor entor .c.   (v°)
Crestiens. / Puis retorna atot cels par le bois desi
au paien qu'il avoit lié a l'arbre. Il le deslia arrament,
puis leva s'espee tote nue sor son chief, si li dist: "Se tu
viens avec moi et tu me mostres Marsile, je te lairai
15   aler vif, et se tu ne le me fes conoistre, je t'ocirrai
orendroit." Li paiens le li craanta, puis ala avec lui, si
li mostra entre les Sarrazins de loing Marsile. "Voiz le la,"
dist li paiens, "sor cel cheval rous, a cel escu reont."
Donc le leissa Rollanz aler et se feri atot les .c.
20   Crestiens entre les Sarrazins. Il en choisi un entre
les autres greignor de toz, si li dona tel cop par
l'aïde de Deu qu'il le trancha par mi a s'espee, et
lui et son cheval. Qant Sarrazin virent ce, erranment
leisserent Marsile el champ a petit de gent et comencerent
25   ça et la a foïr. Rollanz sui Marsile a destre et a
senestre ferant, tant que par la puissance de Deu l'ocist
a un sol cop. Entre les autres furent ocis en cele
bataille li .c. Crestien qui estoient de la compaignie
Rollant, et il meis/mes fu navrez de .iiii. lances, et de   (96)
30   maces et de pierres feruz et defroissiez si qu'il s'en ala
a poine. Qant Baliganz vit que Marsires ses freres fu
morz, il s'en ala d'iluec vers Sarragoce.

LVI

Baudoins et Tierris, si com il vos fu dit devant,
se tapissoient par le boschage, et li autre passerent
les porz. Charles, qui ja les avoit passez, ne savoit
encor ce qui ert avenu detriés lui. Rollanz s'en vint
5   toz seus desi au pié del mont, dolant de la mort de
tant prudomes, et agrevez desi au morir des plaies
et des cous qu'il avoit receuz. Il descendi desoz un
arbre a grant poine de son cheval joste une grant

LV, 8 de R., si oï qu'il s'en aloient fuiant qu'il cov.] A1 L3 P8 Br 2

pierre de marbre qui estoit ilec dreciee en un pré au
10   chief de Roncesvaus. Il avoit encor s'espee qui si
ert bele et bone, qu'en ap[e]loit Durendart. Durendart
dit autretant come "dur cop done," car ançois defausist
braz que l'espee. Il la trest et tint en sa main. Il
l'esgarda molt / piteusement et dist tot em plorant   (v
15   si con vos orroiz ja: "Ha! bele espee luisant, de
longuor covenable, de laor planteive, de force tres
ferme, de heut d'ivoire blanche, de croiz doree
resplandissant, aornee de cez granz nons Nostre
Seignor, "Alpha" et "O," garnie de la devine poissance,
20   qui te gardera desormés? Qui te tendra desormés? Qui
t'avra mes? Qui ert saisiz de toi il n'iert ja veincuz,
ne esbahis, ne espoantez por peor d'anemi ne de fantome,
mes toz jorz de la vertu Deu et de s'aÿde avironez.
Par toi est ocise et destruite la gent paiene, et la
25   loi crestiene essauciee et la loenge de Deu et la
gloire de lui aquise, et par tantes foiz ai venchié par
toi le saint sanc Nostre Seignor Jhesu Crist, et tantes
foiz en ai ocis les anemis Deu, et tant Sarrazin et tant
mescreant detranchié et destruit. Par toi est la jostise
30   Deu aemplie, et li piez et la mains costumiere de larrecin
detranchié.

LVII

Ha! espee bonaüree, desor totes tranchanz,
desor totes agüe, a cui n'en fu onques nule re-   (9
semblable ne ja n'iert. Nus qui de toi fust navrez
ne pooit en avant vivre. Si mauvés hom t'a, ne
5   cremeteus, ne paiens, n'aucuns mescreanz, molt en
sera m'ame dolente." A cez paroles feri Rollanz de
l'espee sor la pierre de marbre trois cous com cil
qui la voloit depecier por ce qu'il cremoit que ele
ne tornast en mains de Sarrazins. En deus parties
10   fendi la pierre, n'onques l'espee ne fu fraite ne
maumise. Adonc comença a soner son cor, se par
aventure aucun des Crestiens qui por la peor des
paiens fust tapiz es bois venist a lui, ou cil qui
avoient les porz passez, par aventure retornassent, et
15   fussent a sa mort, et prissent s'espee et son cheval,

LVI, 30 et li piez ... detranchié *lacking*] A1 L2 P8 V

et ensuïssent les paiens. Adont sona son cor par tel
esforz qu'il le fendi par la force de s'aloine, et
les voines del col et li nerf li rompirent. Icele
voiz del cor porta li angles es oreilles Charle qui
20   avoit fichiees ses tentes el val qu'en apele le Val
Charle vers Gascoigne, ou il avoit .viii. / liues de   (v°)
la ou Rollanz ert. Si tost com li rois oï la voiz del cor,
il s'en merveilla molt et vost donc retorner, qant Guanes,
qui estoit consachanz de l'uevre, li dist: "Sire, ne
25   retornez pas arriere, car Rollanz seut chascun jor boisiner
por noient. Sachiez qu'il n'a mestier d'aïde, ainz cort
aprés aucune beste par cez bois."

LVIII

Ha! si dolereuse traïson qui deust estre comparee
a la traïson Judas. Rollanz se coucha a la terre aprochanz
a la mort, et jut sor l'erbe desirranz d'eue dont il
poïst apaier sa soif qu'il avoit molt grant. Este vos
5   ilec Baudoin son frere. Si tost com Rollanz le vit, il li
proia qu'il li alast querre de l'eue. Il i ala et la quist
ça et la, mes il n'en pot point trover, et qant il vit qu'il
n'en troveroit point, il en vint devant Rollant et vit qu'il
ert pres de mort. Adonc le benesqui, et por la doute des
10   paiens monta sor le cheval Rollant, et prist son cor et
s'espee, si se mist / a la voie vers l'ost. Si tost com   (98)
il s'en parti, este vos Tierri iluec et comença sor lui a
plorer et dist a Rollant qu'il garnesist s'ame de foi et de
confession. Rollanz avoit le jor receu corpus domini et s'ert
15   confessez devant ce qu'il alast a la bataille as prestres
dont assez avoit en l'ost, car tel estoit la coustume ainz
qu'il alassent a la bataille.

LIX

Rollant li verais martirs leva les ielz vers
le ciel et dist: "Sire Jhesu Criz, por cui foi je lessai

LVII, 22 com li rois *lacking*] A1 L2 P8 V – 25 arriere por chose
    nule que vos aiez oïe, car sachiez qu'il n'ont mestier d'aïde. Vos
    savez bien que R. seut chascun jor boisiner por noient. Sire,
    sachiez qu'il cort] A1 L2 P8 V
LVIII, 6 Il i ala . . . ça et la *lacking* A1 L2] *see note* – 13 plorer et
    molt grant duel a fere] A1 L2 P8 V – 15 as prestres . . . a la
    bataille *lacking* A1 L2 P8 V] Br 2; *see note*
LIX, 1 qant r. de pasmoisons leva] A1 L2 P8 V

mon païs et ving en estranges terres et en estranges païs
essaucier crestienté, par l'aïde de toi ai je veincu maintes
5   batailles de mescreanz et soffert por toi maint cop et mainte
trabucheure, et maintes poines et maint reproches, et eschar-
nissemenz, et travalz, et chauz et froiz, et soif et fain, et
moltes angoisses, Sire, a toi coment je m'ame. Sire, com tu
deignas nestre de la Virge Marie por moi, et soffrir mort en
10   la croiz, et el sepulcre estre enseveliz, et au tierz jor
resusciter et monter es sainz ciels qu'en la presence de ta
deïté / ne deguerpis onques, Sire, si deignes tu m'ame deli-   (v°)
vrer de la perpetuel mort d'enfer. A toi me regehis corpaple
et pecheor qui pius pardonerres es de toz les pechiez de
15   cels qui en penitence et en foi te reclaiment. Sire, qui
totes felonies de pecheor en quelconques hore il se convertist
a toi pardones, et a cels de Ninive pardonas lor mesfez
qant il se convertirent, et a la feme reprise en avoutere
delessas ses pechiez, et a Marie Magdeloine les suens, et a
20   monseignor saint Pierre qant tu le regardas, et au larron
merci reclamant aovris paradis, tu me faces pardon! Tot ce
que je ai mesfet me pardone et m'ame met en perdurable
repos! Sire, a cui li cors ne perissent mie por la mort,
ainz sunt mué en mielz; Sire, qui l'ame dessoivree del
25   cors fes vivre en meillor vie et qui deis "Je voil mielz la
vie del pecheor que la mort," je croi de cuer et regehis de
boche que por ce vels tu m'ame mener de ceste vie qu'aprés
la mort la faces vivre en meillor vie, / et l'entendement   (99)
qu'ele a ore avra ele meillor de tant com il a entre
30   l'ombre et le cors."

LX

Rollant prist donc sa pel entre le cuer et les
memeles et dist gemissenment, plains de lermes, si
com Tierris en fu tesmoing qui puis le reconta tot ensi
com il le vit et oï: "Deus, voirs peres, filz de la
5   boneuree Virge Marie, de tot mon cuer regehis et croi
que tu es mis racheterres, et qu'au jor del juïse
resusciterai de terre et en ceste char meismes verrai
Deu mon Sauveor." Ceste parole dist par trois foiz
si qu'il tenoit sa pel et sa char forment. Aprés mist

LIX, 11 resuscitez et montez] A1 L2 P8 V — qui la presence de ta
    deïté ne deguerpis (gurpis A1) o. A1 L2] *see note* — 14 pius es
    et p. P8 V] A1 L2 — 17 pardones *lacking* L2 V] A1 P8

10   sa main sor ses ielz et dist par trois foiz: "Et
cist oeill meismes te verront ensement." Adonc comença
ielz overz a esgarder vers le ciel et a fere croiz
sor son piz et sor toz ses membres. Adonc dist:
"Totes choses terrienes me sunt vius, car or esgart
15   je par la volenté de Deu ce qu'ielz ne vit, n'oreille
n'oï, n'en cuer d'ome n'entra, que Nostre Sires
appareille a cels qui l'aiment." Aprés tendi ses mains
a Deu et fist proiere por toz / cels qui en cele   (v°)
bataille erent mort: "Sire," dist il, "la douçors de
20   ta misericorde soit esmeue sor tes feels qui en ceste
bataille sunt ui mort, qui de lointiens païs en estranges
contrees vindrent combatre a la gent mescreant, et
essaucier ton saint non, et venchier ton precieus
sanc, et esclairier ta foi. Il gisent ore mort por toi
25   par les mains des Sarrazins, mes tu, beau Sire, esleve
par ta pitié lor pechiez et oste des tormenz d'enfer
lor ames! Envoie tes sainz archanges sor els qu'il
ostent lor ames de la region des teniebres d'enfer et
les conduisent el regne celestiel qu'il puissent regnier
30   o tes seinz martirs sanz fin o toi, qui vis et regnes o
Deu le Pere et le Saint Esperit perdurablement in secula
seculorum! Amen."

LXI

En ceste confession et en ceste proiere issi la
boneuree ame del cors Rollant le beneoit martir et fu
portee des angles el perdurable repos, ou ele regne et
est en joie sanz fin, conjointe as compaignies des
5   sainz martirs / par la digneté de sa deserte. Aprés   (100)
ce que Rollanz fu trespassez, se parti Tierris d'iluec
qui tot vit et oï et verais tesmoing en fu.

LXII

Dementres que l'ame de Rollant le beneoit martir
issoit de son cors, je, Torpins, arcevesques, chantoie le
roi le jor messe des feels Deu el Val Charle. Cel jor ert

LX, 17 qu'il aime] A1 L2 P8 V – 20 sor toz cels qui A1 L2] *see
above* p.   – 21 ui *lacking*] A1 L2 P8 V – 29 regnier et
vivre] A1 L2 P8 V
LXI, 6 de lui] L2 P8 V
LXII, 3 le roi *lacking* A1 L2] *see note*

la sezieme kalende de jung. En cele hore, ausi come
5 raviz en l'autre siegle, oï une compaignie chantant
lassus en haut. Si com cil trespassoient, este vos
aprés une torbe de malignes esperiz qui passa par devant
moi ausi com s'il repeirassent de proie toz charchiez.
Je lor dis erramment: "Qu'est ce que vos portez?" "Nos
10 portons," distrent il, "Marsire en enfer, et vostre boi-
sineor enporte Michiels li archanges es ciels et molt
d'autres avec lui." Qant je Torpins oi chanté la messe,
je ving au roi isnelement et si li dis: "Sire, sachiez
certainement que li beneoiz archanges misires saint
15 Michieus enporte l'ame de Rollant et de molt autres
es ciels, mes je ne sai de quel mort il est / morz,   (v
et li deables enportent l'ame de Marsile et de molt
autres en enfer." Si come je Torpins parloie ensint
au roi, ez vos Baudoin sor le cheval Rollant atot
20 le cor et atote l'espee, qui tot aconta si com il
ert avenu et coment il avoit Rollant leissié joste
la pierre. Adonc leva par tote l'ost li criz et li
plors si granz c'onques teus ne fu oïz. Ensint
repairerent arrieres criant et plorant.

LXIII

Premierement trova Charles Rollant, ses braz mis
en croiz sor son piz. Charles chaï errament sor lui
plains de sangloz et de sospirs, et comença molt fort
a plorer et a detuerdre ses mains et sa face a de-
5 pecier et sa barbe a arrachier et ses chevous. A
hauz criz tot em plorant demesureement comença a dire:
"Ha! beaus niés, braz destre de mon cors, honors de
France, espee de jostice, hante noient flechissable,
heaume de salu, semblanz de proesce a Judas Maqabeu
10 et de force a Sanson, chevaliers tres aigres, sages de
bataille, forz desor toz les forz, reaus ligniee,
destruierres de Sarrazins, deffenderres / de Crestiens,   (1
murs de clers, bastons d'orfenins, viande et refeccions
de veves et de povres, releverres de sainte eglise, langue

LXII, 10 et vostre boisineor Michiel li archanges emporte l'ame de
  Rollant es ciels] *see note* – 15 (de *lacking*) molt P8 V] A1
  L2 Br 2
LXIII, 5 chevous a hauz cris tot em plorant. Puis com. son neveu a
  regreter en tel maniere: "Ha!] A1 L2 P8 V

15 mesco[i]nte de mençonges, droituriers en jugemenz, cuens
nobles sor toz François, sires des oz, porquoi t'amenai je
en cez contrees? Porquoi te voi je mort? Porquoi ne
muir je avec toi? Porquoi me lesses tu triste et vain?
Ha! las! chaitis, que ferai je ore de toi? Tu vives
20 avec les angles! Tu aies joie avec les martirs! Tu
t'esjoïsses entre les sainz! Sanz fin plorerai sor
toi ausi com David fist sor Saül et sor Jonathan et
sor Absalon. Tu qui es en joie es cieus nos lesses
tristes el siegle. La sale resplandissanz de joie
25 te tient, et nos li jorz plains de plors. Tu, qui
.xxxviii. anz avoies, ies ore de la terre levez es cieus.
De ce dont li mondes plore s'esjoïst ore la celestial
sale." Par iteus paroles et par autreteus plora
Charles Rollant tant com il vesqui. En cel leu ou
30 Rollanz gisoit mort, fichierent la nuit lor tentes.
Charles fist le cors appareillier et enoindre de basme
et de mirre et d'aloën./   (v°)

LXIV

Tote la nuit veilla l'ost en plors et en proieres,
espris environ lo cors granz luminaires honoreement et
granz feus par les boschages. L'endemain en alerent tuit
armé en Roncesvaus ou la bataille avoit esté, ou li cors
5 de tant prudomes gisoient mort. Il troverent les uns morz
et les autres demi vis. Olivier troverent mort gisant tot
estendu en croiz, lié de .iiii. harz a .iiii. peus fichiez
en terre, escorchié des le col desi as ongles des piez
et des mains de couteaus aguz, et tot deperciez de
10 darz et de saietes et de hanstes et d'espees, et de
cous de bastons tot defroissiez. Adonc leva li criz
granz et li plors, et la voiz des plaignanz et des crianz
iert si tres granz si com chascun ploroit por son ami
que li bois et les valees erent totes ploines de plors
15 et de criz qu'il feisoient.

LXIII, 26 de la terre *lacking*] A1 L2 P8 V
LXIV, 9 et des mains *lacking* A1 L2] P8 V Br 2 − 10 saietes et de
    lances et de cous] L2 P8

LXV

   Charles li rois jura adonc par lo roi poissant
desor toz qu'il ne cesseroit d'aler aprés les
Sarrazins desi la qu'il les troveroit. Il s'esmut
atotes ses genz. Adonc ce tesmoigne / l'estoire   (1
5 que li soleuz s'estut et esloigna li jorz l'espace
de trois jorz. Il errerent tant qu'il vindrent a une
eue qui avoit non Hebir joste Sarragoce. Ilec les tro-
verent, les uns dormanz, les autres manjanz. Adonc lor
corut Charles sore ausi come li leus fameilleus cort a
10 la proie. Ilec ot Torpins tant cous et tantes bleceures
qu'il en fu aprés pires del cors et moins en vesqui.
Ensint le fist la Charles et ses genz c'onques de .iiii.
mile qu'il erent n'en eschapa uns. Adonc s'en repeirerent
et vindrent arrieres en Roncevaus. Les morz et les
15 navrez fist Charles prendre et porter desi au cors
Rollant. Iluec fu donc dit et affermé que tot cest
afferes ert avenu par Ganelon et que ce avoit il fet.
Charles le fist amener devant lui, et Tierris l'en apela
tantost de traïson, et il s'en deffendi par Pinabel qu'il
20 mist por lui. Il s'armerent, et qant il furent armé il
vindrent ensemble, et ne demora gueres que Tierris
l'ocist, si com l'estoire dit qui veritable est.
Qant Charles vit que la verité fu ensi esclairiee, il
fist lier Ganelon par les .iiii. / menbres as .iiii.   (v°
25 plus forz chevaus de tote l'ost et quatre forz homes
seoir desore, si le fist detrere as .iiii. parties del
monde. Sifetement morut de laide mort et de despite.
Aprés ce appareillierent les cors de lor amis, les
uns de basme, les autres de mirre; li un les
30 ovroient et gitoient fors les entrailles, et cil
qui n'avoient les chiers oignemenz les appareilloient
de sel. Selonc ce que chascuns ert, atornoit son ami
por porter l'en plus aeisiement qu'il pooit. Li un
les emportoient sor bieres de fust, li autre sor
35 chevaus, et li autre sor espaules, et li autre entre
lor mains, et li autre en eschieles sor lor cous, et

LXV, 3 les *lacking*] A1 L2 P8 V — 6 trois heures] A1 L2 P8 V; *see
note* — 7 les *lacking*] A1 L2 P8 V — 16 Donc dist et afferma
que] P8 V — 22 qui v. est *lacking*] A1 L2 P8 (est v.) V — 25 et
quatre homes desore] L2; *see variants* — 29 les autres les ov.]
A1 L2 P8 V — 36 cous, et li autre les enf. iluec] A1 L2 V

li un enfooient les autres iluec. Ensint se partirent
de Roncevaus atot lor amis, a granz criz et a granz
dolors.

LXVI

Adonc avoit .ii. cimetires de haute dignité,
l'un a Arle en Aleschans et autre a Bordaus, que
Nostre Sires benesqui par les mains de .vii. evesques.
Li uns ot non saint Maximiens d'Aquitaine, li autres
5   saint Throphins d'Arles, li tierz saint Pols de Nerbone,
li quarz saint Sa/turnins de Tholose, li quinz saint   (103)
Frontins de Pierregort, li sistes saint Martiaus de
Limoges, li septimes saint Antropes de Saintes.
Voirs est que de cez .vii. sainz homes gist grant partie
10   en cez .ii. cimetires, et cil meismes i gisent que
Charles trova morz en sa chapele si com devant fu
dit qant il fu repairiez de la bataille des Navars.
Le cors Rollant le beneoit martir fist Charles porter
a Blaives sor .ii. mules en un lit aorné d'or et covert
15   de pailes, s'espee et son cor avec lui. Ilec le fist li
rois ensevelir molt honoreement el mostier Saint Romain
qu'il avoit fondé et mis chanoines regulers. En la sepolture
fist li rois metre s'espee a son chief et son cor a
ses piez, en l'ennor de Deu et de sa proësce. Puis
20   en porta l'en le cor a monseignor Saint Seurin a Bordeaus.
Mes ne dit mie l'estoire qui cil fu par qui il fu portez.

LXVII

Vos qui l'estoire oez, n'enquerez mie que l'espee
devint, car Deus ne vost soffrir qu'ele fust puis veue
por ce qu'ele ert aornee des sainz nons Nostre Seignor.
Si ne vost Deus qu'ele fust puis trovee que desloiautez
5   n'en fust fete / por lui avoir, et qui vos en dira   (v°)
el, ne l'en creez vos mie. Boneuree est la vile de
Blaives qui de si haut oste est honoree com de Rollant.
Bien se doit eslecier del solaz de son cors. A Belin
le chastel fu portez et enséveliz Oliviers, et Gondel-
10   buef li rois de Frise, et Ogiers li rois de Denemarche,

LXVI, 14 .ii. mules en *lacking* A1 L2] P8 Br 2 Br 3 *(so too most*
   of the III M mss.)

et Arastans li rois de Bretaigne, et Garins li dus de
Loherroine et molt autres. Bieneuree est la vile
de Belin qui de tanz barons est aornee. Ensint furent la
enterré. Et a Bordeaus el cimetire Saint Seurin fu
15   enterrez Gaifiers li rois, et Angeliers, dus d'Aquitaine,
et Lambert li princes de Boorges, et Gerriers, et Guerins,
et Renaut d'Aubespine, et Gautiers de Termes, et Guielin,
et Begues, et bien entor .xv. mile des autres. Hoël li
cuens en fu portez a Nantes sa cité et fu enterrez iluec,
20   et molt autres Bretons. Qant en cez cimetires furent
enterrez, Charles dona por le salu de lor ames en la
remenbrance de Judas Machabeu .xii. mile onces d'or et
autretant d'argent, et vestemenz et poture, et tote la
terre / qui est environ de Blaives .vi. liues, et tot   (1
25   le chastel et tot ce qui i apent neis la mer qui soz
lui est, dona Charles a l'iglise de monseignor Saint
Romain a Blaives en alues por l'amor de Rollant.
Et si comenda as chanoines de l'iglise qu'il ne
feissent nul servise a nule persone laie, mes tant
30   solement que li chanoine, cil qui erent present et a
venir, vestissent chascun an .xxx. povres, et donassent
a mangier, et deissent .xxx. sautiers et trente messes
atotes vegiles et atot le servise des morz plaine-
ment en la memoration de l'ame de Rollant el jor de
35   son trespassement, et por totes les ames de cels qui
en Roncesvaus et en Espaigne erent mort el servise Dame-
dieu et avoient a morir, qu'il fussent parçoniers des
celestieus biens. Ice li promistrent et covenancerent a
tenir et a fere par sairement.

LXVIII

Aprés ce, je, Torpins, l'arcevesques, et Charles,
nos partimes adonc de Blaives atote nostre ost et
venimes a Arles par Gascoigne et par Tholose. Ilec
trovames les Bor/goignons qui de nos estoient departu   (v
5   en Oistrevaus. S'estoient venu ou lor morz qu'ils

LXVII, 12 Renomee est] A1 L2 — 14 Saint Seurin *lacking* A1 L2]
P8 V Br 2 — 18 Bueves] A1 L2 V — 19 cuens de Nantes] A1
L2 P8 V] A1 L2 P8 V — 27 en aumone por A1] P8 V Br 2 — 29 *nule lacking*
A1 L2] P8 V Br 2 — 33 atoz le s.] A1 L2 — 37 et de toz cels
qui crestiens erent a m.] A1 L2 V
LXVIII, 1 Aprés cel jor] A1 L2 P8 V — 5 s'avoient aporté lor morz
en liz et en ch. qu'il voloient enterrer] *see note*

aportoient en liz et en charetes pour eus enterrer en
Aleschans dont Arle est pres. En cel cimetire fu enterrez
par nos mains Estouz li cuens de Lengres, et Salemons, et
Sanses li dus de Borgoigne, et Hernauz de Beaulande, et
10   Auberis li Borgoignon, Guienarz, Estormiz, Hates,
Yvoires, et Berarz de Nubles, et Berengiers, et Naimes
li dus de Baivieres, et bien entor .x. mil des autres, et
Costantins en fu portez a Rome enterrer et maint
autre de Puille. Aprés ce venimes ensemble a Viane,
15   et je, Torpins, remés ilec molt agrevez de plaies et
de cous que je avoie sofferz en Espaigne. Adonc priai
je Charle et requis sor l'amor qu'il avoit a moi,
qu'il me feist savoir le jor de son trespassement s'il
trespassoit ainçois de moi, et je li creantai que je
20   li feroie le mien savoir se je trespassoie ançois de
lui. Je, Torpins, l'arcevesque, remés ensint a Viane,
et li rois qui ert auques affebloiez s'en parti atot sa
gent et vint a Paris. /   (105)

LXIX

    Adonc assembla un concile d'evesques et de hauz
homes a monseignor Saint Denis. Il rendi graces a
Deu de ce qu'il avoit Espaigne conquise a l'ennor de
son non. Li rois dona tote France a monseignor Saint
5   Denise si com saint Pols li apostres et saint Climenz
li apostres l'avoient devant donee a monseignor Saint
Denise. Charles manda et comenda que tuit li roi de
France et li evesque qui estoient present et a venir
fussent obeïssant en Deu au pastor de monseignor Saint
10   Denise, ne rois ne fust coronez en France se par son
conseill non, ne nus evesques dampnez a Rome ne receuz.
Aprés comenda que chascune meison donast .iiii. deniers
par an a edefier l'eglise. Ensint le fist et establi de
tote France; et toz cels qui estoient serf qui volentiers
15   donroient cez deniers relascha. Donc s'estut Charles devant
le cors monseignor saint Denise, si li proia qu'il feist
proiere a Deu por toz cels qui cez deniers ren-
droient volentiers et por cels qui en Espaigne avoient
receu martire.

LXVIII, 21 lui. Ensint le creantames li uns a l'autre] A1 L2 P8 V
LXIX, 17 tot

LXX

Cele nuit aprés s'aparut messires saint Denise
au roi en son dormant, si l'esveilla et li dist: /   (v
"Rois, saches que tuit cil qui par ton amonestement
et par ta proiere sunt mort en Espaigne sunt sauvé,
5   et tuit cil qui les deniers donent et donront a
edefier m'iglise si com tu l'as atirié, de lor greignor
pechiez sunt ja quites par ma proiere." Qant cist
miracles fu revelez par France de par lo roi, de totes
parz aportoient et rendoient les deniers devotement,
10   et cil qui les rendoient volentiers partot estoient
apelé "Franc Saint Denise" por ce qu'il erent delivre
de toz autres servises. De ce mut costume que cele
terre qui devant estoit apelee Galle fu puis apelee
France. Cist moz de "Frans" si dit autretant come
15   "delivres," car desor totes genz doivent estre seignor.
Qant Charle ot ensi esploitié, il s'en ala vers Le
Liege droit a Es la Chapele et fist fere en la vile
bainz d'eue chaude atrempe[e] de froide, et l'eglise
Nostre Dame Sainte Marie qu'il avoit ilec comenciee
20   aorna honorablement d'or et d'argent et de toz autres
aornemenz qu'il covenoit a sainte eglise. Des estoires
de la viez loi et de la novele la fist molt riche/ment   (1
depeindre et son palés autressi qui dejoste l'eglise
estoit. Totes les batailles d'Espaigne fist peindre
25   el palés et les .vii. arz de merveilleuse oevre.

LXXI

Premierement fist Charles peindre gramaire, qui
est mere de totes les arz, et qui enseigne quantes
letres sunt et queles, et coment eles doivent estre
escrites, et par queles letres les parz et les sillabes
5   se devisent, et en quel leu li diptongue doivent estre,
si come dui livre d'ortografie demostrent qui premierement
furent entre les autres. 'Orto' en greu si est 'droit'

LXX, 5 et ont doné] A1 L2 P8 V – 12 vint (*the scribe hesitated*
over the word and wrote vī *followed by a minim and a* t *so*
barred that minim and t *look like* tt; *the scribe of* P6 *copied*
this as vint) P8] A1 L2 – 20 honorablement *lacking*] A1 L2
LXXI, *I recall that the chapters on the seven arts are lacking in*
Br 2.

en latin. 'Grafie,' c'est 'escriture.' 'Ortografie'
si dit autretant come 'droite escriture.' Par ceste
10 art entendent li liseor en sainte eglise ce qu'il
lisent, et cil qui list et ne l'entent si est ausi
come cil qui n'a mie le clef del tresor et ne set
qu'il a dedenz.

LXXII

Aprés fu peinte musique qui enseigne a chanter,
par qui li servise de sainte eglise sunt plus bel, car
par cest art chantent et orguanent./ Qui ceste art   (v°)
ne set, si moine sa voiz ausi come cil qui fet en
5   parchemin torte ligne. N'est mie chanz qui n'est selonc
musique et qui n'est escriz par quatre lignes. Par
ceste art chanta David les saumes el sautier et en la
harpe et en la gigue et el timpanon et es autres estrumenz.
Par cest art furent fet li estrument de musique. Ceste
10 art fu primes trovee par la voiz des angles. Si ne
doivent mie anuier li chant de sainte eglise puis qu'il
vindrent primes des voiz des anges. En ceste art si a
grant sacrement et grant profit, car les .iiii. lignes par
quoi ele est escrite senefient .iiii. vertuz: Prudence,
15 Force, Atrempence, Jostise, et li .viii. ton senefient .viii.
beneurtez qui sunt en l'ame.

LXXIII

Aprés fu peinte dialetique qui aprent a deviser
le faus del voir et a desputer de sens et de parole.
Aprés fu retorique qui enseigne a parler plaine-
ment et droit. Rectorique dit autretant come 'planteif
5   en parole.'
Aprés fu peinte giometrie. Giometrie dit autre-
tant come 'mesure de terre.' Ceste art enseigne a
mesurer / l'espace des monz et des vals et des mers.   (107)
Qui bien set ceste art, il conoist bien quant piez
10 il a ou quantes liues en un champ de terre ou en une
contree. Par ceste art firent li senator de Rome, Rome
et les enciennes citez, et les voies et les liues d'une

LXXII, 2 bel et plus delitable a servir Deu] A1 L2 P8 V — 3 org. li
clerc en sainte eglise] L2 P8 V
LXXIII, 11 Rome et *lacking* A1] *see note*

cité a autre, et li fill Israël en mesurerent la terre
de promission et de lonc et de lé.

LXXIV

Aprés fu peinte artimetique qui parole del
nombre de totes choses. Qui bien set ceste art, il
voit bien quantes pierres il a en un mur ou en une tor,
ou qantes gotes d'eue il a en un henap ou quanz homes il
5   a en un ost.

LXXV

Astrologie fu aprés par quoi l'en set ce qu'en
fet en autres leus, et les biens et les maus qui sunt
present et a venir. Qui bien set ceste art, il conoist
bien s'il a une grant chose a fere qu'il en est a
5   avenir, ou s'il voit .ii. champions en un champ il
saura bien liqueus veintra ou liqueus ert veincuz.
Li senator de Rome conoissoient par ceste art l'occision
des genz et les batailles qui erent avenues es estranges /
païs. Li Troi Roi, et Herodes meismes, conurent en ceste
10   art qant Nostre Sires nasqui par l'estoille qui apparut.
Chascune de cez .vii. arz a un livre estret de soi
dont nigromance est uns. On le puet savoir, mes l'en
n'en puet ovrer se par deable non, et por c'est apelee
arz de voltre; et ses nons le prueve bien, car nigromance
15   dit autretant come noire devinoison, et li titres en est
teus: "Ci comence la mort de l'ame." Ensint furent pointes
ces set arz el palés lo roi en ordre.

(v°

LXXVI

De signis quae
aparuerunt
ante mortem
Karoli Magni

Ne demora gueres aprés que Nostre Sires mostra
signes de sa mort trois anz devant ce qu'il morust,
teus com vos orroiz ci. .vii. jorz se tint li soleuz
et la lune en nerté, et ses nons qui estoit escriz en
5   l'iglise a Ais en pierre a cisel esfaça tot par lui meismes,
et li porches qui estoit entre l'eglise et le palés
chaï par lui meismes un jor de l'Acension, et li

LXXIV, 1 des nombre] A1 L2 P8 − 4 en un pot ou de vin ou en .i.
    henap] A1 L2 P8 V
LXXV, 7 connoissent L2 P8] A1 V − 10 estoire] A1 L2 P8 V −
    12 uns ou l'en puet savoir totes les merveilles] A1 L2 P8 V

p   ponz qu'il avoit fet a Maiance, ou il avoit mis .vii.
      anz au fere par grant estuide sor l'eue, / arst tot   (108)
10   par lui meismes et chaï. Et si com il aloit un jor
      d'un leu a autre li jorz s'en oscurci et une flamme
      de feu trespassa par devant lui si qu'il chaï de son
      cheval d'une part, et la resne qu'il tenoit en sa
      main d'autre. Donc corurent si conpaignon si l'en
15   redrecierent, mes n'ot adonc mie de mal. Aprés ce
      affebloia molt li rois et amaladi tant q'au chief de
      .iii. anz aprocha au lit de la mort. Et qant il se
      santi de la mort aprochier, si li menbra de la proiere
      que Torpins l'arcevesque li ot fete qant il se parti de lui
20   a Viane. Adonc comenda a un suen norri ançois qu'il
      moreust qu'il retenist sor s'amor l'ore et le jor
      de sa mort et qu'il le nonçast Torpin, et cil bonement
      le li craanta. Ne demora mie granment que li rois
      par la volenté de Deu morut.

LXXVII

      En cele hore qu'il trespassa, je, Torpins, estoie
      a Vianne devant un autel ou je chantoie un saume del
      sautier qui si se comence: "Deus in adiutorium meum
      intende." Dementres que je chantoie cest seaume, ez/   (v°)
5   vos par devant moi trespassant une compaignie de
      malignes esperiz qui aloient vers Loherroine. Si
      com il trespassoient, g'en regardai un qui sembloit
      Ethiopien de noireté et ensivoit les autres lentement.
      Je dis a celui: "Ou alez vos?" "Nos alons," dist il,
10   "a Ais por Charle, et si l'enporterons en enfer." Je,
      Torpins, li dis adonc: "Je te conjur de par Deu Nostre
      Seignor Jhesu Crist que tu reviengnes par moi et que
      tu me dies que tu auras fet." Il s'esvanoï de moi et je,
      Torpins, remés ilec mon saume disant. Ne l'oi mie bien
15   finé qant il repairerent a moi. Je demandai a celui a
      cui j'avoie primes parlé: "Qu'avez vos fet?" "Uns
      Galiciens," dist il, "sanz teste vint la et mist es peises

LXXVI, 11 et come flamme] A1 L2 V – 17 .iiii. anz A1 L2] P8
    Br 2 ; *see note*
LXXVII, 5 trois compaignies] A1 L2 P8 V – 8 noireté; *the word is
    not clear in P5; the scribe seems first to have written* norece *and
    then altered it to* noireté; *the scribe of P6 copied the word as*
    noireté – 12 tu t'en viegnes] A1 L2 P8 V

tantes pierres et tanz merriens d'esglises qu'il avoit
fetes que li bien peserent plus que li mal. Ensint le nos
20   a tolu." A cest mot s'esvanoï. Ensint fu demostree la
mort Charle a Torpin l'arcevesque.

LXXVIII

Quinze jorz aprés la mort Charle vint a Viane
le message a cui li rois avoit comendé devant sa mort
qu'il nonçast a Torpin / *le jor de son trespas. Il li*   (1
conta le jor et l'ore, et meyme ce jor et cele hore
5   *avoit Torpins veue la vision. Voirs est qu'al sesme*
jor que Charles acoucha trespassa il dou siecle, receue
tote droiture de sainte yglise, en la tierce hore dou
jor, en la quinte kalandre de fevrier, au sexanteesme et
.xii. anz de son aaige, et au quarantieme et septiesme an
10   *de son regnemant, et a .viii. cenz et .xiiii. anz de l'in-*
carnacion Nostre Seignor. Issi trespassa Karles des poinnes
d'enfer delivrés par monsignor saint Jaque et par sa deserte.
Por ce fait que saiges qui edifie iglise en l'ennor de Deu,
car il edifie as cielx sa propre mansion. Voirs est que
15   *Torpins vesquit petit aprés la mort Karle et trespassa*
du siecle a Vianne. Ses cors fu mis en une iglise
joste la cité outre Rosne. Lonc tens aprés fu
trovez en char et en os en son sarqueu, vestuz d'un
evesqual vestement, si con il fu tesmoigniez d'autre
20   *escripture et de plusors anciens clers qui certainemant*
le sorent, par cui il est mis en escrit et en memoire.
Issi trespassa li arcevesques Torpins aprés son seignor
le bon roi Karle, la cui arme est par la merite de sa
deserte jointe a la celestial compaignie, avec Deu le
25   *Pere, qui vit et regne et regnera sanz fin ou siecle(s)*
des siecles. Amen.

LXXVIII *The text in P5 ends in 1.3, that is, at the bottom of
fol. 108 v°. The text used to complete the Chronicle is that of
A1, of which the rejected readings follow:* 5 a sesme] L2 P8 V –
21 fu mis] L2 P8 V Br 2

Appendix To The Text:

The Supplementary Chapters In MS V

I

Coment li Amiraus entra en Espaigne aprés le mort Karlon.

Ci poés vous savoir et oïr comment il avint en
Espaigne puis la mort Karle. Uns grans sires c'on
apieloit l'aumaçor de Cordes vint avant et dist qu'il
5   voloit ravoir toute la tierre que Karles avoit tolue as
Sarrasins. Dont asambla ses os et ala toute la tierre
gastant par Espaigne cha et la et vint dusques a
monsigneur Saint Jakeme et prist et roba quanqu'il
trova en l'eglisse: livres et calisces, dras de soie et
10   tout riens, et fissent du moustier estables a lor
chevaus et fissent partout leur besoignes vilainnement,
par quo[i] l'une des parties d'iaus morut si que par
desos lor issoit li sans et li boiele par le comman-
dement saint Jakeme, et li autre awloient et li autre
15   moroient de mort sobite. Qu'en diroie jou plus? L'
aumaçors meismes fu entrepris d'autretel maladie
et fu awlés. Mais par le conseil d'un prestre de
saint[e] eglisse commença a apeler l'aïe de Dieu et
dist: "Dieus des Crestiens, Dieus de saint Jakeme,
20   Dieus sains Pieres, Dieus sor toutes cosses, se tu
me rens santet, jou ne mesferai jamais vers toi et
si renoierai Mah[omet] mon Dieu, ne jamais u mostier
Saint Jake reproce ne ferai. A! sains Jakemes,
qui si grans sires es, se tu me rens santé a mes
25   eius et a mon ventre, jou te renderai quanque jou
t'ai reubé ne mes gens." Aprés çou .xv. jours fu
tous garis et li rendi au double quanqu'il

23 MS: ferai a sains J. qui si g. s. es
25 MS: eix

181

avoit pris a l'eglisse et a le ville et as gens
ausi, et issirent de la cité et dist li amiraus que
30   li Dieus as Crestiens estoit Dieus sor tous autres
puissans et sains Jakemes estoit de haute
merite. Li amiraus s'en ala en Espaigne
gastant tant qu'il vinrent en une [v]ille c'om
apieloit Orins ou il avoit une glise de saint
35   Romain. Molt estoit aornee ricement de vaisiaus
d'or et d'argent et de pailes. L'amiraus et ses
gens roberent quanqu'il i trouverent et
gasterent. Et kant herbegié se furent, uns dus
de sa maisnie entra u moustier Saint Roùmain
40   et vit les coulombes de piere rice et bielle qui
sostenoient les maisieres, et avoient doré les
capitiaus. Par couvoitisse prist cil une cugnie et
le feri entre les jointures. Ensi come il feroit
ens a force .i. mal de fier pour l'or avoir
45   du piler, par le volenté de Dieu et de saint
Romain devint pierre li chevaliers et encore
est iluec en sanblance d'omme et est encore
d'autretel couleur com sa cote estoit au jour
qu'il devint pierre, et dient li pelerin qu'il
50   est de maille d'or et qu'ele put. Et quant li
aumaçours le vit, si dist, "Certes, mout fait a
hounourer et a douter li Dieu as Crestiens et
si saint qui aprés lor mort se vengent si
cruelment de lor anemis. Jakemes Sans Tieste me
55   toli l'autre jour mes eius et me santé et
le me rendi; Roumains, cis autres, si a fait
une piere d'uns de mes chevaliers. Mas
Jakemes est plus debounaires que cis Romains,
car il me rendi santé et clarté et cis Romains
60   ne me veut rendre mon chevalier. Il n'i a plus;
fuions nous ent de ci." Lors s'em parti li
aumaçors atoutes ses gens, ne onques puis en
la contrée saint Jakeme ne retorna, ne onques
puis nus Sarasins ne li osa mal faire.

II

Pourquoi Navarois sont apelé.
    Si com l'estoire dist et aferme, Julius Cesar en

55 MS: eix

son tans envoia Nubiens, Escos, Cornualois pour
Espaigne conquere pour chou qu'il ne

5   voloient rendre treu, et coumanda qu'il
tuaissent tous les houmes et as femes ne
fesissent nul mal. Quant il furent arivé, si
arsent toutes lor nés a Baionne et
essillierent toute la tiere dusques a Cesar

10   Auguste. Mais il ne pooient aler avant, car
tout cil dou païs s'asamblerent et vainkirent
et cachierent fors de la tiere. Asés en ocissent
la. Cil qui s'en fuirent en alerent sor la
mer entre Nares et Panpelune et a Baionne

15   et en la tiere de Bisquarre et d'Alerne,
et la fissent molt fors castiaus et ocissent
les hommes et prisent lor femes dont il orent
puis enfans. Cil enfant pres leur perre[s] furent
apellé Navar, et cil sont de Navare et dist

20   autretant Navars comme 'nons vrais' pour çou
qu'il ne furent pas estrait de droit linage.
Nadavare fu une cités qui fu en Aufrique, et
i preecha sains Mahius li apostres, et de celle
cité Nadavare si ont encore nons cil de

25   Navare et auront tous jors, car cil qui les
encaucierent les nomerent ensi. Chi faut et finne
li estoire Karlemainne que Maistres Jehans tranlata.

Notes To The Text

Prol., 14 *chiere tenue.* As was normal in Old French, the adjective used as adverb modifying a feminine adjective or participle agreed with it. Cf. LXVII, 6 var. and 12 var.

I, 14 *Lombardie. Lombardie* means Italy. So the Reichenau Glossary: *Italia-Longobardia.* Mouskés, *Chronique rimé*, insists:

> Or est Ytale Lombardie v. 126

and

> En Ytale, qu'est Lombardie v. 599.

II, 1 *que Charles ert si cremuz.* Here as often in Old French, *que* is used as a relative adverb, no need being felt to express in a declinable form its specific function in the relative sentence. Cf. the note to LXVI, 16-17.

III, 2 *Jahanz de Naples.* The text of the *Descriptio* has *Johannes Neapolis sacerdos* and *Iohannes Neapolitanus.* (ed. Rauschen, p. 104, 1.15, 1.16), which Rauschen glosses simply (p. 220) as *Priester zu Neapel. Neapolis, Naples* is probably the Neapolis of Samaria, the ancient Shechem, the present Nablus, of which the mediaeval French form was *Naples.* Cf. Paul Deschamps, "La toponomastique en Terre Sainte au temps des Croisades" (Clovis Brunel volume, t.I, p. 353).

IV, 13 *de la chasse . . . en issi,* an example of the pleonastic use of *en.*

184

IV, 19   *dont Nostre Sires fu coronez.* The supporting
manuscripts all read *il fu,* the *il* referring to *Deus*
in 1.17, and this understanding of the identity of
God and Christ is consistently manifested in the
Turpin; VIII, 5: *Deus Jhesu Crist;* LX, 5: *Deus,
voirs Peres, filz de la Vierge Marie;* LX, 8: *Deu
mon Sauveor;* LX, 18: *Deu . . . toi qui vis et
regnes o Deu le Pere et le Saint Esperit.* The sec-
ond redactor no doubt wrote *il.* But the manu-
scripts of our sub-group F A2 C1 B2 C2 A3 S,
no doubt in accordance with their common
source, all repeat in 1.19 the *Dieus* of 1.17,
showing that the scribe of P5 was not alone in
thinking that the use of the pronoun left the
meaning unclear. His reading *Nostre Sires* retains
the sense of the passage and reflects his own
style; I therefore retain it here.

VII, 8   *qu'en ne set ou il est.* This use of *que* without a
correlative introducing a consecutive clause is
rather unusual in Old French prose. In this sen-
tence the consecutive force is so weakened that
the *que* is in function little more than a copula-
tive. The sense is "My body lies in Galicia (in
such wise) that it is not known where." See R.L.
Graeme Ritchie, *Recherches sur la syntaxe de la
conjonction "que",* pp. 41 ff., especially p. 46,
and cf. below *que prendre ne la pot* (VIII, 2),
qui pres est de la cité qu'en l'en puet bien veoir
(XX, 4), *que li rois ne le sot* (XXXII, 10). Cf. too
XXXII, 19, where *que* without a correlative
introduces a final clause: *que si anemi ne l'ocient.*

VII, 11   The Latin text here reads (91, xv): *Quapropter
tibi notifico, quia sicut Dominus . . . sic . . .,*
where *quia* introduces a noun clause, comple-
ment of *notifico:* "Wherefore I tell you that just
as God . . . so He has chosen you . . . to free my
tomb." This is the sense given in MSS M, L1, P2,

P3, Br 1 and all the manuscripts of Group III M;
e.g., ignoring irrelevant variants, M: *Pour ce te
fach je sçavoir que ensi comme Dieu . . . aussi . . .*
In these manuscripts the Latin *quia* is repre-
sented by *que*. But the readings in the III R man-
uscripts are characterized by the use of *car,* and
a resulting ambiguity which some scribes
resolved according to their particular under-
standing of its function.

P5	:	*Por ce le te faz je savoir car si com Deus . . . autressi . . .*
P7	:	*Si le te fay assavoir, filz, pour ce que . . .*
A1	:	*Et por ce te foiz a savoir ce, que si con . . . autresi . . .*
L2 ,L3 ,B1 ,O	:	*Pur ceo te faiz jeo saveir kar . . .*

The scribe of P5 took the *car* as causative and
the following clause as adverbial modifying *le te
faz je savoir*. Evidently, he thought the matter
over, for his *le* is added above the line to make it
clear that he understood the complement of *faz
savoir* to be the preceding announcement of St.
James. P7 gives the same sense, but has the con-
junction *pour ce que*. The sub-group L2, L3, B1,
O use *car* but with the function of *que* introduc-
ing a subordinate noun clause. The scribe of A1,
who always uses *que* for *car,* understood the pas-
sage as did the scribe of P5, and added *ce* as the
latter added *le*. The scribe of P1 too read the
same meaning into the passage. But there can be
no doubt that theirs is a misinterpretation; the
sense is not: "I tell you all this because God has
chosen you . . .," but "Because of all this, I tell
you that God has chosen you . . ." I therefore
emend the text of P5, keeping however the *car*
which was evidently the cause of the trouble and
leaving it with the same function as that of *que,*
introducing as complement of *faz savoir* the
clause *t'eslist il . . .* For *car = que,* see Lerch, I,
p. 144.

VII, 16-17   *toz li pueples qui est . . . i iront.* Old French used
the singular or the plural after a collective noun.
The use here of *est*, singular, in the relative
clause and of *iront*, plural, in the main clause, is
justified by the notion of collectivity in the first
case and of plurality in the second. Br 3, F (with
variants), C1 read with P5; A1 has, similarly: *toz
li monz qui est . . . i iront.* The variants show
that the point of view differed according to the
scribes. Cf. XII, 7.

X, 1   For the identification of the towns and territor-
ies listed in Chapters X and XI, which in a num-
ber of cases is still left in doubt, see the studies
by Dozy, Jones, Smyser and David listed in the
Bibliography. In my *Table of Proper Names* I
have relied heavily on all their work. Except
where the forms used by Johannes are almost
identical with the Latin I have put the Latin
form in brackets immediately after the French.

X, 8   *Talavere.* The Pseudo-Turpin lists two *Talaveras,*
97, i and iv, the one no doubt to be identified
with Talavera la Real the other with Talavera de
la Reina, though it is not possible to say which is
which in the Pseudo-Turpin's text. Johannes
omits the second Talavera, probably thinking
that it was a mere repetition of the first.

X, 12   *Luiserne, Ventose qui est en Val Vert.* The pas-
sages in the Latin *Turpin* concerning *Lucerna
Ventosa quae dicitur Carcesa, quae est in Valle
Viridi* (97, v-vi), the legend of the engulfed
Lucerna (99, xvii-101, ii), and the accursed cities
Lucerna Ventosa, Caparra, Adania (101, xi-xiii),
have been much discussed (e.g. Bédier, *Légendes
épiques,* III, pp. 152-166; Jones, *op. cit.,* pp.
275-276; Smyser, *op. cit.,* p. 19, n.l; David, *op.*

cit., III, pp. 25-31). Perhaps the following résumé will serve as a tentative conclusion to these enquiries.

The identification with the surest historical basis is that of Ventosa with Castro de la Ventosa a little to the west of Ponferrada in the valley of the Sil, a valley known in the twelfth century as Vallis Viridis. Carcesa is probably Carteya, situated in Andalucía between Córdoba and Málaga and famous as the seat of Bishop Hesychius, one of seven evangelists who brought Christianity to Spain. Carteya appears in variant forms in the writings of early mediaeval historians; among these are *Carthesia, Carceso, Carcesa* (see *España Sagrada* IV, pp. 12 ff., especially, p. 20). The Pseudo-Turpin used a tradition in which it had been identified, probably because of a confusion (*España Sagrada,* IV, p. 12), with Ventosa. It appears in the ancient breviaries of Córdoba and Seville, printed in the sixteenth century, as *Carthesia Ventosa* and as *Carthesa, id est Ventosa depopulata.* Close by Castro de la Ventosa, to the south and across the Sil on its left bank, lies Lake Carucedo, to which attaches a local legend, perhaps emanating from the nearby monastery of Carucedo, of a village engulfed in its waters. It may be that the name of the lake played a part in the deformation of Carteya or Cartesa to Carcesa and in its transference to the valley of the Sil where it was identified with Ventosa. Lucerna for long seemed to be quite unhistorical, a name which could be attributed to any place where legend told of a pagan town miraculously destroyed. But Luis L. Cortés y Vazquez, in his study "La Leyenda del Lago de Sanabria" (*Revista de dialectología y tradiciones populares,* IV, 1948, pp. 99-114), informs us that a local legend is still told of Lake Sanabria, better known as Lake Castañeda, lying

to the northwest of Zamora, according to which
the lake covers the site of the ancient city of Vil-
laverde de Lucerna. The Pseudo-Turpin, without
making any attempt to simplify the accumula-
tion of names, seems to have set down here a
story as he learned it in all its jumble from pil-
grims who had heard it on the spot.

Johannes is somewhat independent in his
treatment of these passages in his Latin model.
He omits the phrase *quae dicitur Carcesa* and he
shows quite clearly that he regarded Ventosa as a
name separate from, and not in apposition to,
Lucerna. The Latin as printed by Jones reads
(101, xi) *Hae sunt urbes quas . . . (Karolus)
maledixit, et idcirca sine habitatore permanent
usque in hodiernum diem: Lucerna Ventosa,
Capparra, Adania.* Johannes, transposing this
passage to 101, ii, and thus making it follow on
the description of the engulfment of Lucerna,
translates: *Cele cité* (viz. Luiserne) *maudist
Charles et trois autres, Ventose, Capaire, Adanie.*
I might add here that, although Jones prints
Lucerna Ventosa with no mark of punctuation
between the two (99, v and 101, xiii) they are
separated by a dot in the Codex Compostellanus.
So are they too in the C manuscripts and in our
Johannes MS, P5. But this is not true of all the
Latin or of all the Johannes manuscripts. Evi-
dently the scribes were not always certain of
how to understand *Lucerna Ventosa quae dicitur
Karcesa.* Johannes however, arbitrarily or out of
his securer knowledge, took special care to dis-
tinguish *Ventose* from *Luiserne.*

X, 14   *Urance.* The Latin text reads: *Urancia quae
dicitur Arcus* (97, vii). Johannes omits *quae
dicitur Arcus,* but Urance, Urancia, is probably
the Los Arcos mentioned in the *Guide du Pèl-
erin,* and situated just west of Estella. See Jones,
op. cit., p. 276.

X, 16   After the word *nombre* Johannes omits the names *Terraciona, Barbastra, Rozas, Urgellum, Elna, Gerunda, Barquinona,* no doubt because of homoioteleuton: *Terraciona — Terragona.*

X, 19   *Oramalgie.* The Latin name *Hora Malaguae* is not to be found in the C manuscripts; but here it is in Johannes. See above, note 3 to Chap. III.

X, 20   After *Oracotante* Johannes omits *Ubeda* (97, xv).

X, 27   After *Arrabite,* Johannes omits *Maioricas insula* (99, v).

XI, 1   *Tote la terre . . .* This is where the compiler of the chronicle preserved in our MS Br 2 began his borrowing from the Johannes *Turpin.*

XI, 2   After *Portigal,* Johannes omitted *tellus Saracenorum.* This is the reading which is given by the C manuscripts in place of the mystifying *tellus Serranorum.*

XI, 17   The manuscripts of our second redaction seem to have inherited a corrupt text from the first redaction. The Latin reads (101, vi): *Clodoveus namque primus rex Francorum christianus.* In Group I, only M has the correct sense:

M   :   Cleovis qui fu premiers rois crestiens de France

P₁   :   Cloevieus qui premiers roi fu en France

L₁   :   Clodius le premer roy des Creistiens fust

Group II as represented by P2 P3 seems to repeat the error visible in L1 : *qui premerains rois fu des Crestiens,* but Br 1 has: *Glodois qui premiers roy de France fu crestiens.* The corrupt reading which appears in L1 and P2 P3 has passed on to most of the manuscripts of the second redaction. Except for irrelevant variants, P5 A1 L2 L3 O P8 V F A2 C1 read: *C. qui fu li premiers rois des Crestiens.* This too is the reading behind Br 2 : *qui premiers rois de Grieus fu,* where *Grieus* is obviously due to a misreading of an abbreviation *Cr̄iens.* Some scribes knew their history better, and emended their model. This is no doubt true of Br 1 , and also of B1 : *C. qui premiers des rois Crestiens fu,* of Br 3 : *C. qui fu premier roy crestien,* P11 : *C. le premier roy crestien de France,* and the scribe of the common source of B2 C2 A3 S: *C. li prumiers rois de France des Crestiens.* We can see that the corruption which has infected the second redaction consists essentially in the loss of *de France.* Johannes probably wrote: *C. qui fu premiers rois de France crestiens.* The loss of *de France* and the resulting confusion might be explained by a scribe's misreading of an abbreviated form of the phrase: *rois de f. crestiens,* which took the *f.* as a long *s,* attached it to the *de* and so turned the phrase to *rois des crestiens.* Whatever the explanation of the error may be, the nonsense in P5 must be relegated to the variants.

XII, 6
a sa vie. The *a* is used here in a temporal sense, "during." Cf. the Latin: *dum adhuc viveret.*

XII, 7
qui sostient. The verb in the singular with *qui* having as antecedent the collective: *une legion de deables,* is less common in Old French than the plural. Cf. VII, 16 and note.

XII, 11
et errament. The *et* which the scribe of P5 uses here is a particle brought in to enliven the description. It has the force of the English *why* used interjectionally as a form of emphasis, or of the French *voici que.*

XII, 13

P5 and all our controlling manuscripts read *dehors,* and this reading is prevalent throughout our tradition. The Latin *Turpin* has *deorsum* (103, vi); the other French translations render the word quite straightforwardly by *desous.* In our Group I, M L1 read *dehors,* but M adds *et par en bas.* P1 has *lee desous.* In Group II, Br 1 reads *dehors* but P2 P3 read *desous.* The manuscripts in Group III R all have *dehors* except P7 which, however, reflects *dehors* in an attempt at emendation: *assise sur la terre hors de l'eaue, desoubz lee . . .* In Group III M, P8 V read *dehors,* but Br 3 has *quarree dessoubz.* F A2, and so no doubt their common intermediary, have *desous.* So does C1 ; but B2 C2 A3 S all depending on a common exemplar, have *dehors.* Br 2 has *defors.* One can hardly think that Johannes wrote *dejos (dejous)* or *desos (desous)* and that *dehors* is a corruption in form and sense of the one or the other of these words. The explanation, surprising but almost unavoidable, of this complex of variants would be that *dehors* was an error committed by the translator and that the context, calling for a contrast to the *desus estroite* which follows, prompted the more attentive scribes to make an obvious emendation. Cf. the reading of M.

XIII, 6

les aorna. The word *les* is not clear in MS P5, but it looks more like *les* than *la.* The scribe of P6 who copied P5, and for whom the writing in P5 must have been less faded than it is now, took it as *les* and so I follow him. The *les* must refer to the bishops and canons of Saint-Jacques. The Latin (103, xix) has *eamque . . . ornavit,* which is reflected in all our manuscripts except P5 P6 P8 V — and Br 1, which is corrupt here.

XIII, 10

Boorges must reflect a *Bituricensium* in the Latin, an error for *Biterrensis.* See above, Ch. III, n. 3.

XIV, 7

Il fu morz. The formation is unusual; one would have expected *Il morut,* and that is what we do find in P1 L1. The sense is preterite, "He died." In Old French, and especially in Old French prose the perfect was used mainly as a present perfect.

XV, 4

escrois "din." The word in this form occurs in MSS O B1 L3 P5 Br 2 P2 F A2 B2 C2. The variants are interesting: *escrous* A1, *escreus* L2, *cri* L1, *noise* Br 1, *une error* (no doubt for *crior*) V, *criee* Br 3, *escruison* C1.

XV, 12

charoig. The word in P5 comes at the end of a line. Cf. *batail* below, XVII, 1, also at the end of a line.

XV, 18

la rive. The word is clear in P5. The other manuscripts show *aigue, aiue, eue* or *ewe,* but it seems unlikely that in writing *rive* the scribe of P5 misread so common a word in so clear a context. His *rive* must be the word he wanted to write and it can only mean "river" here — another example to add to the single one listed by T. -L. (VIII, 1332) and taken from the Oxford Psalter. The scribe of P6, the fifteenth century copy of P5, changed the *rive* of his model to *riviere,* which may represent a correction or the substitution of a more familiar for a less familiar word.

XV, 18

en uns prés. The plural is probably used to convey the sense of "broad in extent." Cf. A. Henry's note to v.2534 in his ed. of *Buevon de Conmarchis,* and the lines he quotes there from the *Roman de la Violette:*

> Puis les mainnent en mi uns prés
> Grans et larges et descombrés.

XVI, 10   The repetition of the conjunction *que,* unnecessary to the sense, is common in Old French. Mediaeval writers seem to have found it especially called for when a clause intervened between the conjunction and the subordinate which it introduced, as here: *se il combatoit gent a gent.* Cf. *Berte aus grans piés,* ed. A. Henry, vv. 1937-38:

> Bien set que se sa fille fust en bonne santé,
> Qu'ele l'eüst veue ou aucun mant mandé.

XVI, 12   For *li un,* A1 reads *l'un,* a rare example of the elision of *i* in the plural *li.*

XVII, 5   The scribe of P5, very percipiently, changed the *racines* of his model to *tronçons,* but he forgot to change the feminine pronoun *eles meismes* in 1.6 correspondingly to the masculine. The scribe of P6, copying him, made the necessary change. *Tronçons* makes excellent sense, but I think it better to restore *racines* than to correct *eles meismes.*

XVII, 6-7   *et les racines qui remestrent en la terre engendrerent d'eles meismes grant arboie autreteles come longues perches.* Johannes was in difficulty here. The Latin text is: *et radices quae remanserunt in tellure in modum perticarum ex se magna postea generarunt nemora* (III, xi-xiii). The sense is: "and the roots which remained in the ground, later, like cuttings, grew into a large grove of trees." Johannes has mistranslated *perticarum,* taking it as meaning "tree trunks" instead of young planted "slips," or "sets" or "cuttings," a meaning which it had in Latin but which seems not to have remained attached to its French derivative, *perches;* but cf. *FEW* VIII, 279, col. 2 and n. 7. This misunderstanding has led him to misconstrue the Latin syntax. He took *in modum perticarum,* an adverbial phrase of manner modifying *generarunt,* as an adjectival phrase qualifying *nemora: grant arbroie autreteles come longues perches. Autreteles* seems to agree with the sense *arbres* implicit in the collective *arbroie.* Some of our scribes, however, appear to have been dissatisfied with this loose concord; a few of them make *arbroies* plural (L1 P3 V B2), others replace *arbroie* with *arbres* (P1 P6 O Br 2 F P11).

XIX, 2   *Sarrazins et Mors . . .* For these names see David, *op. cit.,* III, pp. 42-44.

XX, 30   The scribe first wrote *par un faus trou.* He "corrected" *trou* by adding an *s* above the line, probably after copying *fez,* but apparently forgot to correct *un* to *uns.* Johannes's translation is a polite rendering of *per latrinas et foramina* (117, xiv).

XXI, 17   *Cil* has no specific antecedent. Johannes, treating the Latin freely, has added the phrase *reclamant . . . Crist* and omitted the clause *interfecit multos illorum* (119, xiv). His *Cil,* rendering the Latin *At illi,* which quite clearly takes up *illorum,* is defined only by the context. No doubt, its strong demonstrative force was felt: "Those (on the other side)."

XXII, 1   *les porz d'Aspre.* Johannes writes *les porz d' d'Aspre* in place of the Latin *portus Cisereos, portuum Ciserei.* He does this consistently (XXV, 4; L, 22; LII, 5) except where he simply omits the proper noun: *les porz* LII, 6; *au pié del mont* LVI, 5. *The Portus Cisereos* or *Ciserei* are the Port de Cize, the pass on the way from Saint-Jean Pied de Port through Roncevaux to Pamplona. The *Porz d'Aspre* represent geographically the Col de Canfranc, or de Somport,

leading from the vallée d'Aspe over the summit
to Jaca. Perhaps Johannes knew one of the
forms of the *Chanson de Roland* in which the
Porz d'Aspre replace the *Porz de Sizer* or *de
Sirie* of the Oxford manuscript. He may have felt
that the name he chose had a poetic reality
which was more important than topography or
the tradition followed by the Pseudo-Turpin.
Whatever his reason, the substitution which he
made was deliberate. It stands in contrast with
the other vernacular translations of the *Pseudo-
Turpin Chronicle.*

XXII, 4

de tote sa cure. The word *cure* occurs only in
the manuscripts of Group III R, but it occurs in
all of them except P7, which omits the whole
phrase. Johannes seems to have written *de tote
sa terre,* for that is the reading in MSS M and P1
of Group I and in MSS P2 and P3 of Group II.
L1 lacks the phrase, Br 1 has *de sa seigneurie.*
Br 2 also lacks the phrase. The manuscripts of
Group III M read almost unanimously *de tout
son pooir.* The word *cure* must be a substitution,
made by our second redactor, for *terre,* which
he probably found in his model written in abbre-
viation *tre,* with *t* very like *c* and it's upright
prolonged in an upward curve to represent *er.* It
is so written in MS M, fol. 104 v°, b. Michel's
scribe baulked at the word and put *pooir* in its
place. But the scribes of the III R manuscripts
wrote it with no apparent hesitation and so it
must have been familiar to them in this concrete
sense of "dominions," a meaning recorded, as far
as I know, with reference only to an ecclesiasti-
cal incumbency or jurisdiction.

XXII, 6

serf . . . de lor chars. The controlling manuscripts
all read *de lor chiés;* cf. the Latin (121, vii):
Soluta servitute proprii capitis. Both *char* and
chief are used here with the meaning "person."

XXIII, 4   *Uns autres Rollanz.* A search for this other
Roland among the mediaeval saints, archbishops,
military heroes and lesser figures who bore the
name might take us to Broceliande – and back
again. Does any reality lie behind this *autres
Rollanz*? behind too the *autres rois* in Brittany
at the time of Arestans (1.11) and behind the
autres dus en Aquitaine at the time of Angelier
(1.14)? I think it would be far more rash to deny
than to assert that there is, though in each case
we are presented with an unsolved problem of
identification. Jules Horrent (*Roncesvalles,*
p. 150, n. 1), working back to this passage in the
Turpin from the Spanish romances in which
Roland gradually degenerates from hero to vil-
lain, finds in it the seed from which that Spanish
tradition was to grow. He interprets the Pseudo-
Turpin's phrase *Alius tamen Rotholandus fuit* to
mean not "another Roland" but "another side
of the same Roland," and understands it as a
covert reference to the tradition of Roland's
incestuous birth. I cannot think that the Pseudo-
Turpin would have made even a veiled allusion
to shame in Roland's lineage. But history does
seem to have known, or created, another
Roland, this one stained with an incestuous ori-
gin. Léopold Delisle has guided us to him. In his
article on "Les ouvrages de Guillaume de
Nangis" in *Mémoires de l'Académie des Inscrip-
tions,* XXVII:2, p. 302, Delisle writes: "Guil-
laume de Nangis rapporte qu'il y a deux
personnages du nom de Roland: le fameux, qui
était comte du Mans, et un autre, qui passait
pour avoir été comte du Gâtinais et qui avait
donné à l'abbaye de Saint-Denis le domaine de
Beaune en Gâtinais," and he quotes from the
Latin text of Guillaume's *Chronique universelle:
Rotholandus, comes Cenomanensis, dominus
Blavii, qui nepos erat Karoli ex Bertha sorore et*

filius Milonis de Angleris; alter namque Rotholandus fuit, quem dicunt aliqui Karolum ex quadam sorore sua genuisse, et hic, ut opiniantur nonnulli, comes Wastinensis fuit et dedit Beato Dyonisio Belnam in Wastineto (Bibl. Nat. Latin MS 4918, fol. 285 r°).

For the tradition of Charlemagne's incest with his sister, Gisèle or Berthe, see B. de Gaiffier, "La légende de Charlemagne. Le péché de l'Emp'ereur et son pardon" in *Études critiques d'hagiographie,* pp. 26 ff.

XXIII, 7   *Genevois.* The Pseudo-Turpin wrote *comes gebenennsis,* which can only be a translation of *cuens de Genves.* It shows that, no matter what place the name represented in the minds of the trouvères — Geneva, Genoa, Gien, Elne — for him it was the Genevois. See the *Table of Proper Names,* s.v. *Genevois.*

XXIII, 8   "Estouz li cuens de Langres" is *filius comitis Odonis* in the Latin (123, xiii) and in MSS M and P1 of our Group I is duly "le fiu Oedon" (L1 omits Estouz entirely). But the phrase is lacking in Group II, and therefore also in Group III.

XXIII, 16-18   *la cité d'Aquitaine.* This unidentified city is mystifying to us and was no less so to Geoffroi du Breuil who expressed his puzzlement to the abbey chapter in Limoges. See Jones, *op. cit.,* p. 350, or better, *Cat. Cod. Hag. Bibl. Par.* II, 466.

XXIV, 15   *Guionarz.* Cf. the Latin *Guinardus* 125, xviii. The scribe of P5 hesitated over the fourth letter and seems deliberately to have made it indistinct. It looks like an ill-formed *o* but could be an *e.* P6, a copy of P5, transcribed the name as *Guiounars,* taking the doubtful letter as an *o.*

The other Renaud manuscripts read *Guienarz;*
the rest of the Johannes tradition hesitates
between *Guimars* and *Guinars.*

XXV, 12   *Vint jors.* The Latin text, and the manuscripts of
our Groups I and II read *octo diebus, .viii. jorz.*
Most of our Group III manuscripts read *vint;* the
second redactor seems to have read *.viii.* as
vint — a common error. For example, L2 has
vint liues for *.viii. liues* at LVII, 21 and at
LXIII, 26 reads *trente et vint* instead of *.xxxviii.*
See also the supplement, p. 170.

XXVIII, 8   *par esgart et par atiremant des .ii. olz.* The
phrase is not in the Latin nor in the manuscripts
of our Group I. It appears in P2 and P3, and its
sense is conveyed in Br 1: *de l'accord de[s]
deux ost[z] .* We may therefore conclude that it
is an addition made by Pierre de Beauvais, from
whom it passed on to our second redactor. In
the context, *esgart* and *atiremant* are similar in
meaning: "the ruling arrived at" and "the
arrangement made." There is synonymic repeti-
tion here as though it was a formula, but I do
not know of its occurrence elsewhere. We might
translate: "according to the terms and arrange-
ments decided upon by the two armies."

XXIX, 11   *qui nos esponent les escritures.* The point of
interest here is the A1 variant: *qui nos esproig-
nent et ensoignent les escritures,* in which
esproignent is a dialectal form of *espreignent,*
from *espreindre.* Cf. *FEW exprimere* and T.-L.
s.v. *espriendre.*

XXIX, 26   The reading in P5 *demostre estre fause,* makes
sense, but it is inferior to the *demostres tu* of the
controlling manuscripts. The Latin reads
(139, ix): *nunc ostendis falsam* with which

demostres tu is in accord; *demostre* is a 1st pers.
sing. and gives the meaning "(your religion), I
show it to be false," which is much less pointed
and dramatic than "you prove it false (by your
own act)." However, the Johannes manuscripts
are very divided on the matter. All the manu-
scripts of Group II read *demostre estre fause,*
and so do MSS Br 2 and, in Group III M, MSS F
A2 P11 C1 C2 A3 S, these last stemming from a
common intermediary. The scribe of L1 in
Group I also understood the verb as being in the
1st pers. and wrote: *ore la treoffe geo malveise.*
All the manuscripts in Group III R except P5
read *demostres tu* and so do P8 *(mostres)* and
B2 in Group III M, and, in Group I, MS P1. The
readings in MSS M and V give us the clue to the
trouble; both have *demoustre tu* showing the
loss in writing, as in pronunciation, of final *s.*
The acceptability of the sense conveyed by
demostre must have led to the dropping of *tu.*
But in no manuscript is *je* supplied as subject of
demostre. The presence of the complement, *loi,*
at the head of the sentence called for the inver-
sion of subject and verb, and here the pronoun
subject was accented so that its absence leaves
the syntax, to say the least, awkward. Grammar
and sense are against the reading in P5 and so I
relegate it to the variants.

XXXI, 13 *et si autre baron.* P5 omits *autre* but the sense is
clearly the one afforded by *autre:* "and his own
particular vassals." Cf. the idea of opposition or
separateness in the modern *nous autres.*

XXXI, 16 MS P1 adds here: *Hernaus de Biaulande haoit sor
tos homes Agolant, car ja .i. jor qui passés estoit
li avoit tote vilonie faite et por che metoit plus
s'entente a lui encontrer.*

XXXI, 19

qu'il ocioient. The 3rd. pers. pl. is used, as often in Old French, for the indefinite. Cf. the A1 variant: *on ocioit,* and cf. LXXII, 3 and n.

XXXII, 2

Por ce que Charles veinqui Ag. senefie que. The first *que* is causal here and is provided with a correlative *por ce* announcing the clause which serves as the subject of *senefie.* As often with this construction the sense is very vague; it is especially so here where the main verb is *senefie.* The movement of the sentence is less from cause to effect than from datum to conclusion. Cf. Ritchie, *op. cit.,* p. 22, pp. 62 ff. and especially pp. 68 ff., and A Henry's note to his *Enfances Ogier,* v. 3741. Our MSS A1 P8 B1 use as correlative simply *ce: Ce que.*

XXXII, 6

totes choses sunt poissanz. The force of the participial adjective is passive: not "exercising power" but "subject to it;" not "powerful" but "possible."

XXXII, 14

il erent repoz. The plural must refer to the aumaçor and his men. Such is the reading in P5 L2 L3 O and in Br 1 *(ilz estoient).* But the scribes of B1 A1, of M, of P2 P3, of Br 2 and of the Michel manuscripts used the singular.

XXXII, 17

par qu'il. This use of *que* for the strong form *quoi* before a vowel is common in Old French. The varied usage shown by the scribes here, where the antecedent to the relative is indefinite, is interesting: *par coi (quoi)* P8 V; *par cui (ki)* A1 L2 — a quite usual use of *cui* with a neuter antecedent.

XXXIII, 23

Nazres. The whole Johannes tradition is in trouble with the place name here. Since it becomes clear as *Nazres* at XXXIV, 1, I do what the

scribe of P8 seems to have done and apply the
obvious correction at XXXIII, 23.

XXXIII, 25   *Babiloine.* Probably not Old Cairo is meant but
              ancient Babylon since at L, 5 the Emir of
              Babylon sends Marsile and Baligant to Saragossa
              from Persia.

XXXVIII, 15   *se.* The *se* in P5 contrasts with the *et* in the other
              Johannes manuscripts. The *se* is a form of the
              adverb *si,* and the sense is "thus."

XL, 14   *soit reprochié.* The construction is impersonal;
              or perhaps the subject is left to be understood in
              au veincu: "may (the fact of his having been
              defeated) be (reproached to him) a cause of
              reproach to him for ever."

XLI, 10   *Li Sarrazin acorurent . . .* The loss of *a lor mort*
              in the Renaut manuscripts is obviously an error;
              it leaves the sense incompletely expressed. The
              reading I have adopted is that of Br 2 which
              agrees with that of P2 P3 (cf. *au mort* Br 1) and
              P1 (cf. *vers leur signeur mort* M) and is essen-
              tially that of the Michel manuscripts.

XLII, 16   *tymbres.* For the *tymbres, tabors, tympans* of
              our manuscripts here and at XLIII, 4, 19, see
              now Albert Henry's edition of *Cleomadés* , Vol.
              II, 693 ff.

XLIV, 12   *Joieuse.* See above, p. 99.

XLV, 13   *edefia les Crestiens.* P5 , with the other Renaud
              manuscripts except P7 , uses the partitive article
              and reads *des Crestiens.* The Latin, 169, xvi,
              with the punctuation as corrected by David, *op.
              cit.,* III, pp. 60 ff., shows *quos in illa patria habit-
              antes repperit Christianos, aedificavit.* The

Michel manuscripts read *les C.* with the exception
of C1 : *edefia illueques Crestiens.* Groups I and II
read *les* except Br 1 : *et y ediffia plusieurs C.*
The *des* seems to be due to Renaud's scribe, but
there seems to be little justification for accept-
ing his reading. Perhaps his *d* is due to the prox-
imity of the *d* in *edefia.* The scribe of A sensed a
difficulty and wrote *l'edefia des C.,* the *l'* refer-
ring to the church of Saint-James. I reject *des*
therefore and print *les.*

    The word *riches* means powerful, and the
general sense of the passage is: "Charles reha-
bilitated the Christians he found in Galicia and
put them in positions of authority."

XLVI, 8   The scribes vary in the way they construct
cuidier here with its complementary object,
some using the direct object, some the preposi-
tional object introduced with *a.* Except for A1 ,
the reading in the Renaut manuscripts is *cuidoit
a,* which I therefore adopt here.

XLVIII, 1 ff.   *destre partie . . . senestre partie:* right and left
as seen from the first and central church, Saint-
Peter's in Rome.

XLVIII, 3-4   *Car il avoient requis . . .* The *il* refers to St.
James and St. John mentioned at the end of
Ch. XLVII. Johannes is not as explicit as the
Latin, perhaps writing with the thought that the
famous story told in *Mark* X, 35-37 would be as
present in the mind of his audience as in his
own. Other Old French translations show a pref-
erence for the version of the story given in
Matthew XX, 20-21.

L, 10   *se despareilla molt del semblant.* T.-L. gives only
a few examples of *despareillier (soi).* We may
note the A1 variant: *desaparoillier (soi),* and also

the fact that MS V constructs the verb with the preposition *a: se desparilla mout a son semblant.*

L, 13   *se il le metoit en eise de Charle.* Johannes has dealt very freely with the Latin here (cf. 179, xxiv ff.); the sentence in ll. 11-16, *Marsiles l'onora . . . et sis pooirs,* is his addition. The phrase in P5 is supported by Br 2 V F B2. B1 reads: *. . . a aise de Charlon;* L2 L3 : *sil m. eise de Karlon* and C1 : *se il li m. son cuer en aise de K.* The *de* is respective (cf. *poissanz de braz et d'espee, sage d'armes,* XXIII, 7, 13) and the phrase means: "if he put him at ease with respect to Ch.," that is, in the context, "if he relieved him of Ch." A number of our manuscripts show that some scribes preferred the prepositional phrase *en aise (enaise) de, a aise (aaise) de,* followed by an infinitive. So M: *s'il le m. en aise de prendre Ch.;* P2 P3 : *s'il le m. a aise (en aisse* P3*) de Ch desconfire;* A1 C2 A3 : *s'il le m. en aise de Ch. occirre.* The *prendre* in M is suspect, for P1 has: *s'il l'en voloit metre en saisine* and L1 : *s'il veusist sei mettre em aÿe endreit de Ch.,* and *desconfire* is equally suspect in P2 P3 for Br 1 reads: *s'il le m. en l'amour de Ch.* These readings do not suggest that *occirre* was lost in some manuscripts, but that it, or *prendre,* or *desconfire,* are additions in others. But I hesitate to draw this conclusion, for a little later in the Latin, and in a different context (181, v-vi), occurs the phrase: (the presents were given to Ganelon) *ut pugnatores in manibus illorum traderet* ad interficiendum. Is *ad interficiendum* the *prendre, desconfire, occirre* of our texts transposed by Johannes? There is no sure answer and so I print the phrase as it is in P5 Br 2 V F B2 supported by the readings in L2 L3 B1.

LV, 5   *a quatre forz arz.* The *a* is instrumental. Cf. 1.22 below: *le trancha par mi a s'espee.* The scribes of L2 P8 V preferred *de*, as did the scribe of P5 at XLIV, 12: *trancha de Joieuse s'espee la perche.*

LVI, 28   *tant Sarrazin et tant mescreant,* an example of the use of the acc. sing. with adjectival *tant.*

LVI, 30   One may wonder why the scribe of P5 omitted the last phrase of the Chapter. The serious and critical attention with which he worked would perhaps justify our attributing to him the thought that the punishment of thieves was not an exploit of a dignity befitting Durendal, whose fame was won in the service of God against the misbelievers. His omission may be due simply to homoioteleuton: *aemplie - detranchie.*

LVIII, 6   The Latin here reads (195, ix ff.): *Qui cum aquam huc illucque quaereret nec inveniret, videns eum morti proximum . . .* The sense of this passage has come down faithfully, though with many variants, through Group I to Group II. It appears in P2, P3 as: *Et il* (sc. Baudouin) *i ala. B. la quist ça et la mais n'en trova point. Il s'en vint devant R. et vit . . .* The reading in the Renaud manuscripts shows the omission of *Il i ala et la quist ça et la.* The reading in the Michel manuscripts shows the loss of *et la quist ça et la.* Br 2 shows the loss of *i ala et.* It would seem then that the whole sentence was in fact in the original of the second redaction and that homoioteleuton in *ala, et la* has caused the omission of the second part of the phrase in the Michel manuscripts and of the first part in Br 2. Renaud's scribe must be responsible for the omission of the whole sentence, for it is characteristic of all the manuscripts in our Group III R. One can hardly think that he made the omission intentionally, for the sentence adds a dramatic detail to this well-known and much-liked episode.

Perhaps it is not too speculative to imagine that his model was written with some twenty-one letters to a line and that the passage lay before him in this wise:

il li alast querre de l'eue.
il *i ala et la quist ça et la*

and that his omission is to be explained by his having jumped the second of these lines because it began so similarly to the first. However that may be, I think it necessary to restore the reading of the second redaction and have done so on the basis of the readings in MS Br 2 and the manuscripts of Group III M.

LVIII, 15-17   The restored sentence is in conformity with the Latin. Its loss is due to the repetition of the phrase *a la bataille,* and occurs not surprisingly in many of our manuscripts: P1 Br 1, all of the Renaud manuscripts, which proves that Renaud's scribe passed over it, and, in Group III M, P8 V C1. I restore the sentence on the basis of Br 2, supported by Br 3, F A2, B2 C2 A3 S.

LIX, 11-12   The Pseudo-Turpin wrote here (197, vi-vii): *et caelos, quos tui numinis praesencia numquam deseruisti, voluisti adire.* The reading corresponding to the relative clause is throughout our tradition corrupt:

Group I
M   : que la presence de ta deïté ne te deguerpi onques
L1   : que la p. de ta d. ne guerpistes o.
P1   : *is mutilated here; only* deguerpi *in the 3rd. pers. is clear.*

Group II
P2 P3   : que la p. de ta d. ne deguerpi o.
Br 1   : *passage lacking.*

Group III R : qui la p. de ta d. ne deguerpis
 : (guerpis A1 , O) o. P7 : et ne
 : deguerpis o. la presente deïté

Group III M
P8 : que li p. de te d. ne me guer-
 pisse o.
V = P2 P3 (guerpi)
Br 2 : que la presence de ta deïté ne
 deguerpesis o.
Br 3 : *passage lacking*
C1 : et le p. de le d. ne deguerpi o.
B2 C2 S : et la pr. de la d. ne te guerpi o.
A3 : : et ne li presente *(sic)* de le d.
 ne te deguerpi o.
F A2 (*and so* P10 P11) *omit the passage.*

It would seem simplest to accept the reading in
V, which agrees with P2 , P3 here, as that of the
translator and as the one which was handed
down to the second redactor. But this would
ignore the difficulty caused by *deguerpis
(guerpis)* in the 2nd. pers., which corresponds to
the Latin *deseruisti* and which appears in L1 , in
all the III R manuscripts and in Br 2 . The con-
fused readings, with their obfuscations of the
sense, can perhaps best be explained by the loss
of *en* (rendering the Latin ablative *praesentia*) in
*qu'en (qu'en la presence de ta deïté ne deguerpis
onques),* possibly written *quē,* or perhaps the
loss of *o* in *qu'o.* The loss of *en* would explain
the *deguerpi* of P2 P3 V as an emendation com-
ing near to the proper meaning. I have restored
the lost *en* to the text. Our scribes were clearly
not of a quality to perceive the christological
doctrine involved in the sentence. The Pseudo-
Turpin himself was of a different caliber, and
had in mind the traditional dogma clearly
expressed for example in Eucherius on *John*
III, 13, *Instructionum ad Salonium Liber Primus*

(Migne, L, 801): *Secundum carnem in terra erat,
secundum Deitatem caelum non deerat.* Cf. St.
Augustine, *Confessiones* Lib. IV, XII, 19: *Illuc
enim abscessit, unde numquam recessit.*

LIX, 17   *Ninive.* See for the allusion *Prophetia Jonae,*
c. III.

LIX, 20   Johannes here uses *regardas* to render *(et Petro
lacrimanti) relaxasti.* See *Glossary,* s.v.

LXII, 2-3   The Latin text reads (203, viii-ix): *Dum . . . et
ego Turpinus . . . adstante rege, defunctorum
missam eodem die . . . celebrarem.* For *eodem
die* some of our manuscripts show *le jor,* the *le*
having demonstrative force, and for *adstante
rege* some of them show *le roi,* the oblique case
with dative force. But in none of our manu-
scripts do we find both *le jor* and *le roi.* Thus in
Group I, Group II, Group III M and Br 2 *le jor*
is lacking; examples, M: *chantoie le roi messe
des fais* (sic; *feus* P1) *Dieu;* P2 P3 : *chantoie
messe le roi des feus Dieu;* P8 *cantoie le messe le
roi des feus Diu.* In Group III R there is no men-
tion of *le roi* , e.g. P5 : *chantoie le jor messe des
feels Deu.* The presence of *le roi* in the III M
group and the presence of *le jor* in the III R
group is proof that Johannes wrote *chantoie le
jor le roi messe . . .* and that the second redactor
reproduced him correctly. An explanation of
our problem might be that in *le roi le jor, jor*
and *roi* could look so similar in manuscripts that
scribes, glancing from model to copy and from
copy back to model, simply overlooked one of
the terms. However that may be, I restore *le roi*
omitted in P5 .

LXII, 10-11   Here the Latin reads (203, xv): *tubicem vestrum
(vestrum* is Hämel's correction) *cum multis*

Michael fert ad superna. Except for L1, the
manuscripts of Group I and II have the sense of
the Latin, e.g. M: *et vostre buisineour Rollant
emporte Michiel (Micheaus li angles* P2, P3) *et
mout d'autres es chius.* The erroneous reading in
P5, *et vostre boisineor Michiel li archanges
emporte l'ame de Rollant es ciels* which, with
irrelevant variants, is shared by most of the man-
uscripts of Groups III R and III M, shows that in
spite of the clash of case forms, the epithet
buisineor was applied to St. Michael, with the
thought no doubt of the Saint in his traditional
role as sounder of the last trump, and that a new
complement to the verb was supplied to replace
it. L1 in Group I has committed the same error:
e Michael vostre businur emporte R . . . en ciel.
Among the manuscripts of Groups III R and
III M however, A1 in III R and Br 3 and C1 in
III M, give the right sense: *et Michiaus li
archanges emporte vostre busineor es ciels* A1 ;
*et Rouland vostre buisinier est pourté ou ciel
par Michiel l'a.* Br 3 ; *et de vostre buisineeur
porte Mikieus li a. l'ame es chieus* C1 . These three
manuscripts show no other sign of possible con-
tamination; their readings here must be con-
sidered as independent and correct emendations
of a corrupt text. The corruption, towards which
we see as it were a natural tendency in L1 , must
be due to the second redactor himself. Johannes
no doubt wrote, *et vostre buisineor emporte
Michieus . . . es cieus.* The second redactor
missed the aptness of *buisineor* as applied to
Roland and writing at a time when the function
of the case endings was being replaced by word
order, he made Michael the hornblower and
supplied as complement *l'ame de Rollant,* plac-
ing it after the verb. For most of the scribes who
copied him this made perfectly clear though
wrong sense. But the barbaric syntax evidently

put the more cultured scribes on their guard
and so we have the emended texts in A1, Br 3
and C1. I relegate the passage in P5 to the
rejected readings and print an attempted restora-
tion of the text.

LXIII, 10   *Sanson.* The reading in A1 is *Sanson Forti* (in
                 P7: *Sampson Fortin*), which is not an unusual
                 denomination of Samson in mediaeval writings.
                 The *Forti,* it has been suggested, is probably due
                 to a scribe's unintelligent reproduction, from
                 some collection of exempla, of a phrase like *in
                 Samson fortitudo* with *fortitudo* abbreviated as
                 forti. Cf. however Professor Margaret Pelan,
                 "The Nomina Suffix – tin(e)" in *Modern
                 Language Review* XLIX, 1954, p. 15, n. 2, p. 19.

LXV, 5   *esloigna.* T.-L. gives few examples of *esloignier*
                 used intransitively with the meaning of "
                 "lengthen, be prolonged," and none of the use
                 in a temporal sense. Our controlling manuscripts
                 show a preference for *alonger* and *aloignier.*

LXV, 6   *trois jorz.* The reading *trois hores* in P5 is a
                 mark of the scribe's conservative and pondered
                 manner. His reserve was shared by the scribe
                 responsible for the copy of the Michel text
                 which gave rise to the sub-group of manuscripts
                 F A2 B2 C2 A3 S (C1 lacks the whole passage).
                 But there is no doubt that the main *Turpin* tra-
                 dition, Johannes's translation included, specified
                 three days.

LXV, 27   *de laide mort et de despite.* We have here a noun,
                 mort, qualified by two co-ordinate adjectives
                 linked with *et,* one placed before the noun and
                 one after.

LXV, 37   *et li un enfooient les autres iluec.* I print the
                 reading of A1 L2 V, which corresponds to the

Latin: *alter alterum sepeliebat* and which is supported by B1 O A2 B2 C2 , and really by C1 : *et li autre enfueent illueques les autres.* The reading which I adopt is *a lectio difficilior;* it is worth noting that the *lectio facilior* which we have in P5 Br 2 Br 3 is the reading which has come down to us in Groups I and II — an illustration of the degenerate state in which the original translation and the first redaction survive.

LXVI, 4   *Maximiens d'Aquitaine.* The reading in the Latin manuscripts here is *Maximinus Aquensis* (213, xiv). Saint Maximinus of Aix has been discussed by Jean-Remy Palanque in the *Analecta Bollandiana,* LXVII, 1949, pp. 377 ff. Palanque was willing to accept Maximinus as the name of the first bishop of Aix, but concluded that we cannot be sure of the identity of the saint who bore that name and held that office. The Johannes manuscript tradition makes it quite clear that our translator wrote here *Maximiens d'Aquitaine.* We can hardly think that Johannes misread his Latin model as *Maximianus Aquitanensis,* and it would be gratuitous to suppose that this was a variant reading in the Latin manuscript he had before him. His substitution must be deliberate and so we have to ask who was his St. Maximian of Aquitaine and why did Johannes prefer to put him instead of Saint Maximin of Aix among the seven famous bishops who according to tradition had been sent from the Holy See to establish Christianity in Gaul. Perhaps his *Maximiens d'Aquitaine* was the Maximianus who became bishop of Trèves and who was an Aquitanian born. *Aquitaniae originem duxit provinciae (AA. SS.* Maii VII, p. 21). Just before his death, his *Vita* tells us, he went back from Trèves to Aquitania to see his brothers and there shortly afterwards he died and was buried in a place unknown. The *Vita* goes on to tell the story of how a determined band of Trevires discovered his tomb and surreptitiously took his body away to Trèves while the uncouth and drunken Aquitanian guards slept. Johannes's expression *d'Aquitaine* is itself strange unless used with such a connotation as I have suggested, and it may be that Johannes preferred him to Saint Maximinus of Aix as being of greater interest for that region of south-western France in which so many of the scenes of the *Pseudo-Turpin Chronicle* were laid. It remains possible however that Johannes had in mind, more than did the Pseudo-Turpin himself, that mysterious *cité d'Aquitaine* which he had described in XXII, 16 ff., *urbs Aquitaniae* (123, xxii), in which case his Saint Maximien must be considered lost to history with all other traces of that unidentifiable Aquitania.

LXVI, 16-17   *qu'il avoit fondé et mis chanoines regulers.* The two relative sentences, coordinated with *et,* are introduced by a single *que* which is made to serve as direct object of *avoit fondé* and also as a relative adverb, loosely fulfilling the function of indirect object of *avoit mis.* Wolf-Dieter Stempel has quoted examples from Villehardouin and Clari showing this indifference to case on the part of the relative pronoun *que* (*Untersuchungen zur Satzverknüpfung im Altfranzösischen,* p. 219). See too Sneyders de Vogel, *Syntaxe historique,* § 129, 2.

LXVII, 5   *por lui avoir.* The *lui* is used as the feminine form, as often when *li* and *lui* had become confused in pronunciation. Cf. the V variant at LXX, 23: *dejoste lui* where *lui* replaces *eglise.*

LXVII, 16

Lambert. Johannes omitted him at XXIV, 10 between Ogier and Costentins, obviously because of homoioteleuton — the repetition of *cum* — *milibus heroum* (125, xiii).

LXVII, 18

Begues. P5 writes *Bueves,* but no Bueves is mentioned elsewhere in the manuscript tradition of the *Turpin,* and *Begues* is the name at XXIV, 14.

LXVII, 31

vestissent . . . .xxx. povres et donassent a mangier. An example of the laxity with which Old French used a single complement with two co-ordinate verbs, the one governing a direct, the other an indirect, complement.

LXVIII, 5-7

The Latin text reads (217, vii-ix): *(Burgundiones) qui . . . venerant cum mortuis suis et vulneratis quos lectulis et bigis secum illuc adduxerant ad sepeliendum eos in cimiterio Aylis Campis* (see variants). Our Groups I and II show superficial variants here but no manuscript is in difficulty with the sense. So, e.g., P2 reads: *S'estoient venu atout lor mors qu'il aportoient en lis et en charretes pour enterrer . . .* Only O among the manuscripts preserving the second redaction has kept the sense of the passage: *Si esteient venuz ileuc ou lur morz . . .* All the other manuscripts in Group III show that there had been a corruption in their common source which the scribes emended as best they could. The reading in O offers such an emendation and it comes close to what Johannes had no doubt actually written. The nature of the corruption shows behind the readings in MSS L2 L3 B1: *S'estoient venu lur morz . . .* Evidently all our Group III texts reflect the loss of the preposition *atout (lor morz)* or perhaps of *o, ou,* possibly overlooked because of its juxtaposition to the final *-u* of *venu.* The readings in our controlling manuscripts

show other forms of emendation. So do those in
Br 2: *portant lor mors* and Br 3: *et pourtoient
leurs mors.* The scribe who wrote the common
source of the whole subgroup C1 B2 C2 A3 S F
P11 A2 found a less happy solution to his prob-
lem: *Si estoient venu veoir lor morz!* The indica-
tion is then that a preposition has been lost
before *lor morz* and so I emend the text of P5
according to the reading in O.

LXVIII, 9   *Sanses.* Johannes omitted *Sanses* with *Lambert*
at XXIV, 10. See note to LXVII, 16.

LXX, 2   *par qui.* The use after a preposition of *qui* with
an antecedent naming a thing is not infrequent
in Old French. Cf. Sneyders de Vogel, *Syntaxe
historique,* § 114. A1 keeps the form *cui;* P8
and V prefer *coi.*

LXX, 5   *donent et donront.* Most of our manuscripts
keep the tenses here as they are in the Latin:
dant et daturi sunt (219, xxii); but the scribe of
P5, and also the scribes of M and P8, seem to
have considered the matter and concluded that
the present and the past are the tenses called for
by the present tense of the main verb: *sunt ja
quites.* However, the Pseudo-Turpin no doubt
meant to encourage future contributors and so I
feel obliged to reject the reading in P5 and to
keep the Pseudo-Turpin's forms as expressing
what he meant to say.

LXXII, 3   *chantent et orguanent.* The 3rd. pers. pl. is used
to express the idea of an impersonal subject. Cf.
n. to XXXI, 19. The scribe of P5 changed the
form by introducing as subject *le clerc.* So did
the scribes of M P1 A1. In C1, we find *on: cante
on et organe on.*

LXXIII, 11   The Latin texts show various readings here
(225, xv): *senatores romani ceterasque urbes
antiquas componentes; senatores romani ceteras
urbes a.c.; senatores urbis Romae, Romam ceter-
asque urbes a.c.; senatores romani Roman ceter-
asque urbes a.c.* Evidently, the juxtaposition of
romani, or of *Romae,* to *Romam* tended to cause
the loss of *Romam.* The same tendency has left
our whole Johannes tradition without *Rome* as
complement to the verb. The C manuscripts
offered to Johannes: *senatores romani Romam
ceterasque urbes a.c.* In our MSS M L1 Br 1 P5
A1 (I recall that P2 P3 P7 Br 2 lack the chapter)
we find: *firent li senatour de Romme les
anchiennes cités.* But this reading is really an
attempted emendation of a corrupt text, as is
shown by the passage in L2: *firent li s. de Rome
et li ancien les citez.* The *et* is a relic of the
authentic reading; this is proved by the scribe's
effort to accommodate the syntax to its inclu-
sion. L3 too retains the *et,* but in a further cor-
rupted context: *furent li s. de Rome et les
ancienes citez.* B1 omits the passage. The key to
their difficulty lies in the reading of O, which is
also that of P1: *firent li s. Rume e les anchiennes
cités* (*autres cités* P1), an emendation surely,
behind which lies the authentic reading: *firent
li s. de Rome Rome et les a.c.* The III M manu-
scripts read roughly with V: *Par cest art sorent
li s. de Rome les a.c.* The reading in P8 (see
variants) is due to the scribe's desperate effort to
make sense with *furent* for *surent.* Br 3 is also
innovative: *et [par] cest art sceurent li s. de
Romme anciennement les miles et les lieues . . .*
But in this group again, MSS C1 B2 C2 A3 S F
A2 all proceeding from an independent copy of
the Michel text, show the persistent and authen-
tic *et: seurent li s. de Rome et des autres
chités . . .* I have no doubt that Johannes

rendered *senatores romani Romam ceterasque urbes antiquas componentes* by: *firent li senateur de Rome Rome et les anciennes cités.*

LXXV, 14

de voltre. The reading *de voltre* is perfectly clear in P5 L2 L3 O. The Latin has (227, xix, var.) *ars adulterina dicitur,* for which M reads: *est appellee aoultere,* P1: . . . *ars aultere,* L1: . . . *de avoterie* and Br 1 (again I should recall that P2 and P3 and also P7 Br 2 lack the whole chapter): . . . *d'avotre* with the literal sense respectively: "adultery" or "adulterous," "of adultery," "of an adulterer." Among the manuscripts of Group III R, B1 omits the sentence; P6, the copy of P5, has *d'avoutire* replacing *de voltre,* and A1 has art *de noire* which may be a misreading of an unclear *de voitre* induced by the *noire devinoison* of l. 15. All the III M manuscripts have *ars de dyable,* with the exception of Br 3 which has avoided the phrase: *Mais nul n'en peult user que par le deable et pour tant est son nom nigromance qui vault autant a dire comme noire division.* I think we must accept the evidence of P5 L2 L3 O that *voltre* is a real word, an aphetic form of *avoltre.* The only other example I know is *voustre* listed by Godefroy, VIII, 308 c. He took it from a document of 1454 and commented: "peut-être forme *d'avoutre.*"

LXXVI, 17

.iii. anz. That the reading in P5 is erroneous is assured not only by the evidence of Br 2 and most of the III M manuscripts, but also by the reading *trois anz* in LXXVI, 2 which conforms to the Latin 233, viii. The order of events as presented in the Latin here has been much changed in our translation.

LXXVIII, 13

qui edifie iglise. Cf. the Latin: *qui ecclesiam aedificat* (235, ix). The variant reading *maison*

et (or *ou*) *eglise, "monastery and church,"*
appears in M and L1, in P2 and P3, and, among
the manuscripts of the second redaction, in the
sub-group L2 L3 B1 O, and in Br 2. The whole
passage is lacking in P1 and Br 1. The phrase
eglises ne mostiers appears also in the *Grandes
Chroniques* (Viard, op. cit., p. 295). The read-
ings in M L1 and P2 P3 suggest that Johannes,
who often used hendiadys (cf. *his auditis mirac-
ulis* "iteus miracles et teus marveilles," VIII, 12
and Fischer, *op. cit.,* pp. 44 ff.) translated
ecclesiam by *maison et eglise.* Yet it is not easy
to see why some scribes later omitted *maison.* It
seems more likely that *maison* is a later addition
made independently by a number of scribes. The
word represents perhaps more than synonymic
repetition; rather, it completes the sense with
the inclusion of monasteries along with
churches. Perhaps those who added *maison* were
themselves monks; but it needed no special
interest to make some copyists include regular
foundations along with the secular as benefac-
tions which would help to save the souls of
those who made them.

Notes to the Supplementary Chapters

Supp. Chap.
I, 33

une [v]ille . . . The reading *ille* is corrupt. The Latin text has (247, ix): *ad villam quae vulgo dicitur Orniz* (var: *Ornix, Orinz*). All the Old French translations have *vile,* except the *Grandes Chroniques* where we find *cité*. The identity of the Spanish St. Romain presents a problem. Cf. the *AA.SS,* Feb. III, pp. 746 ff. Here the lives, authentic or otherwise, show that the relics of a St. Romain were visited by pilgrims in quest of healing *apud Orichios in parva aedicula,* or *in agro Aurichiensi in Lusitania.* Vázquez de Parga identifies the saint and his church with San Román de Hornija (*Hispania* I, 1940, p. 130 and 134) in the province of Valladolid. The church, according to Vázquez belonged to the monastery of San Pedro de Montes in the western part of León and close to the Way of St. James. Reiffenberg seems to have been in no doubt about the matter. Where the Mouskés text reads:

> Tant qu'il vinrent a une vile
> Que la gens apieloit Ornis (vv. 12278-79)

he simply glosses *Ornis* "Orense."

I, 50

The texts in MSS 2137, 17203 read together here: *et dient li pelerin qui l'ont veue* (*veu* MS 17203) *qu'ele* (*il* MS 17203) *est de male oudeur et si put.* The Latin has simply (249, i): . . . *quod lapis ille fetorem emittit.* The reading in MS 2137, is no doubt the correct one.

II, 18

pres leur perre[s] "(were called Navarrese) after their fathers." The text in MS 17232, fol. 59 v°,

218

a, reads *apriés.* Cf. T.-L. I, 472, quoting *Floris et Liriopé*, v. 1379:

> *Aprés son aiuel par chiertei*
> *L'ont Bel Narcisus apelé.*

II, 20   The form *nons* in *nons vrais* is an example of the extension of agreement to an adverb qualifying an adjective.

Glossary

The list contains only words which might present some difficulty to non-specialists or some interest to specialists.

acompaigna – XXII, 16, *pret. 3 of* acompaignier; *v. trans. to recruit, to band or gather together (around him).*

afeitier (soi) de – *Prol. 10, to enrich itself with, to adorn itself with, perhaps pejoratively: to put on. At LIV, 7 MS L2 shows for* por esfacier lor pechiez *the variant* p. afaitier l. p. *The sense here is atone for, an extension of the meaning accommodate, reconcile, make at one. Cf. T.-L. I, 173.*

alues – LXVII, 27, *freehold.*

amiraus – *App.,* Suppl. Ch. I, 1, *emir; see Table of Proper Names.*

apaier – LVIII, 4, *appease, quench. P5 alone has* apaier; *variant:* apaisier.

aparoil – *see* appareillier.

appareillier – XVI, 13, XVIII, 9, 10, LII, 1, *v. trans. Make ready, prepare;* LXV, 28, 31 *embalm;* a. (soi) LI, 15; p. p. appareilliees (de) XXV, 18 *ready* (for); *pres. subj. 3* aparoil VII, 13.

apriens – VII, 9, *p. p. of* apriendre; *oppressed.*

arz – LV, 5, *withy, thong; variant form:* harz LXIV, 7.

atirement – XXVIII, 8, *arrangement, terms agreed upon; cf. FEW* XVII, 326b.

atriver (soi) – IX, 1, *to be pacified, to come to terms, to end hostilities.*

aumaçor – XIX, 4, 10, XXXI, 21, XLII, 2, XLIV, 16, App., Suppl., Ch. I, 3 *et passim, a Saracen title: "commander," "chief." The title is the application to use as a common noun of the name* Almanzor, al-Mansur, *"The Victor," the sobriquet applied to Ibn Abi 'Amir, commander in Andalucía under the caliph Hisham II. See also* Cordres *in the Table of Proper Names.*

ausint – *see* ensint.

220

autressint – XXXII, 22, XXXIV, 7, XLIII, 6, 10 *likewise, similarly. The scribe of P5 preferred this form, but cf.* autressi XLII, 13 *and cf. variants* autresi, ausi.

awloient – App. Suppl. Ch. I, 14 *went blind; imperf. indic. 3rd. pers. pl. of* awler, *a form of* avogler.

boisineor – LXII, 10 *hornblower.*

boisiner – LVII, 10 *to sound the horn.*

bugle – V, 7 *wild ox;* cuir de bugle *oxhide.*

car – VII, 11 *that; subordinating conj. introducing a noun clause; see note.*

cerchierent – I, 3 *pret. of* cerchier *to journey through, to visit.*

chars – XXII, 6 serf de lor chars *serfs in their persons, serfs in personal bondage; see note.*

complaignenment – II, 8 *literally, "complainingly." The adverb is formed on the gerund* complaignent *which itself retains the adverbial sense of the Latin form in* – ndo, *with the adverbial ending,* -ment. *Cf.* erramment, LXII, 9, gemissenment LX, 2.

corage – XVIII, 15, XXII, 20 *nature, disposition, spirit;* XXIII, 3: de grant c. *stout-hearted.*

cure – XXII, 4 *dominions; see note.*

darreain – XI, 9 *(noun) the last time;* XXV, 9 au darrien *(adv.) last, last of all;* XXX, 6, *(adj.) last*

darreanetez – XII, 20, *last days, end.*

darrien – *see* darreain.

despareillier (soi) de – L, 10 *to diverge from, to be in contrast to, to belie; see note.*

despite – LIV, 13, LXV, 27 *despicable, shameful; the p. p. of* despire *used adjectively; see note to* LXV, 27.

destruiemenz – XVII, 9 *loss, hurt, damage. Cf. the variant* detriement *and the* detrimentum *of the Latin text.*

detriés – XX, 6 *behind.*

deviser – L, 20, LI, 1 *decide;* LXXIII, 1 *divide, discern (cf. the variant* discerner); LXXI, 5: deviser (soi) *to be divided, separated, distinguished.*

discrez – III, 5 *discriminating, versed in, skilled.*

edefier – XLV, 13 *to build up, to rehabilitate;* LXXVIII, 13, 14 *to build.*

einsi – *see* ensint.

eise – L, 13 metre aucun en eise d'aucun *to put someone at ease with respect to someone, to relieve someone of someone; see note.*

empire — III, 14 *pomp;* atot son pooir et atot son empire *in all his power and splendor.*

emprés — VI, 1 *after.*

ensi — *see* ensint.

ensint — XVI, 8, XXI, 4, XXII, 9 et passim *thus, in this way. This is the almost constant form of the adv. in P5, but cf. einsi* XVII, 15, ensi XLI, 13, ausint XVIII, 18, XLVII, 13, XLVIII, 10; issi LXXVIII, 22. *With similar consistency the controlling manuscripts show the variants* issi A1, ainsi L2, ensi P8 V.

escharnissemenz — LIX, 6 *mockery, insults.*

escheles — XIII, 5 *bells.*

escrois — XV, 4 *din; see note.*

esgart — XXVIII, 8 *decision, ruling.*

esloigna — LXV, 5 *pret. of* esloignier, *used intransitively, lengthen, be prolonged; see note.*

esperiz — XV, 2 *awakened, startled.*

eslecier (soi) — LXVII, 8 *rejoice, be glad.*

feels — LX, 20 tes feels *thy faithful;* LXII, 3: messe des feels Deu *the Missa Fidelium.*

fesse — V, 9 *the swaddling clothes in which the Christ child was wrapped in his cradle.*

gitoient jus — IX, 5 *threw down (their arms). The variant* gieter puer *also was a standard phrase with the same meaning.*

guanchirent sor — LII, 15 *turned upon; pret. of* guanchir, guenchir.

harz — *see* arz.

heut — LVI, 17 *the cross-guard of a sword.*

honniz — XV, 19 *a form of* oni *flat*

issi — *see* ensint.

laor — LVI, 16 *breadth.*

lues — XXVIII, 4 *then and there.*

maisieres — App., Suppl. Ch. I, 41 *walls.*

merriens — LXXVII, 18 *lumber, timber.*

mont — XLIV, 13 tot en un mont *all of a heap.*

mut — *pret. of* movoir XLII, 7 *moved, set out;* Prol. 22 Ch. mut a aler *proceeded to go, set out on his way;* LXX, 12 de ce mut costume *thence arose the custom. In written form, as in meaning,* mut *closely resembled* vint *from which the scribes often failed to distinguish it; cf. variants.*

non – *name* XXII, 3: par non de bataille (causa bellandi) *for the sake of, with a view to, purposing, intending.*

norriçons – VII, 4 norriçons Deu (Christi alumpnus) *disciple. The occurrence of the word with this meaning in a manuscript of ca. 1250 is noteworthy; cf. FEW VII, 253a.*

orguanent – LXXII, 3 *sing to the accompaniment of an organ, sing (in general).*

perruchoi – XV, 11 *a stony place;* cf. T.-L. VII, 781. *The FEW lists* perruchai *and* perruchois *each as a hapax, 13th. century* (VIII, 317b). Perruchoi *occurs in P5, its copy, P6 and in B2. The form preferred by the scribes is* perroi, *but A1 B1 Br 2 read* perron.

planteive – XVIII, 5 *(a city) of plenty, rich.*

poissant – XXXII, 6 *possible; see note.*

pres – App., Suppl. Ch. II, 18 pres leur perres *(named) after their forebears; see note.*

prez – LI, 13 *ready.*

privez – XXII, 16 *personal friends, associates.*

que que – Prol. 3 *whatever; an indefinite pron. used with concessive force.*

regarder – XXX, 10, LIX, 20 *to have regard, consideration, for; see note to LIX, 20.*

regehir (soi) – LIX, 13 *to declare oneself, to confess oneself;* regehir LIX, 26 *declare, avow.*

repairier – XVIII, 6, XX, 16 *to return;* L, 3 to reside; en repairier (soi) XX, 20 *to return, to go back.*

reprises – XVII, 2, XXI, 9 *rooted, sprouting; p. p. of* reprendre *to take root, to sprout, to put forth buds or leaves.*

repondront – XII, 21 *3rd. pers. pl. fut. of* repondre, *from* repondĕre, *to bury, to hide.*

repost – LII, 11 *hiding, lurking, the p. p. of* repondre.

repostement – XX, 3 *secretly, in hiding, hidden.*

rive – XII, 12 *shore;* XV, 18 la rive qui a non Cee *river; see note.*

saus – XIV, 15 *saved (in the religious sense).*

veve (de) – XXIV, 1 *deprived of, bereft of.*

voltre – LXXV, 14 *an aphetic form of* avoltre (avoutre) *adulterer, bastard;* arz de voltre *a false or illegitimate art; see note.*

ydres – XII, 1 *idols.*

Index of Proper Names

For many of the place names obscured in transmission the Latin form is given in brackets as it appears in the C manuscripts, Bibl. Nat., Latin MS 3768 and Brit. Mus., MS Harley 6358. For the often recurring *Charlemagne* the abbreviation *Ch.* is used.

Aaron. *Moses's brother, whose rod flourished,* V, 4. Cf. *Numbers,* XVII.

Absalon. *David's son,* LXIII, 24.

Abule *(Abula). Abla,* X, 22, XLII, 6.

Acension, un jor de l'. *Ascension Day,* LXXVI, 7.

Acinte *(Accintina). Guadix el Viejo,* X, 22.

Adamie. *See* Adanie.

Adan. *Adam,* XXXVIII, 1.

Adanie *(Adania),* X, 19. Adamie, XI, 15. *Jones, op. cit. p. 280, suggests Alhama. David, op. cit., III, p. 26, refuses to make any identification.*

Agabe. *See* Agabie.

Agabie une ille *(Agabiba insula). Zerbi in the Gulf of Tunis,* X, 28. Le roi d'Agabe *(Agabiae, variant form of* Agabibae *in the mss.),* 'XIX, 7, XXI, 21.

Agiens. *Agen,* XIX, 11, XX, 2, 26.

Agolanz. *A pagan king from Africa,* XIII, 7. *The war against him, his defeat and death,* XIV *to* XXXII.

Ais. *See* Es.

Alandaluf *(Alandaluf). Andalucía,* XI, 2. Andaluf, XII, 3. *Given to the Germans in Ch.'s army after the conquest,* XLV, 7. (The final *f* is a scribal error for long *s.*)

Alavars *(Alavarum). The inhabitants of Álava,* XI, 4. *See too* Avaire.

Alcemore *(Altamora). Zamora,* X, 11.

Alcocors *(Alcoroz). Alcoraz,* X, 20.

Alerne, la tiere d' *(terram Alavae). Suppl. Ch.* II, 15. *See* Avaire.

Aleschans. *The Alyscamps at Arles,* LXVI, 2, LXVIII, 7.

Alixandre. *Alexandria,* XIX, 6. *See also* Burabeaus.

Alixandres. *Alexander the Great,* LIV, 9.

Algate *(Algati). Alegón,* X, 19.

Almarie. *Almería,* X, 30.

Alphinors *(Aphinorgium). King of Maiorgues (q.v.), in Agolant's army,* XIX, 8.

Amiraus, li. *Title applied to the aumaçor de Cordes, incipit to suppl. Ch.* I.

224

* (It is noteworthy that, except for three references to the Way of St. James, the saint's name is not mentioned in Chapters XIV to XLIV.)

Provost taken there for burial, LXVIII, 13. *Its voice in the matter of episcopal appointments subordinated to that of Saint-Denis,* LXIX, 11. *The senators of R. skilled in the use of geometry,* LXXIII, 11. *They practised astrology,* LXXV, 7.

Rosne, *The Rhone.* LXXVIII, 17.

Rune. *Another name for the Arga (q.v.) at Pamplona (cf. Bédier, Lég. ép. III, 293).*

Saintes. XX, 33, XXIII, 19. *See also* Antropes.

Saint Fagon. *Sahagún,* XXI, 11.

Salamanche *(Salamancha). Salamanca,* X, 10.

Salancadis. *The name given to the statue of Mohammed at Cádiz,* XII, 3.

Salemons. *Estouz' companion,* XXIV, 5. *Buried in the Alyscamps,* LXVIII, 8.

Samuel. *One of two Hebrew messengers sent by Constantine to Ch.,* III, 5.

Sanses. *Duke of Burgundy; buried in the Alyscamps,* LXVIII, 9. *See note to text.*

Sanson. *The Sampson of the Book of Judges,* LXIII, 10.

Sarragoce *(Sarragocia). Saragossa "qui est apelee Cesarraguste,"* X, 14. *Its territory given after the conquest to the Greeks and Italians in Ch.'s army,* XLV, 6. *Residence of Marsile and Baligant, and scene of Ganelon's betrayal,* L, 4 ff. *Baligant flees there after Roncevaux,* LV, 32.

Scene of Ch.'s final victory, LXV, 7. *Cesar Auguste. The Scots, Nubians and Cornish invaders reach there and are repulsed, Suppl. Chap.* II, 9 ff.

Sarrazines. *The Saracen women sent by Marsile to Ch.'s army,* LI, 8, 20, 21, LIV, 3, 7.

Sarrazins. VII, 9 *et passim. The Saracens. Distinguished from the Moors etc., as a contingent in Agolant's army,* XIX, 2.

Sative *(Sativa). Játiva,* X, 21, XLII, 6.

Saturnins de Tholose, saint. *St. Saturninus, bishop of Toulouse. One of the seven bishops who blessed the cemeteries at Arles and Bordeaux,* LXVI, 6.

Saül. *King of Israel,* LXIII, 23.

Sebile *(Sibilia). Seville,* X, 22, XLII, 5. *See also* Ebraÿns.

Segobe *(Segobia). Segovia,* X, 10.

Segunce *(Seguncia). Siguenza,* X, 10.

Septe *(Septa). Ceuta,* X, 30.

Sepunilege *(Sepuiuilega). Sepúlveda,* X, 10.

Sessoigne. *Saxony,* II, 3.

Seurin, monseigneur saint. *Saint-Seurin in Bordeaux. Roland's horn surreptiously taken there from his tomb in Blaye,* LXVI, 20. *The heroes buried in its cemetery,* LXVII, 14 ff.

Sire. *Syria. Fernagu comes from there to Spain,* XXXIII, 24.

Sorges *(Sanctum Johannem Sorduae).* Saint-Jean de Sorde, XIII, 11.

Symeon, saint. V, 10. *See Luke II, 28.*

Tailleborc. *Taillebourg. Scene of the miracle of the lances,* XXI, 8.

Talavere *(Talaveria). Talavera,* X, 8. *See note to text.*

Termes. *Termes-en-Termenés. See Bédier, Lég. ép.* I, 390-391. *See also* Gautier.

Terragone *(Terragona). Tarragona,* X, 16.

Thalamanche *(Thalamanca). Talamanca,* X, 7.

Thezepins *(Texephinus). "li rois d'Arrabe," in Agolant's army,* XIX, 5. *See also* Arrabe.

Tholete. *See* Tolete.

Tholose. *Toulouse.* LXVIII, 3. *See also* Saturnins.

Throphins. *St. Trophimus, bishop of Arles, one of the seven bishops who blessed the cemeteries of Arles and Bordeaux,* LXVI, 5.

Thierri. XXIV, 15. *Escapes alive at Roncevaux,* LIII, 14. *Hides in the forest,* LVI, 1. *Comforts the dying Roland,* LVIII, 11. *Witness of Roland's last moments,* LX, 3, LXI, 6. *Ch.'s victorious champion against Pinabel,* LXV, 18, 22.

Tiescheterre. *Germany,* I, 14, VI, 7.

Tiois. *The Germans. Given Andalucía after the conquest by Ch.,* XLV, 8.

Tolete *(Toleta). Toledo,* X, 10. *Galafres knights Ch. there,* I, 9. Tholete. *Charles learned Arabic there when exiled in his youth,* XXVI, 10.

Torpins, l'arcevesques de Rains. *Passim. Eye witness and chronicler of Ch.'s wars in Spain, Prol. 12. Referred to in the first person:* XXII, 17, XLVI, 10, LXII, 2 ff., LXVIII, 15, 21, LXXVII, 1 ff. *Referred to in the third person: Prol.* 12, IX, 12, LII, 7, LXV, 10, LXXVI, 19, 22, LXXVII, 21, LXXVIII, 3, 5 *and in the passage which narrates his death:* LXXVIII, 15, 22.

Torquace. *St. Torquatus, a disciple of St. James; the miracle recurring on his feast day,* X, 33 ff.

Tortose *(Tortosa). Tortosa,* X, 17.

Troi Roi, li *(Magi). The Three Kings; knew by astrology when Christ was born,* LXXV, 9.

Tude *(Tuda). Tuy,* X, 4.

Turgel *(Turgel). Trujillo,* X, 11.

Turs *(Turci). Turks,* XXXIII, 25.

Ubete *(Uzeda). Uceda,* X, 7.

Uline *(Ulmas). Perhaps one of the towns named "Olmos." Or perhaps "Olmedo" in the province of Valladolid,* X, 8.

Urance *(Urancia). Los Arcos.* X, 14. *See note to text.*

Urie *(Yria). Iria Flavia, the modern El Padron,* X, 4. Yrie. *Made subject to the archbishop of Compostella,* XLVI, 8.

Usime *(Visunia). Viseu,* X, 3.

Val Charle, le *(Vallis Karoli). The Val Carlos, leading down from Roncevaux to Saint-Jean-Pied-de-Port,* LVII, 20, LXII, 3.

Valance *(Valencia). Valencia,* X, 21.

Val Vert *(Vallis Viridis). Val*